**Herkimer County
Community College Library
Herkimer, New York
13350**

1. Books may be kept for three weeks and may be renewed once, except when otherwise noted.

2. Reference books, such as dictionaries and encyclopedias, are to be used only in the Library.

3. A fine is charge for each day a book is not returned according to the above rule.

4. All injuries to books beyond reasonable wear and all losses shall be made good to the satisfaction of the Librarian.

5. Each borrower is held responsible for all books drawn on his card and for all fines accruing on the same.

D1219574

Android Apps
with Eclipse

Onur Cinar

Apress®

Android Apps with Eclipse

Copyright © 2012 by Onur Cinar

ISBN-13 (pbk): 978-1-4302-4434-9

ISBN-13 (electronic): 978-1-4302-4435-6

President and Publisher: Paul Manning
Lead Editor: Steve Anglin
Development Editor: James Markham
Technical Reviewer: Pierpaolo Cira
Editorial Board: Steve Anglin, Ewan Buckingham, Gary Cornell, Louise Corrigan, Morgan Ertel, Jonathan Gennick, Jonathan Hassell, Robert Hutchinson, Michelle Lowman, James Markham, Matthew Moodie, Jeff Olson, Jeffrey Pepper, Douglas Pundick, Ben Renow-Clarke, Dominic Shakeshaft, Gwenan Spearing, Matt Wade, Tom Welsh
Coordinating Editor: Katie Sullivan
Copy Editor: Marilyn Smith
Compositor: Bytheway Publishing Services
Indexer: SPI Global
Artist: SPI Global
Cover Designer: Anna Ishchenko

Distributed to the book trade worldwide by Springer Science+Business Media, LLC., 233 Spring Street, 6th Floor, New York, NY 10013. Phone 1-800-SPRINGER, fax (201) 348-4505, e-mail orders-ny@springer-sbm.com, or visit www.springeronline.com.

For information on translations, please e-mail rights@apress.com, or visit www.apress.com.

Apress and friends of ED books may be purchased in bulk for academic, corporate, or promotional use. eBook versions and licenses are also available for most titles. For more information, reference our Special Bulk Sales–eBook Licensing web page at www.apress.com/bulk-sales.

The source code for this book is available to readers at www.apress.com. You will need to answer questions pertaining to this book in order to successfully download the code.

Dedicated to my son Deren, my wife Sema, and my parents,
Zekiye and Dogan, for their love, continuous support, and always encouraging me to pursue my
dreams.

I could not have done this without all of you.

–Onur Cinar

Contents at a Glance

Contents

About the Author

Onur Cinar has more than 17 years of experience in design, development, and management of large-scale, complex software projects, primarily in mobile and telecommunication space. His expertise spans VoIP, video communication, mobile applications, grid computing, and networking technologies on diverse platforms. He has been actively working with the Android platform since its beginning. He has a Bachelor of Science degree in Computer Science from Drexel University in Philadelphia, Pennsylvania. He is currently working at Skype as the Senior Product Engineering Manager for Skype clients on the Android platform.

About the Technical Reviewer

Pierpaolo Cira has been working as a software developer, software architect, and system integrator at the University of Salento in Italy since he was 19. He has been involved in many e-business, knowledge management, e-learning, and e-tourism research projects, in collaboration with companies such as Oracle and IBM. He also collaborated on the design and development for the first Semantics for Business Vocabulary and Rules (SBVR) editor, based on the Eclipse Plug-in Development Environment (PDE). He writes technical articles for IT portals, and is involved in several high school and public administration educational activities. Currently, he is working on the public web systems for the University of Salento, based on Liferay and Alfresco.

Introduction

Android is one of the major players in the mobile phone market, and its market share is continuously growing. Android is the first complete, open, and free mobile platform, and it offers endless opportunities for mobile application developers. As with all other platforms, having a robust and flexible development environment is the key for the platform's success.

Eclipse is the most adopted integrated development environment (IDE) for Java programmers. And now Eclipse is the preferred IDE for Android app developers.

Android Apps with Eclipse provides a detailed overview of Eclipse, including the steps and illustrations to help Android developers quickly get up to speed on Eclipse and to streamline their day-to-day software development.

Who This Book Is For

This book is for both beginners and intermediate developers who would like to quickly come up to speed on Android development using the Eclipse IDE.

What You Will Learn

This book covers the following topics:

- How the Android platform works and the basics of Android application development
- How to use the most popular Java IDE, Eclipse, to develop Android applications
- How to install and configure Eclipse for Android development
- How to leverage Eclipse with the Android Native Development Kit (NDK) for C/C++ needs
- How to leverage Eclipse for scripting using Android's Scripting Layer for Android (SL4A)
- How to debug and troubleshoot Android applications using Eclipse

Downloading the Code

The source code for this book is available to readers from `http://www.apress.com`.

Contacting the Author

Readers can contact the author through his *Android Apps with Eclipse* site at
`http://www.zdo.com/android-apps-with-eclipse`.

Android Primer

In this chapter, we will briefly cover the Android platform from various angles. We will start with Android's history, to better understand the motivations behind its formation. Then we will explore the Android platform architecture's fine combination of technologies that empower the platform to deliver a superior mobile experience. We will emphasis the multilayer Android security framework, which employs both software and hardware to keep the platform secure. We will briefly review the service application programming interfaces (APIs) that are provided through the Android framework for user-level applications to interact with the platform. Finally, we will discuss Android application deployment and distribution.

Android History

Android Inc. was founded in Silicon Valley, California, in October 2003, with the idea of providing a mobile platform that is more aware of the user's location and preferences.

Google acquired Android Inc. in August 2005 as a wholly owned subsidiary of Google Inc. Google's main intention was to provide a fully open platform, backed by Google technologies, for both the users and the application developers.

In November 2007, the Open Handset Alliance was founded as a consortium to develop an open standard for mobile devices. Open Handset Alliance began its journey by announcing the Android platform. In less than a year, new members started joining this consortium.

Android became an open source initiative that is led by Google under Open Handset Alliance's umbrella. The goal of the Android open source project is to provide an open platform to improve the mobile experience of users.

Android is the first complete, open, and free mobile platform.

- *Complete:* The Android platform is a robust, secure, easily upgradable, mobile platform with a comprehensive framework and well-defined interfaces. It allows application developers to develop and fully blend their applications into the platform. It also provides compatibility and certification programs, so device manufacturers can design highly compliant devices.

- *Open:* The entire Android platform has been developed and provided under open source Apache licensing terms. Android does not distinguish between preloaded applications and third-party applications. Developers have full access to device features and services while developing applications.

- *Free:* The Android platform does not charge any licensing, royalty, membership, or certification fees to develop applications on the platform. Android platform source code and software development kits are provided free of charge to application developers. The software development platform is widely available on many desktop operating systems, allowing application developers to develop applications using the operating system of their choice.

Today, Android is one of the major players in mobile phone market. Based on the recent market analysis, on average, 700 thousand Android devices are activated daily, and more than 200 million devices are already activated. Android currently has 48% of the mobile phone market share, and it's growing rapidly.

Android Versions

The first beta of the Android platform was released on November 5, 2007. Since then, it has been through a number of updates and bug fixes. Although bug fixes are usually transparent from the application developer's perspective, updates usually mean changes and additions to the framework API. For that reason, besides the Android platform version numbers, a second version number, called the *API level*, is used to identify the framework API that is supported.

Since April 2009, each Android version has been released under a codename based on desserts, such as Éclair, Froyo, and Gingerbread. This introduced a third versioning scheme to the Android platform, making things even more cryptic for first-time Android application developers. When speaking of Android application development, you will often hear people say things like "my application requires Éclair and above," "this method requires at least API level 9," and "my phone got the Android 2.1 update." Understanding which version and which API level they are referring to, as well as which new APIs are part of which Android platform version, can easily become a cumbersome memory exercise. You can use Table 1-1 as a reference to map between these three version schemes.

> **NOTE:** Since the Android platform is continuing to evolve, Table 1-1 may not cover the latest platform revisions. For an up-to-date listing, refer to the API Levels section of the Android Developer Pages, at
> `http://developer.android.com/guide/appendix/api-levels.html`.

Table 1-1. *Android Release Dates, Revisions, API Levels, and Codenames*

Release Date	Platform Version	API Level	Codename
November 5, 2007	Beta		
September 23, 2008	Android 1.0	1	
February 9, 2009	Android 1.1	2	
April 30, 2009	Android 1.5	3	Cupcake
September 15, 2009	Android 1.6	4	Donut
October 26, 2009	Android 2.0	5	Éclair
December 3, 2009	Android 2.0.1	6	Éclair
January 12, 2009	Android 2.1	7	Éclair
May 20, 2010	Android 2.2	8	Froyo
January 18, 2011	Android 2.2.1	8	Froyo
January 22, 2011	Android 2.2.2	8	Froyo

Release Date	Platform Version	API Level	Codename
November 21, 2011	Android 2.2.3	8	Froyo
December 6, 2010	Android 2.3	9	Gingerbread
February 9, 2011	Android 2.3.3	10	Gingerbread
July 25, 2011	Android 2.3.5	10	Gingerbread
September 2, 2011	Android 2.3.6	10	Gingerbread
February 22, 2011	Android 3.0	11	Honeycomb
May 10, 2011	Android 3.1	12	Honeycomb
July 15, 2011	Android 3.2	13	Honeycomb
September 20, 2011	Android 3.2.1	13	Honeycomb
August 30, 2011	Android 3.2.2	13	Honeycomb
October 19, 2011	Android 4.0.1	14	Ice Cream Sandwich
November 28, 2011	Android 4.0.2	14	Ice Cream Sandwich
December 16, 2011	Android 4.0.3	15	Ice Cream Sandwich
February 4, 2012	Android 4.0.4	15	Ice Cream Sandwich

As shown in Table 1-1, there are 15 API levels that you should consider while developing your applications. The API level determines the size of your audience as well, so picking this number wisely is very important while developing a new Android application.

The Android mobile phone market is highly fragmented. By simply looking at the release dates, you might think that most of the Android user base is running at least Android 3.0, since it has already been around for a year; however, this is not true. Due to the fragmentation, the release dates are far from giving a clear view of Android versions in use. Figure 1-1 is the latest version distribution chart from Android Platform Versions Dashboard (`http://developer.android.com/resources/dashboard/platform-versions.html`).

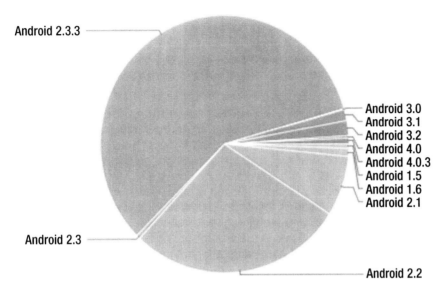

Figure 1-1. *Distribution of Android versions based on market data*

As you can see in Figure 1-1, most of the Android user base is currently running Android 2.3.3, Gingerbread. This means that your application needs to support API level 10 as a minimum in order to reach the majority of the Android users. It also means that you won't be able to use the latest API features introduced in the newer versions of the Android platform in your application. In this book, we will be developing our examples using Android 2.3.3.

The variety of versions is a common problem for Android developers. Most application developers develop packages for different API levels. This resolves the problem, but it means that different code branches need to be maintained.

In March 2011, Google introduced the Support Package as a solution to the versions problem. The Support Package is a set of static libraries that allows application developers to develop Android applications that support multiple Android platform versions. The main goal of the Support Package is to simplify the process of supporting multiple Android versions from a single code base. You can find more information about the Support Package at `http://developer.android.com/sdk/compatibility-library.html`.

Android Platform Architecture

Android is more of a complete software stack for mobile devices than an operating system. It is a combination of tools and technologies that are carefully optimized for mobile needs.

Android relies on the well-proven Linux kernel in order to provide its operating system functions. For the user-space application, Android relies on the Java Virtual Machine technology by employing the Dalvik virtual machine. The Android Zygote application process, through service preloading and resource sharing, boosts the application startup times and allows efficient use of scarce memory resources on mobile platforms. All these successful technologies play an important role in the success of the Android platform, as illustrated in Figure 1-2. In addition to these tools and technologies, the Android runtime provides a unique computing environment that is tailored for providing a smooth mobile experience to end users, while streamlining mobile application development for developers.

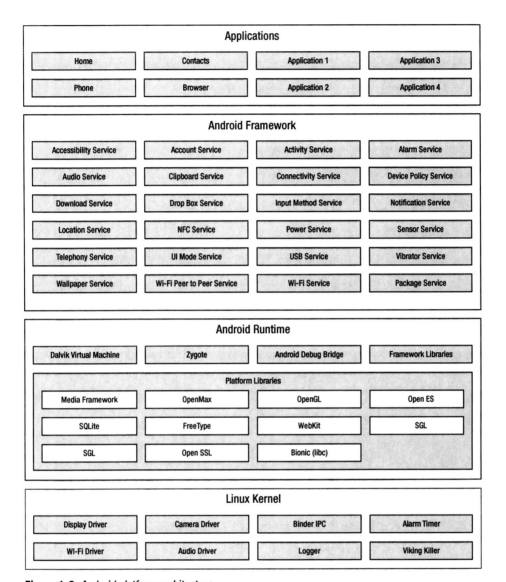

Figure 1-2. *Android platform architecture*

Hardware Abstraction Layer

Android relies on the Linux kernel as its hardware abstraction layer (HAL), and also to provide its operating system functionality. During the course of Android development, multiple improvements have been made to the Linux kernel code in order to tune it for mobile needs. The following are the most notable features:

- Alarm timer
- Paranoid network security
- Binder
- Wakelocks
- Android shared memory (Ashmem)
- Process shared memory (Pmem)
- Low memory killer (Viking Killer)
- Logger

Although application developers are not expected to interact with these low-level components directly, knowing their roles in the overall Android platform is important.

Alarm Timer

Android is designed to run on mobile platforms, where the only power to the device is provided through batteries. Android goes into a variety of sleep modes in order to efficiently use the limited battery resources. While the device is in sleep mode, the applications need a way to wake up the system in order to perform certain periodic tasks. On Android, this is achieved through the alarm timer kernel module. It allows a user-space application to schedule itself to run at some point in the future, regardless to the state of the device.

The **android.app.AlarmManager** class in Android runtime allows the user-level application to interact with the alarm timer through API calls. The Alarm Manager allows the applications to schedule an intent using the alarm timer (intents are discussed in the next chapter). When the alarm goes off, the scheduled intent is broadcast by the system to start the application. The Alarm Manager holds a CPU wakelock (described a little later in this chapter) as long as the application is busy executing code in its broadcast receiver's **onReceive** method. This guarantees that the device will not go into sleep mode again until the application is finished performing its task.

The alarm timer retains the scheduled alarms while the device is asleep; however, this list is cleared if the device is turned off and rebooted.

Paranoid Network Security

Network security is one of the most important requirements of any mobile platform. In order to provide an extensive level of security, Android handles this requirement at the lowest possible layer as a kernel modification. Through this implementation, Android restricts access by the group of the calling process. Applications should request the necessary permissions in advance, in order to be part of these network groups. Otherwise, the network access of these applications will be blocked within the kernel.

Binder

The Android platform architecture makes heavy use of interprocess communication (IPC). Applications communicate with the system, phone services, and each other by using IPC.

> **NOTE: Interprocess communication (IPC)** is a mechanism to allow applications to exchange data with each other and also with the operating system itself.

Although Android relies on the Linux kernel for its operating system-related functionality, it does not use the System V IPC mechanism that is provided through the Linux kernel. Instead, it relies on an Android-specific IPC system, which known as Binder.

Binder technology originated with the engineers at Be Inc. as a part of the Be Operating System (BeOS). The development of Binder continued at PalmSource as a key foundation of the Cobalt system, and later was open sourced as a Linux kernel module under the name OpenBinder project. Android's Binder implementation is a complete rewrite of the OpenBinder project in order to comply with the Apache License. Binder communicates between processes using a kernel module, as shown in Figure 1-3.

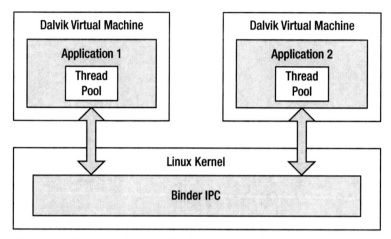

Figure 1-3. *Binder kernel module allowing two applications to communicate*

Binder's user-space code maintains a pool of threads in each process, and these threads are used to process incoming Binder requests as local events. Binder is also responsible for tracking the object references across processes. Additionally, Binder provides an extra level of security, by transmitting the user and group ID of the calling process with each Binder request.

Binder is a key construct in the Android platform. It is the central messaging channel across the entire Android platform. Android applications communicate with the system, services, and each other through the Binder interface.

Although Binder is implemented as a low-level service, application developers are not expected to directly interact with it. The Android runtime provides the **android.os.IBinder** interface as the API to communicate with other processes through Binder. Android provides the Android Interface Definition Language (AIDL), which is tuned for Binder.

AIDL allows you to define the programming interface that the client and server will use to communicate with each other. As with many other operating systems, on Android, the processes are not allowed to access the memory of another process directly. AIDL provides the functionality to decompose the objects into primitives that Binder can understand and use across project boundaries.

Threading is one of the most important parts of interacting with Binder:

- Calls made from the local process are executed in the calling thread. Binder calls are synchronous and will block the current thread until the request is processed. If the request is expected to take a long time to complete, the request should not be made from the application's main thread. This would make the application hang, and may result in the application being terminated by the Android platform. Binder also supports nonblocking requests through the oneway attribute.

- Calls from a remote process are dispatched from the thread pool provided by the local process. The service code is expected to be thread-safe, since the requests can be executed by any of these threads.

Android SDK provides the necessary code generators to translate programming interfaces that are defined in AIDL into actual Java classes. Application developers are only expected to provide the implementation for the generated interface and the Android service that will provide the interface to the clients.

Wakelocks

Android is designed to operate on mobile platforms with scarce resources. Because of this, Android devices go into sleep mode very frequently. Although this allows the system to use the available resources efficiently, it is not preferable for the device to go into sleep mode while the kernel or an application is in the middle of an important process. Wakelocks were introduced as a kernel patch in order to allow an application to prevent the system from going into sleep mode while it is performing a task.

Two types of wakelocks are supported by the Android platform:

- An idle wakelock prevents the system from entering a low-power idle state.

- A suspend wakelock prevents the system from entering a full-system suspend state.

Application developers interact with wakelocks through the `android.os.PowerManager.WakeLock` interface. To use this interface, the application should request `android.permission.WAKE_LOCK` in advance.

Wakelocks should be used with caution. Preventing the device from going into sleep mode will increase the power consumption, which will eventually cause it to run out of battery power. An application should hold the wakelock during important operations, and immediately release it as soon as the operation is complete.

Android Shared Memory

Android shared memory (Ashmem))is a POSIX-like shared memory subsystem on the Android platform that is implemented as kernel module. Ashmem is highly tuned for mobile needs, and it provides better support for low-memory devices. Ashmem supports reference-counted objects that can be shared among multiple processes.

Process Shared Memory

In addition to Ashmem, Android provides a second type of shared memory subsystem, known as process shared memory (Pmem). Pmem is used for sharing large amounts of physically contiguous memory among processes. Pmem is mostly used by the Android media engine to deliver large media frames between the media engine and the application processes.

Low Memory Killer

Low memory killer, also known as the Viking Killer, is one of the other Android-specific enhancements in the Linux kernel. This feature allows the system to reclaim memory before it runs out of memory.

In order to start an application, the device must first read the application code from the persistent storage to random-access memory (RAM). Since this is a time-consuming and costly process, Android attempts to keep the application processes around as long as possible. But eventually, it will need to remove them from RAM when the memory runs low.

The order in which applications are removed to prevent running out of memory depends on the importance of an application, which is gauged by the current state of the user's interaction with that application:

- An application with a foreground activity, which the user is currently interacting with, is considered the most important one.

- An application with a visible activity, which is not currently interacting with the user but still visible, is also considered important.

An application with a background activity, which is no longer visible to the user, is not considered important, since its current state can be saved and later restored when the user navigates back to the activity.

Android starts with the least important application when removing processes from memory. An empty process is one that has no activities, services, or broadcast receivers. These types of applications are considered as the least important, and Android starts removing them first.

The threshold values for each of these application states are configured using the **/etc/init.rc** system configuration file. Table 1-2 lists these thresholds.

Table 1-2. *Memory Threshold Values for Removing Applications from Memory*

Application State	Memory Threshold
Foreground application	6MB
Visible application	8MB
Hidden application	20MB
Content provider	22MB
Empty application	24MB

The low memory killer service gets this information through **ActivityManagerService**.

Logger

Logging is the most important part of troubleshooting, but it is tricky to achieve, especially on mobile platforms, where the development and the execution of the application happen on two different machines. Android has an extensive logging system that allows system-wide centralized logging of information from both the Android system itself and the applications.

The Android logging system is implemented as a kernel module known as the logger. A set of API calls and user-level applications are also provided to interact with the logger module.

The amount of information being logged on the platform at any given time makes the viewing and analysis of these log messages very difficult. In order to simplify this procedure, the Android logging system groups the log messages into four separate log buffers:

- *Main:* Main application log messages
- *Events:* System events
- *Radio:* Radio-related log messages
- *System:* Low-level system debug messages for debugging

These four buffers are kept as pseudo-devices under the **/dev/log** system directory. Since input and output (I/O) operations on mobile platforms are very costly, the log messages are not saved in persistent storage; instead, they are kept in memory. In order to keep the memory utilization of the log messages under control, the logger module puts them in fixed-sized buffers. Main, radio, and system logs are kept as free-form text messages in 64KB log buffers. The event log messages carry additional information in binary format, and they are kept in a 256KB log buffer.

A set of user-level applications is also provided to view and filter these logs, such as the logcat and the Dalvik Debug Monitor Server (DDMS) tools, which we will examine in chapter 5.

The Android runtime provides a set of API calls to allow applications to easily send their log messages to the logger. Application log messages are sent through the following classes:

- **android.util.Log**: This class is used to send application log messages. It provides a set of methods to specify the priority of the message, as well as a tag to indicate which application is generating this log message.

- **android.util.EventLog**: This class is used to send event log messages in binary format.

- **android.util.Slog**: This class is used by the Android runtime components to send system log messages. It is not part of the Android API, and it is not accessible from the applications.

Zygote

On most UNIX-like operating systems, the application that is known as Init is considered as the parent of all processes. Init gets started after the kernel successfully boots. Its primary role is to start a set of other processes based on the system configuration.

Zygote, also known as the "app process," is one of those core processes started by Init when the system boots. Zygote's role within the Android platform is very similar to that of Init. Its first task is to start a new Dalvik virtual machine instance and initialize the core Android services, such as the following:

Power service

Activity service

Package service

Content service

Alarm service

Window service

Content providers

Telephony service

Battery service

Watchdog

After starting these services, Zygote starts working on its second task, which is where its name comes from.

> **NOTE:** Based on its dictionary definition, **zygote** is the initial cell formed. In single-celled organisms, the zygote divides to produce offspring.

As noted earlier, on Android, every application runs within its dedicated virtual machine instance. In addition, Android applications rely on a set of class and data objects that needs to be loaded into memory first for the application to perform its task. This introduces a large overhead when starting a new application. Despite this overhead, Android needs to keep the startup time as small as possible in order to provide a highly responsive user experience. By the use of *forking*, Zygote resolves this problem in a fast and efficient way.

In computing, forking is the operation to clone an existing process. The new process has an exact copy of all memory segments of the parent process, although both processes execute independently, as shown in Figure 1-4. Copy-on-write is an optimization strategy used in forking that delays copying the memory by allowing both processes to share the same memory segment until one of them tries to modify it.

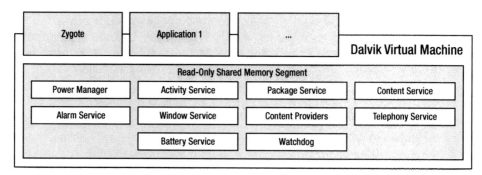

Figure 1-4. *Zygote and other applications sharing read-only components of the Android framework*

Since the Android runtime classes and data objects are immutable by the applications, this makes them ideal candidates for copy-on-write optimization during forking.

Zygote preloads the Android runtime objects and waits for requests to start new applications. When a new request arrives, instead of starting a new virtual machine instance, it simply forks. This allows the new application to start very quickly while keeping its memory footprint low.

Dalvik Virtual Machine

Java is a general-purpose, object-oriented programming language that is specifically designed for platform-independent application development with the goal of "write once, run anywhere." Java achieves this by compiling the application code into an intermediate platform-independent interpreted language called *bytecode*. During runtime, this bytecode is executed through another Java entity known as the Java Virtual Machine.

Virtual machines are native applications that run on the host computer and interpret the bytecode. In order to optimize the runtime of complex applications, most virtual machine implementations also support the just-in-time (JIT) feature, which allows on-the-fly translation from bytecode to native machine code. This allows long-running applications to execute much faster, since the interpretation of the bytecode is needed only at the beginning of the application execution.

One of the biggest challenges most mobile platforms face is the lack of applications. In order to resolve that problem from the very beginning, Android relies on the well-proven Java programming language, which already has a very large developer community, as well as applications, tools, and components that will facilitate application development.

Android also relies on a highly customized virtual machine implementation that is tuned for mobile needs. Dalvik virtual machine is Android's customized Java Virtual Machine for mobile platforms.

Dalvik virtual machine is very different from other Java Virtual Machine implementations. Most virtual machine implementations on the desktop platform are developed based on the stack-based virtual machine model. Dalvik virtual machine is based on the register-based virtual machine model due to the mobile needs. Register-based virtual machines require longer instructions to interpret; however, the actual number of instructions executed is very low compared to stack-based virtual machines. This makes register-based virtual machines a much better choice for mobile environments, where the computing power is a scarce resource.

Since Dalvik virtual machine requires a different type of bytecode to interpret, it does not support the standard Java class files, and it relies on its own format, which is known as Dalvik Executable (DEX). The Android software development platform comes with a set of tools to postprocess the compiled Java class files into DEX format.

DEX format is also a much more compact way to store compiled Java application code on the mobile platform. Standard Java applications are formed by multiple class files that are stored separately. DEX merges all class files into one big DEX file, as shown in Figure 1-5. This minimizes the footprint of the application code.

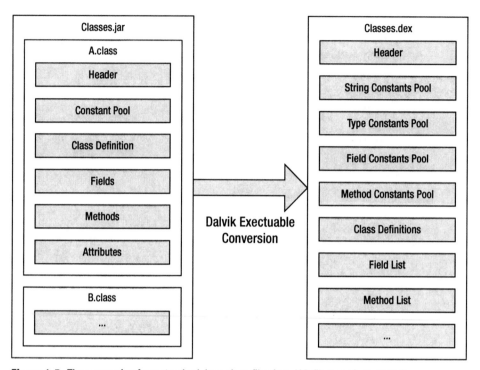

Figure 1-5. *The conversion from standard Java class files in a JAR file to a single DEX file*

The constant pools in the DEX format allow string, type, field, and method constants, and everything else in the code, to be stored in a single place, using indexes to those lists instead of the full names. This reduces the size of the class files almost 50%.

The Android platform runs each application in its own dedicated virtual machine instance as a sandbox. This puts high requirements on the platform, since multiple virtual machines are expected to run simultaneously within a limited CPU resource environment. Dalvik virtual machine is specifically tuned to work in this type of environment.

File System

The file system is a very crucial piece of the operating system. Especially on mobile platforms, file system plays an important role in satisfying the expectations of the operating system.

Mobile devices rely on flash-based storage chips. Android relies on Yet Another Flash File System (YAFFS2) as its primary file system. YAFFS2 is an open source file system implementation designed and written by Charles Manning for the Linux operating system. YAFFS2 is a high-performance file system specifically designed to work on NAND-based flash chips. It is a log-structured file system that takes data integrity as a high priority.

In addition to the file system, the structure of how the operating system files and components are organized plays an important role in Android as well. Mobile platforms are expected to be easily upgradable and also highly secure in order to protect user's confidential information. Android addresses this requirement by relying on organizing itself using multiple partitions. By keeping different parts of the operating system in different partitions, Android provides a high level of security and also makes the platform easily upgradable.

The partitions used depend on the device manufacturers. Here is a list of the most common ones:

- **/boot**: This partition includes the boot loader and the Linux kernel that is needed to boot the device. This partition is not writable by the user applications, since modifying the content of this partition may cause the device not to boot anymore.

- **/system**: This partition contains all the Android system files and applications that are preloaded on the device. During an upgrade, this partition is replaced by the latest version of the Android platform. This partition is not writable by user applications, although the Android Market application can make this partition writable temporarily in order to update the preloaded applications.

- **/recovery**: This partition keeps a recovery image, which is an alternative boot partition. It provides maintenance functionality in order to recover the system or to do other tasks, such as making system backups. This partition is also not writable from user applications.

- **/data**: This partition keeps the user's applications and also the user's data, such as the contacts, messages, and settings. When the device is factory reset, this partition is erased.

- **/cache**: This partition is used to store frequently accessed files. On most Android devices, **cache** is not a partition on the flash media, but rather a virtual partition stored in RAM. The content of this partition does not persist when the device reboots.

▨ **/sdcard**: This is a mount point, rather than a partition, on the internal storage. The SD card that is attached to the device is mounted under this name. This mount point is not always accessible to the applications, since it may be directly mounted on a host PC when the device is connected through the USB connection.

Although Android does not expect application developers to use these partitions directly, knowing their purpose can be very useful during Android application development.

Security

As with many other mobile platforms, the biggest requirement for Android, from the users' perspective, is the security and integrity of users' applications and data. Android is designed with security in mind.

The Android architecture provides security at multiple layers of the platform. This extensive security framework is also exposed to the developers through the Android runtime. Security-savvy developers can easily rely on these APIs in order to provide a high level of security for their application and the data it uses. Developers less familiar with the security are already protected by the default security settings.

Android provides a high level of security by using multiple security features from both the hardware and the software. Although it is designed to work on a variety of hardware platforms, Android still takes advantage of hardware-specific security capabilities such as the ARMv6 eXecute-Never feature.

The Android platform is built on the top of the Linux kernel. The Linux kernel itself has been used in many security-sensitive environments for many years. The Linux kernel provides Android several key security features, such as the following:

▨ A user-based permission model

▨ Process isolation

▨ Secure IPC mechanism

▨ Ability to remove unnecessary functionality from the kernel itself

The Linux kernel is designed for multiuser platforms. Although Android is a single-user environment, it still takes advantage of the user-based permission model. Android runs the applications within a virtual machine sandbox, and treats them as different users on the system. By simply relying on the user-based permission model, Android easily secures the system by preventing the applications from accessing other applications' data and memory.

On Android, services and hardware resources are also protected through the user-based permission model. Each of these resources has its own protection group. During application deployment, the application requests access to those resources. If the request is granted by the user, the application becomes a member of these resource groups. The application won't be allowed to access any additional resources if it is not a member of that resource's group.

In addition to the security features provided by the operating system, Android also enhances the Android platform binaries using ProPolice to protect them from stack buffer overflow attacks.

File system protection is also one of the new Android features available since Android 3.0. It allows Android to encrypt the entire storage media using the AES-128 algorithm. This prevents other people from accessing the user's data without knowing the key used.

Device administration is one of the other security features available since Android 2.2. It allows administrators to remotely enforce security policies and to erase the device remotely when the device is lost or stolen.

Services

The Android platform is not limited to only the features provided from the Linux kernel. The Android runtime comes with a lot of services for application developers. The following are the major services provided.

- **Accessibility service**: This service is provided through the `android.view.accessibility.AccessibilityManager` class. It is a system-level service that serves as an event dispatcher for accessibility events and provides a set of APIs to query the accessibility state of the system.

- **Account service**: This service is provided through the `android.accounts.AccountManager` class. It is a centralized registry of the user's online accounts. It allows applications to access online resources using the user's accounts after user approval.

- **Activity service**: This service is provided through the `android.app.ActivityManager` class. It allows the application to interact with the activities running in the system.

- **Alarm service**: This service is provided through the `android.app.AlarmManager` class. It allows applications to register with the Alarm service in order to schedule execution at some point in the future.

- **Audio service**: This service is provided through the `android.media.AudioManager` class. It allows applications to control the volume and the ringer mode.

- **Clipboard service**: This service is provided through the `android.content.ClipboardManager` class. It allows applications to place data in the system clipboard and retrieve it from the clipboard.

- **Connectivity service**: This service is provided through the `android.net.ConnectivityManager` class. It allows applications to query the state of the network connectivity. It also generates events when the network connectivity changes.

- **Device Policy service**: This service is provided through the `android.app.admin.DevicePolicyManager` class. The device administration API provides device administration features at the system level. It allows development of security-aware applications that are useful in enterprise settings.

- **Download service**: This service is provided through the `android.app.DownloadManager` class. It handles long-running HTTP downloads. Applications may request a URI to be downloaded to a particular destination file using this service. The Download service takes care of the HTTP interactions and retrying downloads after failures, connectivity changes, and system reboots.

- **Drop Box service**: This service is provided through the `android.os.DropBoxManager` class. It provides system-wide, data-oriented log storage. It collects data from application crashes, kernel logs, and other sources. The data does not get sent anywhere directly, but debugging tools may scan and upload entries for processing.

- **Input Method service**: This service is provided through the `android.view.inputmethod.InputMethodManager` class. It allows applications to interact with the input method framework (IMF) through the provided methods.

- **Notification service**: This service is provided through the `android.app.NotificationManager` class. It allows applications to notify the user regarding events that happen. The services running in the background communicate with the user only through this service.

- **Location service**: This service is provided through the `android.location.LocationManager` class. It allows applications to obtain periodic updates of the device's current location.

- **Near Field Communication service**: This service is provided through the `android.nfc.NfcManager` class. It allows applications to use the near field communication (NFC) features of the device.

- **Package service**: This service is provided through the `android.content.pm.PackageManager` class. It allows applications to retrieve information related to application packages that are currently installed on the system.

- **Power service**: This service is provided through the `android.os.PowerManager` class. It allows applications to control the power state of the device. It allows applications to hold wakelocks to prevent the device from going into sleep mode while performing a task.

- **Sensor service**: This service is provided through the `android.hardware.SensorManager` class. It allows applications to access the device's sensors.

- **Telephony service**: This service is provided through the `android.telephony.TelephonyManager` class. It allows applications to interact with the telephony functionality of the mobile device. It also generates events for applications to watch telephony state changes.

- **UI Mode service**: This service is provided through the `android.app.UiModeManager` class. It allows applications to control the user interface (UI) modes of the device such as disabling the car mode.

- **USB service**: This service is provided through the `android.hardware.usb.UsbManager` class. It allows applications to query the state of the USB and to communicate with devices through USB devices.

- **Vibrator service**: This service is provided through the `android.os.Vibrator` class. It allows applications to control the vibrator on the device.

- **Wallpaper service**: This service is provided through the `android.service.wallpaper.WallpaperService` class. It allows applications to show live wallpapers in the background.

- **Wi-Fi Peer-to-Peer service**: This service is provided through the `android.net.wifi.p2p.WifiP2pManager` class. It allows applications to discover available peers and establish peer-to-peer connections through the Wi-Fi network.

- **Wi-Fi service**: This service is provided through the `android.net.wifi.WifiManager` class. It allows applications to manage Wi-Fi connectivity. Applications can list and update the configured networks, access the results of access point scans, and establish and tear down connections.

Android Deployment and Distribution

Because the Android platform is a free platform, it does not charge any licensing, royalty, membership, or certification fees to develop and distribute applications on the platform.

The Android platform lets application developers decide how to distribute and monetize their applications. Application developers can distribute their applications as freeware, shareware, advertisement sponsored, or paid.

The Android platform comes with a default marketplace, Google Play, previously known as the Android Market, which is an online store developed by Google for Android devices. Unlike the Android platform, the Android Market application is not open source. It is available only for devices that comply with Google's compatibility requirements. The client portion comes preloaded on Android devices under the name Market. Users can use this application to search and download Android applications. The Market application also keeps the installed Android applications up to date by informing the user of software updates.

Application developers use the server part of the Android Market. Through the web-based interface, application developers can upload their applications for publication.

The Android Market runs a set of tests on the distributed applications, but it does not take any responsibility for the applications downloaded from the Android Market. During installation, the Android Market application displays a list permissions requested by the application and gets the user's implicit permission before proceeding with installation.

Although most Android devices come with Google's Android Market application preloaded, other application distribution channels are supported by the Android platform. GetJar and Amazon Appstore are two alternatives for Android application distribution.

Summary

We started this chapter with a brief summary of Android's history and the existing Android versions. We then explored the core of Android platform and the Linux kernel, and briefly reviewed the Android-specific changes and additions to the Linux kernel to deliver a superior mobile platform.

We explained the reasons behind Android's choice of the Java technology as a foundation for Android applications, and the unique features provided through Dalvik virtual machine to optimize the Java technology for mobile computing. We explored Zygote, the application process that enables Android applications to have quick startup times and small memory footprints. We also studied the Android multilayer security framework. We then presented a brief overview of the Android framework services that allow applications to interact with the Android platform. Finally, we discussed Android development and distribution.

In the next chapter, we will focus on the Android application architecture.

Chapter **2**

Application Architecture

Understanding the architecture of an Android application is key for solid application development. In this chapter, we will start exploring the Android application architecture.

First, we will briefly review the fundamental components that are provided by the Android framework, such as activities, services, broadcast receivers, content providers, and the user interface components. Then we will examine both the activity and service life cycles in great detail. Next, we will go through the procedure to package an Android application for deployment. Finally, we will study the Android manifest file, and its role and importance in Android application development.

Android Components

The main difference between Android and other mobile platforms is the definition of an application.

Other mobile platforms define an application as a stand-alone program that runs within its own sandbox, with limited interaction with the surrounding platform. Mobile platforms provide APIs to allow applications to use the platform services and data stores, such as an address book, to offer a rich user experience. However, this communication is always one-directional, meaning applications may use platform services, but the platform and other applications cannot access services provided in another application.

On Android, applications are like modules. Each application is formed by a set of components, and these components can be accessed by both the platform and other applications. Each new application on Android expands the platform and opens up more opportunities for other application developers by providing a new set of components. Application developers do not need to decide on a set of APIs or a contract in order to achieve interoperability between their applications.

Four main components are defined by the Android framework: activity, service, broadcast receiver, and content provider. Each application does not need to use all of these components, but using them properly allows the application to fully blend into the platform.

Activities and Intents

The *activity* is the most important component of an application. It corresponds to a display screen. Users can interact with Android applications only through the activities. An application may be formed by one or more activities. Each activity allows the user to do a specific task. In order to be modular, it is expected that each activity does a single task.

Users initiate a new activity by its intention to do a certain task. These intentions are captured in Android framework as *intents*. The intent is an abstract description of an operation to be performed. It provides a late runtime binding between different components using a passive data structure.

Android keeps a mapping from intents to activities, and initiates the correct activity based on a given intent. For certain intents, there may be more than one activity that can do the task. In such cases, Android presents the user with a list of these activities to choose from.

A complex task may involve more than one activity. In that case, the activities are kept in an activity stack as the user moves from one activity to the other.

To better understand the concept of an activity, let's imagine a simple use case where the user is sending an e-mail message:

1. The user presses the Compose E-Mail button on the screen.

2. The code captures the user's intention to compose an e-mail message into an Intent object, and gives this intent to the Android framework.

3. Android goes through its registry and pulls the activity that can satisfy this intent, and adds the new activity to the top of the activity stack. Upon starting, the activity takes up the entire screen.

4. The user presses the Select Recipient button. The user's intention gets captures in a new Intent object, and the Android framework goes through its registry again and starts the Contact List activity.

5. The user chooses one or more recipients from the list and selects the Done button. The activity returns the user's selection to the Android framework as a result, and removes itself from the activity stack by making the previous activity visible again.

6. Upon receiving the result from the Android framework, the Compose E-Mail activity populates the user interface accordingly with the list of selected recipients.

7. After completing the message, the user clicks the Send button, and the e-mail gets sent.

8. The Compose E-Mail activity removes itself from the activity stack, and the user is returned to the screen where he or she started.

An application is not limited to using just its own activities. During a task flow, the application can make use of other activities that are provided by either the platform or other applications. For example, to select a contact from the user's address book, the application can use the activity that is already provided by the platform instead of writing a new one. This approach promotes reuse of activities and also provides consistency throughout the platform.

Activities are designed for interacting with the user. When they are no longer visible to the user, Android may terminate them at any time in order to free memory resources. For that reason, activities are not good for performing tasks that are expected to take a long time to complete, such as downloading files from the Internet. The Android framework provides the service component for running these types of tasks.

Services

Services run in the background. Services do not provide a user interface, and they cannot directly interact with the user. Android does not limit their lifetime, and it allows them to continue running in the background as long as the system has enough resources to perform the foreground tasks. Applications can provide activities to interact with the user in order to control the service.

For example, suppose that we are developing a music player application. We would like to let the user select a music file and listen to it while continuing to use the device. An initial activity can interact with the user to select the song; however, the activity cannot play the song directly, since the activity's lifetime is limited by its visibility. We will need to have a service that will run in the background, so that the application can continue playing the songs while the user is doing other tasks with the device. At any given time, the user can start an activity to control the service, since the service itself cannot interact directly with the user.

As with activities, an application is not limited to its own services. Applications can also use services that are provided either by the platform or by other applications. For example, to receive Global Positioning System (GPS) coordinates continuously, the application may start the GPS service that is provided by the platform.

Services are also started through intents. By design, only a single instance of a service can run at any given time. The Android framework starts the service when the first request arrives, and then delivers the subsequent requests to the already running instance.

Sometimes services may need the user's attention. Notifications are used by the services to inform the user about the current status of the service. For example, in our music player application, when the new song starts playing, a notification with the name of the song can be displayed on the notifications bar to inform the user.

Broadcast Receivers

Applications not only interact with the user, but they also interact with the platform and other applications by generating and consuming events. On Android, these events are also delivered in the form of intents.

In order to receive certain types of events, the application may register for a set of intents by providing a *broadcast receiver*. When a matching event is generated in the system, Android delivers the event to that broadcast receiver.

For example, suppose that we would like to have our application start automatically when the phone is turned on. In our application, we specify that the application is interested in receiving the device startup event. When the device is starting, it broadcasts the event. Only the interested applications receive this event through their broadcast receiver.

Content Providers

Content providers allow Android applications to exchange data with the platform and with other applications. Unlike the other components, content providers do not rely on intents. Instead, content providers uses a standard interface in the form of a content URIs, and provide access to the data as one or more tables that are similar to tables found in a relational database. The structure of these tables is communicated to the external applications through the `Contract` classes. `Contract` classes are not part of the content provider framework. Content provider developers are expected to define and make the `Contract` classes available to external applications.

When an application issues a content provider query, Android goes through a registry to match the given URI with the appropriate content provider. The Android framework checks to make sure that the application has the necessary privileges, and sends the request to the corresponding content provider. The response goes back to the requesting application in the form of a cursor. The application then retrieves and manipulates the data through the interface provided by the cursor.

Views, Widgets, Layouts, and Menus

View objects are the basic units of the user interface on the Android platform. A *view object* is a data structure whose properties store the layout parameters and the content of a rectangular region on the screen. It provides the methods necessary to handle its drawing and layout measurement.

A *widget* is a view object that allows the application to interact with the user. The Android runtime provides a rich set of widgets to enable application developers to easily develop comprehensive user interfaces. Android application developers are not limited to using the widgets provided by the Android runtime. By deriving new view objects, developers can create new widgets from scratch or by basing them on an existing widget. A widget is provided through the base class `android.view.View`.

A *layout* is used to express view hierarchy and how each view component should be positioned on the display. Since the size, resolution, and orientation of Android devices vary greatly, the layout allows application developers to dynamically position the view components based on the device's specifications. The Android runtime provides a rich set of layout components that allow views to be positioned based on a different set of constraints. A layout is provided through the base class `android.view.ViewGroup`. The following are some of the common layout objects:

- *Frame layout:* This is the simplest type of layout object. It is provided through the `android.widget.FrameLayout` class. It is a basic layout that can hold only one view object that will occupy the entire space that is covered by the frame view.

- *Linear layout:* This layout allows assigning weights to view objects and positioning them accordingly. It is provided through the `android.widget.LinearLayout` class. It can position view objects either vertically or horizontally based on its configuration. All view objects are stuck following each other. Margins can be introduced using the configuration parameters. Also, a single view object can be nominated to fill the entire empty display area.

- *Table layout:* This layout allows the view objects to be positioned in a table-like format in rows and columns. It is provided through the `android.widget.TableLayout` class. Although it follows a table format, it does not provide borders around the cells. Also cells cannot span columns.

- *Relative layout:* This layout allows view objects to be relatively positioned on the display. It is provided through the `android.widget.RelativeLayout` class. It is one of the most advanced layout components.

In addition to widgets and layouts, application menus are also very important for user interface development. An application menu provides a reliable interface for application functions and settings.

Menus are revealed using the hard and soft menu buttons on Android devices. Menus are slowly losing their importance and being replaced by action bars on the later versions of the Android platform. Beginning with Android 3.0, host devices are no longer required to provide a hard menu button.

Android user interfaces are formed by combining views, widgets, layouts, and menus as appropriate for the application's functionality. The Android framework allows applications to define their user interfaces dynamically as a part of the application code, or they can rely on an XML-based user interface definition language that is specific to the Android platform. This XML-based language allows view code to be designed and managed outside the actual application logic. In addition, application developers can design different user interfaces for both portrait and landscape display without changing the application logic.

Android applications can control and populate the view objects from the application code. Due to the user interface architecture of the Android platform, the user interface is expected to be modified only from the main UI thread. Modifying the user interface from an application thread is not supported and can cause problems during the application runtime. The Android runtime provides an enhanced message queue system that allows application developers to schedule user interface-related tasks through the main UI thread.

Although Android applications can manipulate the view objects, applications with extensive user interface and data model components may be harder to develop due to the complexity of keeping the user interface aligned with the data model. In order to resolve that problem, the Android runtime provides adapters to bind data to views. This allows user interface components to automatically reflect any changes to the data model. The view objects `android.widget.Gallery`, `android.widget.ListView`, and `android.widget.Spinner` are good examples of the use of adapters for data binding to view objects on the Android platform.

Resources

Android architecture encourages users to externalize the application resources from the application source code as much as possible. By externalizing resources, Android applications can use different sets of both graphics and text resources based on the device configurations as well as the current locale. The following resources are currently supported by the Android platform:

- Animation resources
- Color resources
- Drawable resources
- Layout resources
- Menu resources
- String resources
- Style resources
- Value resources

Application resources are placed in the res directory in applications. There are different subdirectories to group different resources.

During compile time, Android generates a resource class to allow the application to refer to these resources in the code.

Data Storage

The Android platform provides multiple ways to save persistent application data. The following are some of the alternatives:

- *Shared preferences:* This approach allows applications to store data as key/value pairs. The Android framework comes with utility functions to allow developers to maintain shared preferences easily. Shared preferences support only primitive data types, and applications should do any marshaling needed to convert the data into primitive types. The Android platform also guarantees that the shared preferences will be saved, even if the application is killed.

- *Internal and external storage:* This approach allows application developers to store any type of data as plain files on the platform. The Android framework provides a set of utility functions to allow application developers to easily do these file operations without knowing the actual location of these files.

- *SQLite databases:* Using a SQLite database allows application developers to store and retrieve structured data easily. SQLite provides a relational database within the application's process space. Although SQLite functionality is provided through native libraries, the Android framework includes a set of utility functions and classes to allow application developers to easily interact with the SQLite database.

Android Life Cycles

The Android application life cycle is much more complicated than the life cycle of desktop applications. The life cycle of desktop applications is directly controlled by the user. Users can choose to start and terminate an application at any given time. However, on Android, the platform manages the application's life cycle in order to efficiently use the scarce system resources.

Activity Life Cycle

The activity life cycle is the group of states that an activity goes through from the time it is first created until it is destroyed.

The Android framework provides a set of life cycle methods that allow the application to make the appropriate adjustments when the activity life cycle changes. For example, if the activity is no longer visible to the user, there is no reason for it to consume CPU cycles for showing animations on the screen. In that case, the application is expected to stop doing any CPU-extensive operations in order to let the foreground application get enough system resources to provide a smooth user experience.

Seven life cycle methods are defined in the android.app.Activity class:

```
public class Activity {
    protected void onCreate(Bundle savedInstanceState);
    protected void onStart();
    protected void onRestart();
    protected void onResume();
    protected void onPause();
    protected void onStop();
    protected void onDestroy();
}
```

Figure 2-1 illustrates the activity life cycle state machine with these methods.

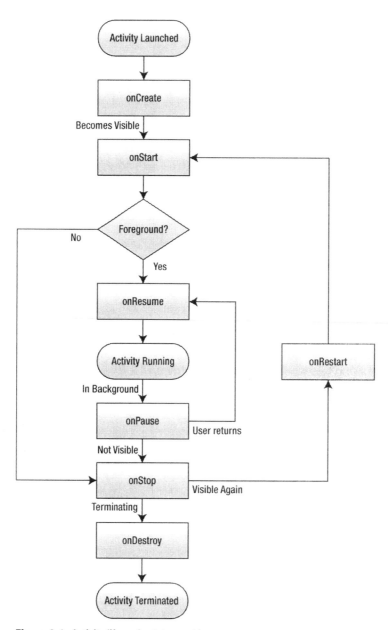

Figure 2-1. *Activity life cycle state machine*

These activity life cycle methods work as follows:

- onCreate: This method is called when the activity is created. It initializes the activity and creates the views. This method also takes a Bundle object that contains the frozen state from the activity's previous run. The activity uses this bundle to restore its previous state. This method call is always followed by onStart.

- onStart: This method is called when the activity becomes visible. It is followed by a call to onResume if the activity comes to the foreground. It is followed by onStop if the activity becomes hidden.

- onRestart: This method is called when the activity is being redisplayed to the user. It is followed by onStart.

- onResume: This method is called each time the activity comes to the foreground to interact with the user.

- onPause: This method is called when the activity is going into the background, but has not been terminated yet. This callback is mostly used to save any persistent state. It is also a good place to stop any CPU-extensive operations and release any system resources, such as the camera. When the application is in the paused state, the system may decide to terminate the application at any time if it needs to reclaim resources for the foreground application. For that reason, the application is expected to save its current state during this call, since it may not have a second chance. Depending on the user's interaction with the foreground application, this call is followed by either onResume or onStop.

- onStop: This method is called when the activity is no longer visible to the user. It is followed by a call to onRestart if the activity is coming to the foreground or with a call to onDestroy if the activity is terminating.

- onDestroy: This method is called when the activity is being destroyed. This may be because the activity is finishing or because the system needs to free resources. The application is expected to release its resources at this time.

> **NOTE:** When overriding these life cycle methods, do not forget to call up to the superclass. Android itself also needs to closely monitor these life cycle events in order to function properly.

The activity should finish up by saving its state within the onPause method, although the onStop and onDestroy methods follow it. The Android platform guarantees that the application process will not be terminated while the application is performing any work in the onPause method; the application may be terminated while executing the onStop or onDestroy method. However, you should be very careful to not spend too much time in the onPause method, since both the Android platform and the user are waiting for this method to complete before bringing the next activity into the foreground. Spending too much time in the onPause method will make the system look irresponsive to user's requests.

Service Life Cycle

The service life cycle is similar to the activity life cycle but with a few big differences. Because services do not interact with the user directly, their life cycle does not depend on the user's actions, as is the case with activities. Since visibility is not a concern for services, the life cycle methods onPause, onResume, and onStop do not apply to them.

Three life cycle methods are defined in the android.app.Service class:

```
public abstract class Service {
    public void onCreate();
    public int onStartCommand(Intent intent, int flags, int startId);
    public void onDestroy();
}
```

Figure 2-2 illustrates the service life cycle state machine with these methods.

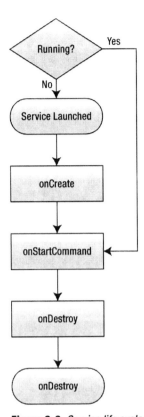

Figure 2-2. *Service life cycle state machine*

These service life cycle methods work as follows:

- onCreate: This method is called when the Context.startService(Intent) method is used by the application and the service was not running already. Since the services are singleton by design, the service gets only one onCreate call during its lifetime.

- onStartCommand: This method is called each time the Context.startService(Intent) method is used by the application. A service may end up processing multiple requests, so it is possible for the service to receive multiple onStartCommand calls during its lifetime. If the service is already busy processing the previous request, it is expected that the service will queue this new request.

> **CAUTION:** When more resources are needed for the foreground application, the Android platform may decide to destroy a running service, and then later restart it when the resource condition improves. If your service needs to store persistent data in order to continue functioning properly after the restart, it is best to store such data during an onStartCommand call.

- onDestroy: This method is called when the service is about to be destroyed by the Android platform.

Packaging

The Android Package File (APK) file format is used to package and distribute Android applications. APK files are actually archive files in ZIP file format. They partially follow the JAR file format, except for the way that the application class files are packaged. APK files contain the following:

- META-INF/MANIFEST.MF: This is the JAR manifest file for the package file itself.

- META-INF/CERT.SF: This contains SHA1 hashes for the files that are included in the package file. The file is signed by the application developer's certificate.

- META-INF/CERT.RSA: This is the public key of the certificate that is used to sign the CERT.SF file.

- AndroidManifest.xml: This is the application's manifest file. It is one of the most important components of Android applications, and we will briefly explore it in the next section.

- classes.dex: This is the application class files in DEX format.

- assets: This is special in that its contents are not compressed while the APK file is generated. This allows the Android platform to provide a file descriptor directly to the APK file during runtime, so the application can easily access the resources without extracting them to the device. Android developers are expected to keep large resource files in the assets directory in order to minimize the application's footprint on the installed device.

- `res`: This directory contains the application resources.

- `resources.arsc`: This contains the view definitions and the string resources.

APK files are signed with a certificate whose private key is held by the application developer. The certificate identifies the author of the application, as well as the integrity of the files contained in the APK file. Compared to many other mobile platforms, Android does not require these certificates to be signed by a certificate authority. Android developers can generate and use self-signed certificates to sign their applications.

The Android platform uses the certificates during software updates in order to make sure that the update is coming from the same author as the one who created the application that is already installed on the system. In addition to the updates, the Android platform also relies on the certificates while granting signature-level permissions to the applications during installation.

Android Manifest

Android applications are described to the system through a manifest file called `AndroidManifest.xml`. All Android applications are expected to have this file in their root directory. The Android manifest file presents essential information about the application to the system in order to let the Android platform correctly run the application's code and to grant the necessary privileges during installation.

The Android manifest file provides the following information to the system:

- It includes the name, package name, and the version number of the application.

- It indicates the minimum version of the API required for running the application.

- It describes the application's components (activities, services, broadcast receivers, and content providers) and their capabilities in terms of the intents that they can handle.

- It declares which permissions are required in order to access protected parts of the Android runtime and also interact with other applications running on the system.

It declares the permissions that other applications are required to have in order to interact with this application's components.

It lists the libraries that the application must be linked against during runtime in order to operate.

The Android manifest file is an XML-formatted plain text file. Here is an example of an AndroidManifest.xml file:

```xml
<?xml version="1.0" encoding="utf-8"?>
<manifest xmlns:android="http://schemas.android.cm/apk/res/android"
    package="com.apress.example"
    android:versionCode="1"
    android:versionName="1.0.0">

    <application android:icon="@drawable/icon"
        android:label="@string/app_name">

        <activity android:name=".MyActivity"
            android:label="@string/my_activity">

            <intent-filter>
                <action
                    android:name="android.intent.action.MAIN" />

                <category
                        android:name="android.intent.category.LAUNCHER" />
            </intent-filter>
        </activity>

        <activity android:name=".MyPrivateActivity">
        </activity>
    </application>

    <uses-permission
        android:name="android.permission.CAMERA" />

    <uses-feature
        android:name="android.hardware.camera" />

    <uses-sdk
        android:minSdkVersion="5"
        android:targetSdkVersion="9" />
</manifest>
```

Summary

This chapter introduced the Android application architecture by briefly reviewing the most fundamental Android components, including activities, services, broadcast receivers, content providers, and other user interface components. We tried to shed light on one of the most confusing concepts of Android development: the activity and service life cycles. Then we explored the procedure to package Android applications and took a closer look at Android manifest files. The next chapters show examples of these concepts in action.

## Chapter 3

Eclipse Primer

Eclipse is the integrated development environment that we will be using throughout our journey into Android development. Eclipse is much more than a simple code editor. It is a highly powerful and complex platform for tools. From that perspective, this chapter is a very important one, as we will establish the framework for the following chapters by setting up the proper working environment for Eclipse.

This chapter will provide an introduction to Eclipse, emphasizing the most frequently used Eclipse components. Becoming familiar with Eclipse is the key to a smooth Android development experience.

Eclipse History

In 1995, Sun Microsystems released the first public implementation of the Java programming language to the public. Java's arrival divided the developer community in two groups: one centered on Microsoft technologies and tools, and the other centered on the Java platform.

Visual Studio was Microsoft's tool platform that provided access to all Microsoft technologies in an integrated fashion. There were numerous successful Java development tools in the market, but they were not as closely integrated as Microsoft technologies.

In the late 1990s, IBM was a major player in Java. IBM's main goal at the time was to bring developers closer to Java middleware. IBM knew that the ideal development environment must consist of a heterogeneous combination of tools from IBM, third parties, and customers' internal tools. IBM's Object Technology International (OTI) lab, the folks behind the VisualAge products family, had extensive experience building integrated development environments. As the first step, VisualAge for Java Micro Edition was developed as a reimplementation of the integrated development environment purely using the Java programming language. Later, the VisualAge for Java Micro Edition code was used as the basis for the Eclipse platform.

IBM was already aware that simply having IBM products on this new platform was not enough to achieve broad adoption by the developer community. Having integrated third-party tools was the key to the success of the Eclipse platform. In 2001, IBM decided to adopt the open source licensing and operating model for the Eclipse platform. IBM, along with eight other organizations, established the Eclipse consortium. The main operating principal for the consortium was to drive the marketing and relations for the Eclipse platform, while leaving the control of the Eclipse source code to the open source community.

In 2003, the Eclipse platform, with its quickly growing set of open source and commercial extensions, was becoming popular with developers. In 2004, Eclipse Foundation, a nonprofit organization with its own professional and independent staff, took over the full control of the Eclipse platform. Eclipse is now the leading Java development environment. Due to its unique and extensible architecture, it also is being used as a development environment for many other programming languages.

Eclipse Architecture

As an Android developer, you will not need to interact with the internals of the Eclipse platform. However, knowing its architecture will make it much easier for you to conceptualize and understand how Eclipse works in general.

The Eclipse platform is primarily designed for building integrated development environments. It is a highly extensible platform, rather than a custom tool for a specific set of tasks.

The Eclipse platform defines the mechanisms and the rules, and allows tools to be built on the top of them by providing a set of well-defined APIs. The Eclipse platform is structured around the concept of plug-ins, as illustrated in Figure 3-1.

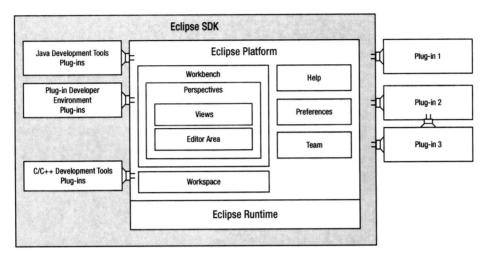

Figure 3-1. *Eclipse platform architectural overview*

Plug-ins are the smallest unit of the Eclipse platform. They are structured bundles of code that contribute a set of functionality to the platform. Plug-ins can be developed, distributed, and deployed individually. The Eclipse platform allows the plug-ins to be extensible as well. Plug-ins can provide a set of extension points, through a well-defined API, for other plug-ins to expand their functionalities.

Each subsystem in the Eclipse platform is based on a set of plug-ins. For example, the Java Development Tools for Eclipse is a set of plug-ins that provide Java development functionality to the platform in an integrated fashion. Java Development Tools plug-ins are also extensible.

In this book, we are going to use Android Development Tools plug-ins. These expand the existing Java Development Tools in order to provide Android-specific development tools and functionality.

Eclipse platform's core, also known as the Eclipse runtime, is responsible for providing the infrastructure where the plug-ins can work and interoperate. The Eclipse runtime also provides any utility servers that will make development of new plug-ins easier for developers. At the time of writing, the latest version is Eclipse Indigo 3.7.2.

In the following sections, we will set up the proper working environment for Eclipse.

Installing the Java Development Kit

Eclipse is a Java-based application, and it requires a Java Virtual Machine in order to run. You will need to install the Java Development Kit (JDK), and not just the Java Runtime Edition (JRE), prior to installing Eclipse. Multiple JDK flavors are supported by Eclipse, such as the IBM JDK, OpenJDK, and Oracle JDK (formerly known as Sun JDK). In this section, we will assume that you are installing the Oracle JDK, the original JDK implementation, which supports a broader range of platforms.

The version of the JDK needs to be compatible with the Dalvik virtual machine as well, since we will be using Eclipse for Android development. At the time of writing, the Dalvik virtual machine supports Java compiler compliance levels 1.5 and 1.6. Although the newer versions of the JDK can be configured to work at those compliance levels, it is much easier to start with the corresponding JDK version, JDK 6, instead.

Using your favorite web browser, navigate to http://www.oracle.com/technetwork/java/javase/downloads/index.html. As shown in Figure 3-2, you will be presented with a list of download options.

Figure 3-2. *Java download page on Oracle's web site*

Since we would like to download JDK 6 rather than the latest version of the JDK, scroll down to the Java SE 6 section on the download page. At the time of writing, the latest version of JDK 6 is Update 31. Click the Download button next to JDK 6 to proceed.

Currently, the Oracle JDK does not provide an installation package for the Mac OS X platform, since the installer is distributed through Apple's software updates. For all other major platforms, Oracle JDK installers are listed on this page, as shown in Figure 3-3. The installation procedure for each operating system varies. In order to make the installation experience as smooth as possible, we will be covering the three major operating systems—Windows, Mac OS X, and Linux—in the following sections.

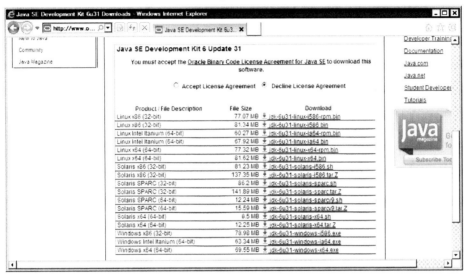

Figure 3-3. *List of Oracle JDK installation packages for major operating systems*

Installing the JDK on Windows

The Oracle JDK comes as an executable installer for the Microsoft Windows operating system. The installation wizard will guide you through the process of installing the JDK on your machine, as shown in Figure 3-4.

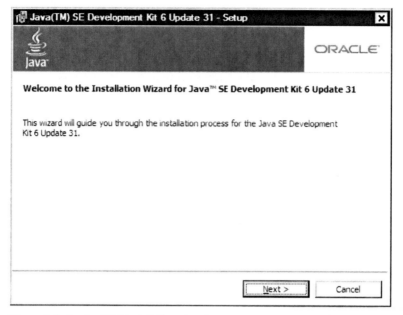

Figure 3-4. *Oracle JDK 6 installation wizard*

The installation wizard will first install the JDK, and then the JRE. During the installation process, the wizard will ask for the destination directories, as well as the components to be installed. You can continue with the default values here. Make a note of the installation directory for the JDK part.

The installation wizard will automatically make the necessary system changes. The JDK will be ready to use upon completion of the installation process.

On Windows, the installation wizard does not automatically add the Java binary directory into the system Path variable, so you'll need to do this. Go to the Control Panel and choose System (or from the Start menu, select Run, and execute sysdm.cpl) to open the System Properties dialog. Switch to Advanced tab, and click the Environment Variables button, as shown in Figure 3-5.

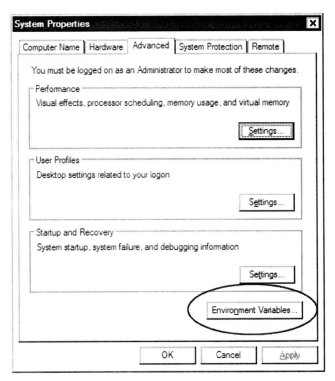

Figure 3-5. *Advanced tab of the System Properties dialog*

As shown in Figure 3-6, the Environment Variables dialog is separated into two parts: the top one is for the user, and the bottom one is for the system.

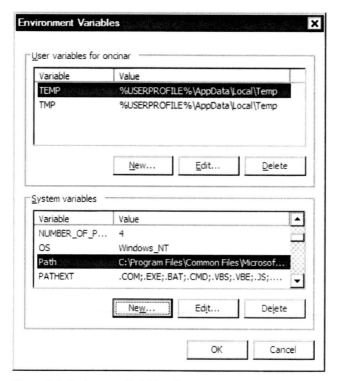

Figure 3-6. *Environment Variables dialog*

In the System variables pane, click the New button to define a new environment variable. Set the variable name to JAVA_HOME, and set the variable value to the JDK installation directory, as shown in Figure 3-7. Click the OK button to save the variable.

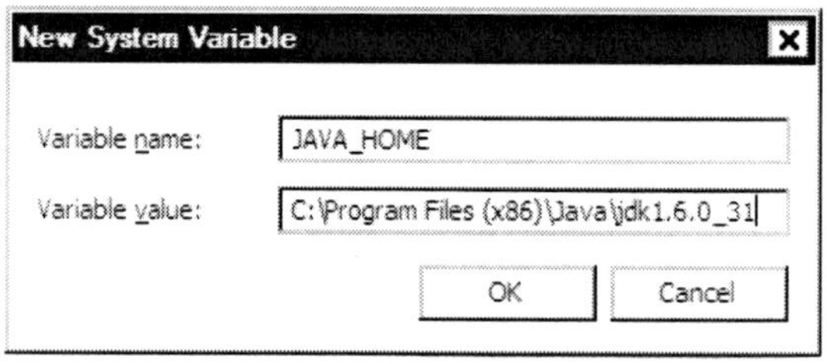

Figure 3-7. *Setting the JAVA_HOME system environment variable*

In the list of system variables, double-click the Path variable, and append ;%JAVA_HOME%\bin to the variable value, as shown in Figure 3-8.

Figure 3-8. *Setting the Path system environment variable*

Now the JDK is easily reachable from the command prompt. In order to validate the installation, open a command prompt window by choosing **Start ▸ Accessories ▸ Command Prompt**. Using the command prompt, execute `javac -version`. If the installation was successful, you'll see the JDK version number, as shown in Figure 3-9.

Figure 3-9. *Windows command prompt showing the JDK version*

Installing the JDK on Mac OS X

The Apple Mac OS X operating system ships with the JDK already installed. It is based on the Oracle JDK but configured by Apple for better integration with Mac OS X. New versions of the JDK are available through the Software Update window, as shown in Figure 3-10. Make sure that JDK 6 or later is installed on the host machine.

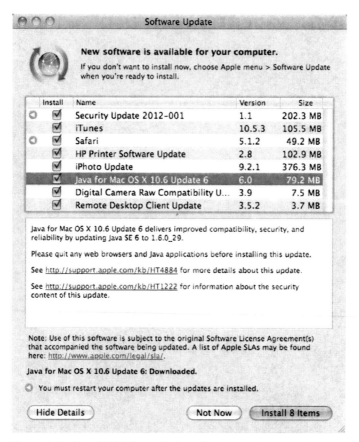

Figure 3-10. *Mac OS X Software Update window showing the JDK*

Installing the JDK on Linux

The JDK installation procedure varies based on the Linux distribution. Due to the licensing terms of the Oracle JDK, it is not included in any Linux distribution. Certain distributions come with a stub application, which allows you to install the Oracle JDK without going through the web download process. As shown in Figure 3-3 earlier in the chapter, Oracle's web site provides two types of installation packages for Linux systems:

▓ The installation package with a name ending with -rpm.bin contains a set of installable packages in Red Hat Package Manager (RPM) format. If you are using a Linux distribution, such as Red Hat Enterprise Linux, Fedora, CentOS, SUSE, or openSUSE, you can download this installation package.

▓ The installation package with a name ending with .bin contains a self-extracting ZIP archive file. This installation package works on any Linux distribution, although it will require some manual system configuration after the installation.

In this section, we will assume that you are running a Linux distribution with RPM support.

After downloading the RPM-formatted installation package, open a terminal window. As shown in Figure 3-11, first invoke chmod +x jdk-6u31-linux-i586-rpm.bin to enable the execution bit on the installer. To start the installation, invoke sudo ./jdk-6u31-linux-i586-rpm.bin on the command line. Depending on the version of JDK, replace jdk-6u31-linux-i586-rpm.bin with the appropriate file name.

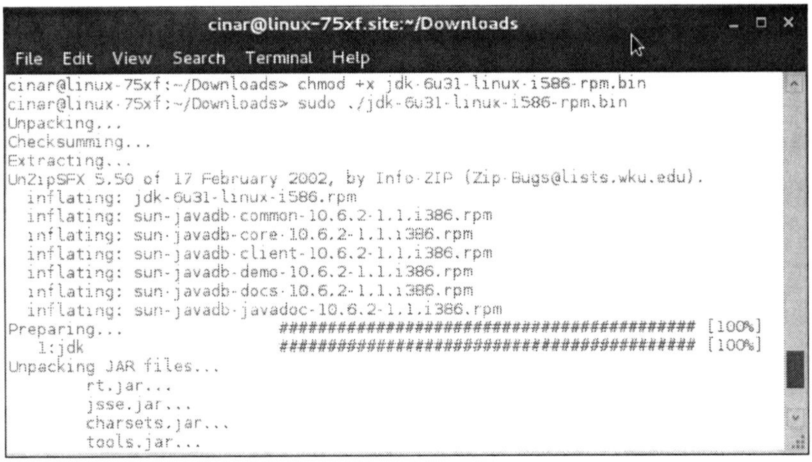

Figure 3-11. *Installing the Oracle JDK on Linux*

NOTE: On the Linux operating system, installing a software package requires super-user (root) permissions. The sudo command will prompt for a password to grant super-user permissions prior to starting rpm.

Installing Eclipse

Installing Eclipse is a fairly straightforward process, although the installation procedure for different operating systems varies. In this section, we will again cover the three major operating systems: Windows, Mac OS X, and Linux.

Using your favorite web browser, navigate to the Eclipse web site, `http://www.eclipse.org`, as shown in Figure 3-12 (the site may look different by the time you are reading this). Throughout this book, we will be using the latest version of Eclipse. At the time of writing, the latest version is Eclipse Indigo 3.7.1.

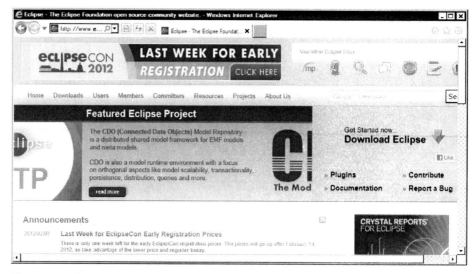

Figure 3-12. *The Eclipse web site*

Follow the link for the download page. As shown in Figure 3-13, you will be presented with a long list of downloadable Eclipse flavors for the operating system of your choice (in this case, Windows). From this list, Eclipse Classic is the most basic Eclipse package that you can download. It contains only the Eclipse platform and the Java Development Tools (JDT). You can certainly start from this package and later install other plug-ins of your choice.

Figure 3-13. *Eclipse download page*

Other Eclipse packages in this list simply contain a set of frequently used plug-ins prepackaged with the Eclipse platform for major programming languages. You can find a detailed comparison of these packages at http://www.eclipse.org/downloads/compare.php.

Installing Eclipse on Windows

The Eclipse installation package for Microsoft Windows comes as a ZIP archive file. Simply right-click the file and choose **Extract All…** from the context menu.

As shown in Figure 3-14, Windows will prompt for the destination directory to extract the files. In this section, we will assume that the destination directory is C:\, the root of the C drive.

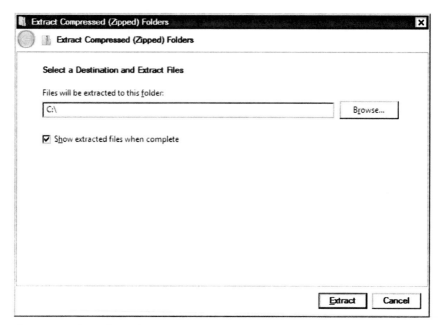

Figure 3-14. *Extracting the Eclipse ZIP package to its destination*

When the process completes, Eclipse will be installed in the C:\eclipse directory, as shown in Figure 3-15. You may now consider making a shortcut to the Eclipse application.

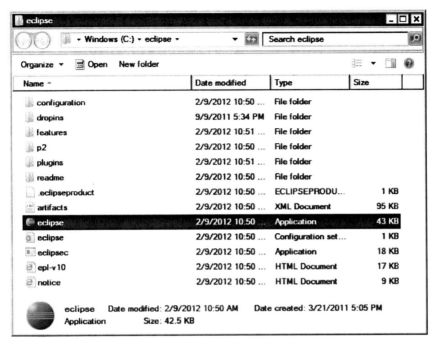

Figure 3-15. *Eclipse files after installation*

Installing Eclipse on Mac OS X

The Eclipse installation package for Mac OS X comes as a GZIP compressed TAR file. When the download completes, Eclipse will show up in your Downloads directory. Depending on the version of the operating system, you may need to double-click to extract the archive file, if it is not already extracted.

You can drag-and-drop Eclipse into your Applications directory from the Downloads directory, as shown in Figure 3-16.

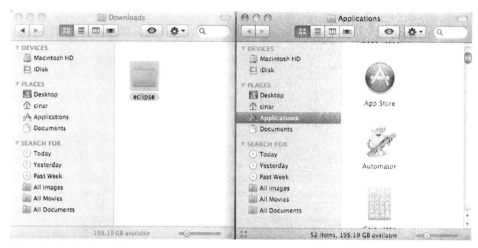

Figure 3-16. *Moving Eclipse from the Downloads directory to the Applications directory*

Later, you can also add Eclipse to your dashboard for easy access.

Installing Eclipse on Linux

The Eclipse installation package for Linux comes as a GZIP compressed TAR file. Open a terminal window and change directory to the destination where you would like install Eclipse, as shown in Figure 3-17. To extract Eclipse files, issue tar zxf eclipse-java-indigo-SR1-linux-gtk.tar.gz on the command line by replacing the file name depending on the version of Eclipse.

Figure 3-17. *Installing Eclipse on Linux*

Eclipse is now ready to use. You may find it convenient to make a shortcut to the Eclipse application for easy access.

Exploring Eclipse

You are now ready to start using Eclipse. In this section, we will start exploring
Eclipse and the terminology it uses.

Workspace

When you start Eclipse, you will be prompted to choose the workspace
directory, as shown in Figure 3-18. In Eclipse terminology, *workspace* is the
directory where your projects, source code, and Eclipse settings will be stored.

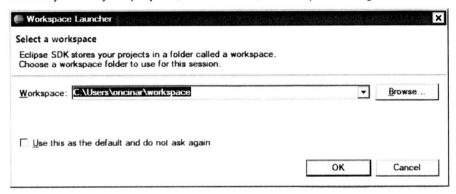

Figure 3-18. *Eclipse workspace selection dialog at startup*

If you move forward with the default setting, Eclipse will make a new directory
named workspace under the user's home directory. In the Workspace Launcher
dialog, you can also set this workspace as the default, and Eclipse will not
prompt for it again next time.

Workspaces are very useful for organizing your projects. For example, I
simultaneously work in two main workspaces: one for work-related projects and
another for my garage projects. However, many Eclipse developers are just fine
working with a single workspace.

After you choose your workspace, Eclipse will greet you with the Welcome
screen, as shown in Figure 3-19. Here, you will find useful links to Eclipse
resources such as tutorials and examples. In the top-right corner, click the
Workbench link to get to the main screen.

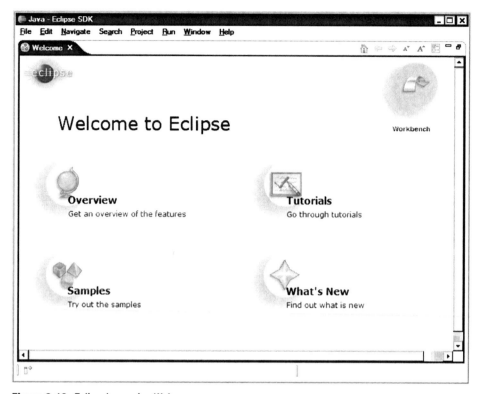

Figure 3-19. *Eclipse's opening Welcome screen*

TIP: You can go back to the Welcome screen at any time by choosing **Help** Welcome.

Workbench

In Eclipse terminology, *Workbench* refers to the desktop development environment. It is the name given to the Eclipse window shown in Figure 3-20. Each Workbench contains a set of perspectives with their respective views, editors, menu, and toolbar items.

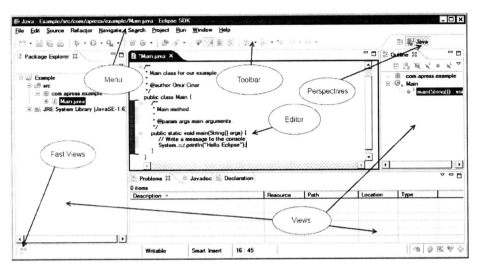

Figure 3-20. *Eclipse Workbench*

You can open more than one Workbench at a time. To open a new Workbench, choose **Window** ➤ **New Window**.

Perspectives

A *perspective* defines the set of views and the layout of views in the Workbench. Each perspective is designed to facilitate accomplishing a specific type of task:

- **Java perspective**: This perspective combines views, menus, and toolbars that are commonly used while developing Java applications.

- **Debug perspective**: This perspective contains views that are related to troubleshooting and debugging Java applications.

Eclipse comes with predefined perspectives for common tasks. You can also modify perspectives and define new ones based on your requirements. To do so, select **Window** ➤ **Customize Perspective**.

You can use the perspective switcher, as shown in Figure 3-21, or select **Window** ➤ **Open Perspective** to switch between perspectives at any time.

Figure 3-21. *Perspective switcher*

Eclipse will also make recommendations to change perspectives when you initiate a new task, such as debugging a project. This allows automatic switching between perspectives depending on the current task.

Editors

Editors allow you to edit source code and resource files. Eclipse supports multiple editor flavors depending on the file types. For example, the source code and the XML resource files are handled with different editor types.

Most file types are already mapped with the correct editors in Eclipse. If Eclipse cannot find an internal editor for a specific file type, it relies on the operating system to find an external editor. For example, if you try to open a PNG formatted graphic file, since Eclipse does not have an internal graphic editor, it will launch the default editor for PNG files by relying on the operating system's mapping. Depending on the type of the active editor, only the relevant toolbar and menu items are shown.

Any number of editors can be open at once. Editors are presented as separate tabs in the editor area, as shown in Figure 3-22. Only one editor can be active at any given time.

```
/**
 * Main class for our example.
 *
 * @author Onur Cinar
 */
public class Main {
    /**
     * Main method.
     *
     * @param args main arguments.
     */
    public static void main(String[] args) {
        // Write a message to the console
        System.out.println("Hello Eclipse");
    }
}
```

Figure 3-22. *Editor area*

You can split the editor area into multiple tab groups by right-clicking the editor tab, choosing **Move ➤ Editor** from the context menu, and moving the detached editor to your preferred corner location.

Views

Views provide alternative presentations for the project and the editors, allowing easy navigation and access to information within the Workbench. For example, the Outline view provides a list of the methods and variables in the currently edited source file, allowing easy navigation within the editor.

Eclipse comes with dozens of views. To open a new view, choose **Window ➤ Show View**. As shown in Figure 3-23, the drop-down menu shows only the most frequently used views. For a full list, choose **Other**....

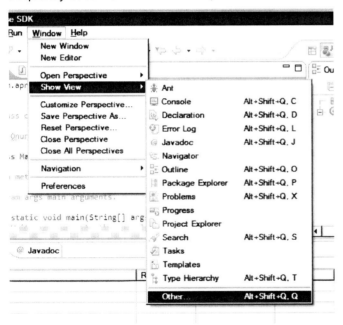

Figure 3-23. *Choosing a view*

Depending on the layout of the perspective, views can be visible at all times, stacked in a tabbed notebook, or minimized. Views may have their own toolbars and menus embedded in the view area.

Fast Views

Fast views are hidden views that can be quickly opened and closed using the Fast View icon on the status bar in the bottom-left corner of the Workbench, as shown in Figure 3-24.

Figure 3-24. *Fast View icon on the status bar*

Clicking the Fast View icon brings up a drop-down menu, as shown in Figure 3-25.

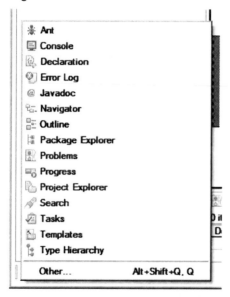

Figure 3-25. *Fast view drop-down menu*

Fast views work like other views, but they don't take up any screen space when they are not in use. You can make any view a fast view by dragging and dropping it to the Fast View icon.

> **TIP:** Alternatively, the same type of behavior as fast views can be achieved by minimizing the views. Minimized views are displayed in a toolbar-like fashion. They are much easier to activate than fast views, since each minimized view is easily identifiable by its icon, which is always visible on the display.

Quick Views

Quick views are hidden views that are shown on the top of the editor area when triggered through a key combination. Quick views are designed to provide easy access to information about the element under the cursor or the currently active editor. Quick Outline view and Quick Type Hierarchy view are examples.

Menus

Eclipse comes with different kinds of menus. Some of these menus are harder to discover than others. The most visible one is the main menu across the top of the Workbench, as shown in Figure 3-26.

Figure 3-26. *Main menu*

Views may also have their own menus, as indicated by a downward-facing triangle icon on the view's toolbar, as shown in Figure 3-27. Click this icon to display the view's menu.

Figure 3-27. *A view menu*

Child windows in the Workbench also provide a menu, also known as the system menu, for window-related operations. This menu can be activated by right-clicking the window's title bar, as shown in Figure 3-28.

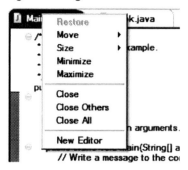

Figure 3-28. *A system menu*

Editors and most views also provide context menus for various sets of tasks. You can access this menu by right-clicking anywhere on that view, as shown in Figure 3-29.

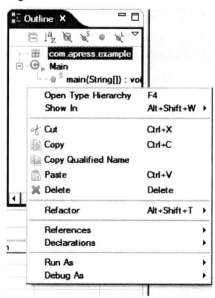

Figure 3-29. *A view menu*

Toolbars

Toolbars provide shortcuts for common tasks. The Workbench contains multiple types of toolbars. The most important one is the toolbar below the main menu at the top of the screen, as shown in Figure 3-30. This toolbar contains icons for the most frequently used Eclipse tasks.

Figure 3-30. *Top toolbar*

Depending on the editor or view in focus, the toolbar items may toggle between enabled and disabled states to reflect the availability of the task in the current context.

Another toolbar appears in the bottom-right corner of the Workbench. It contains shortcuts to the resources mentioned in the Welcome screen.

Views may also have toolbars. These toolbars are located within the view, directly below the view title, as shown in Figure 3-31.

Figure 3-31. *Outline view toolbar*

Eclipse also provides a toolbar to provide easy access to minimized views, as shown in Figure 3-32.

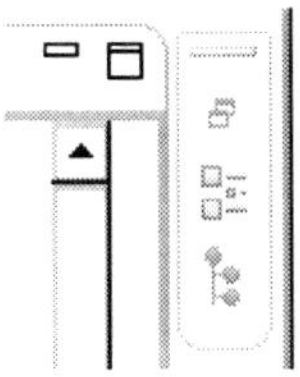

Figure 3-32. *Toolbar for minimized views*

Projects

A *project* is the largest structural unit in Eclipse, which is used to group and organize related files, folders, resources, settings, and other artifacts. For example, a Java project is a group of source files, resources, and settings.

Projects available in the current workspace are presented to the user through the Project Explorer view, as shown in Figure 3-33.

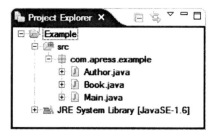

Figure 3-33. *Project Explorer view*

Projects can either be open or closed. When a project is in the closed state, it requires less memory, it is not examined during builds, and it is not editable in the Workbench. It is always a good practice to close projects to improve the build time of the active project.

To create a new project, choose **File ➤ New Project** from the top menu bar. You will see the New Project dialog with a list of available project types, as shown in Figure 3-34.

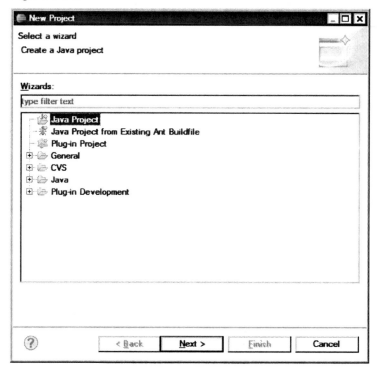

Figure 3-34. *New Project Wizard dialog*

Summary

In this chapter, we first walked through the steps for setting up the proper working environment for Eclipse on Microsoft Windows, Mac OS X, and Linux systems. Next, we briefly reviewed the Eclipse architecture to better conceptualize how the Eclipse platform works in general. Then we explored the most frequently used user interface components. such as workspaces, the Workbench, perspectives, editors, and views.

This chapter established the foundation for subsequent chapters. In the next chapter, we will explore the navigation, refactoring, prototyping, and other advanced features provided by the Eclipse platform.

References

The following references were used for this chapter:

- A Brief History of Eclipse,
  `http://www.ibm.com/developerworks/rational/library/nov05/cernosek`

- About the Eclipse Foundation, `http://www.eclipse.org/org/`

- Eclipse Platform Technical Overview,
  `http://www.eclipse.org/whitepapers/eclipse-overview.pdf`

- Eclipse documentation,
  `http://help.eclipse.org/indigo/index.jsp`

Mastering Eclipse

In the previous chapter, we explored the most frequently used Eclipse components. However, Eclipse has much more to offer.

Large and complex projects, especially when multiple developers are involved, can quickly become difficult to follow and navigate. In this chapter, we will explore the advanced Eclipse navigation features, such as outlines, type and call hierarchies, and markers, that help developers easily find their way around the code.

Besides the navigation, day-to-day software development also involves a lot of time-consuming and redundant tasks, such as writing the getters and setters for each member field, refactoring the code, and updating all the references to it. In this chapter, we will explore the extensive code generators and code manipulators that are provided by Eclipse to handle these labor-intensive tasks. Employing these powerful features enables developers to code much faster, as they can dedicate more time to the actual application.

Navigation

Navigating between different components of a complex project, or even within a large source code file, can easily become a very time-consuming exercise. Being able to navigate easily in a complex project is one the biggest requirements of any graphical development environment. Eclipse provides many advanced functions to streamline the day-to-day development experience; however, most of these nice features are hidden in the platform. Here, you'll learn how to use some of the navigation features, including working sets, Outline view, Type Hierarchy view, Call Hierarchy view, markers, and search.

Working Sets

Working sets allow further grouping of elements, such as projects, files, resources, and breakpoints, for display and operational purposes. Working sets are one of the most important features of Eclipse to facilitate the navigation within the workspace. Working sets can be used as filtering criteria for many views, and also to build a certain portion of the workspace using the build system.

By default, every element in the workspace is considered to be a member of the Window working set. In order to define a new working set, first select an element, such as a file on the Workbench, and then right-click to activate the context menu and choose **Assign ➤ Working Sets...**, as shown in Figure 4-1.

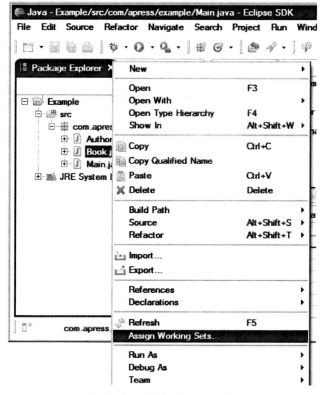

Figure 4-1. *Choosing Assign Working Sets from the context menu*

The Working Sets Assignments dialog will appear, showing a list of existing working sets. Click the New button on the right to define a new working set.

Eclipse will display the New Working Set wizard, starting with a list of available working set types that are applicable to the selected element. In the example in Figure 4-2, we have selected a Java source file, and the available working set types are populated based on that source. Select the type of the working set and click Next to move to the next step.

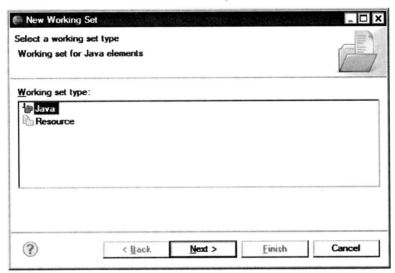

Figure 4-2. *Starting the New Working Set wizard*

In the next step, give a name to this new working set. You can also add other elements to it, as shown in Figure 4-3.

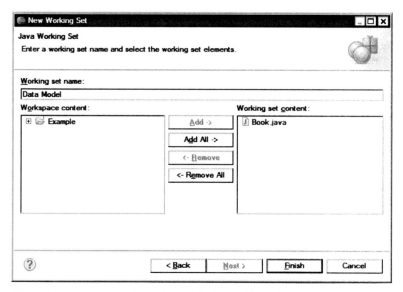

Figure 4-3. *Naming and adding elements to the working set*

When you select Finish, the Working Set Assignments dialog will be shown again, this time with the newly defined working set in the list and checked, as shown in Figure 4-4.

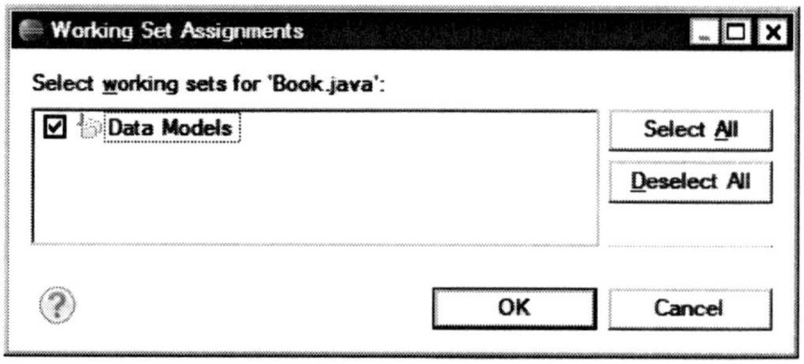

Figure 4-4. *Working Set Assignments dialog showing the new working set*

This new working set can be used as filtering criteria in multiple places. As an example, let's filter the content of the Package Explorer view with the newly defined working set. Select the view's drop-down menu by clicking the expansion arrow icon on the Package Explorer's toolbar, as shown in Figure 4-5. Choose Select Working Set... to set the working set to use. Recently used working sets get added to the context menu also for easy access.

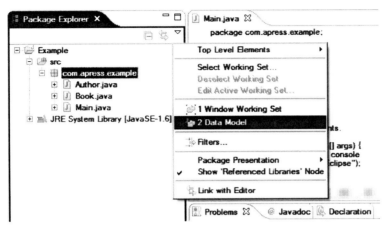

Figure 4-5. *Package Explorer view menu*

Now the Package Explorer view will filter its content to reflect only the elements that are members of the selected working set, as shown in Figure 4-6.

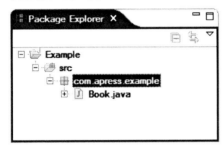

Figure 4-6. *Package Explorer view filtered by a working set*

Outline View

The Outline view provides a structural view of the currently open file in the editor. It allows quick navigation through the content of the editor. The Outline view toolbar offers options for filtering and ordering the view's content.

The content of the Outline view is editor-specific. Some editors, such as the plain text file editor, do not support Outline view. While using the Java editor, Outline view shows classes, variables, and methods in the current Java file as structural elements, as shown in Figure 4-7.

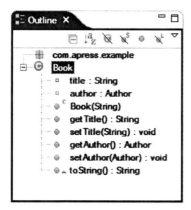

Figure 4-7. *Outline view of a Java file*

The Outline view is visible by default in the Java perspective. To add the Outline view to another perspective, choose **Window ➤ Show View ➤ Outline**.

There is a quick view alternative to the Outline view, known as the Quick Outline view. This view is not visible by default. To display it, press Ctrl+0 on Windows and Linux, or Command+O on Mac OS X. It will appear in the editor area, as shown in Figure 4-8.

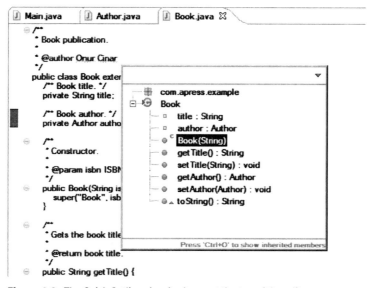

Figure 4-8. *The Quick Outline view is shown at the top of the editor.*

By default, the Quick Outline view shows the class fields and methods. Pressing Ctrl+0 a second time expands this list to cover inherited fields, methods, and types. Inherited elements are displayed in gray to make them easily distinguishable.

The Quick Outline view also supports automatic filtering by allowing the user to type the initial letters of the element to narrow its content. Like other views, the Quick Outline view has its own drop-down menu to allow further customization.

Type Hierarchy View

The Type Hierarchy view is Java-specific and shows subtypes and supertypes of the selected Java object. It allows you to discover the type hierarchy quickly and navigate through the types.

In order to launch the Type Hierarchy view, you will need to first select a Java object from either the Package Explorer view or the editor. After selecting the object, you can open the Type Hierarchy view in three ways:

- Press F4.

- Right-click and choose **Open Type Hierarchy** from the context menu, as shown in Figure 4-9.

- In the top menu bar, choose **Window ➤ Show View ➤ Type Hierarchy**.

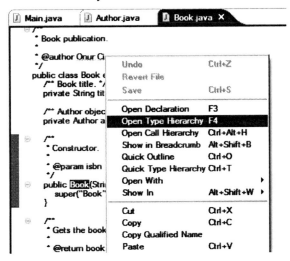

Figure 4-9. *Selecting Open Type Hierarchy from the context menu*

The Type Hierarchy view is separated into two panes, as shown in Figure 4-10. The top pane shows the type hierarchy for the selected Java object. The bottom pane shows the member list.

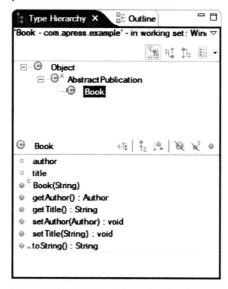

Figure 4-10. *The Type Hierarchy view is separated into two panes.*

The Type Hierarchy view has its own menu, which can be activated by clicking the expansion arrow in the top-right corner. From this menu, you can further filter the type hierarchy by a working set.

In addition to the menu, the Type Hierarchy view has two toolbars: one for each pane. The toolbar for the top pane provides icons to switch between subtype hierarchy, supertype hierarchy, and complete type hierarchy. The toolbar for the bottom pane provides icons to filter and sort the member list.

Double-clicking any element in this view allows you to automatically open it in the editor area.

As with the Outline view, a quick view alternative is available. To open the Quick Type Hierarchy view, press Ctrl+T on Windows and Linux, or Command+T on Mac OS X. It appears at the top of the editor area, as shown in Figure 4-11.

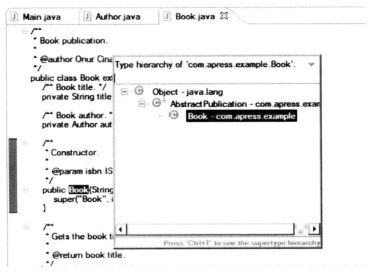

Figure 4-11. *Quick Type Hierarchy view displayed in the editor*

Call Hierarchy View

Another Java-specific view is the Call Hierarchy view, which shows the callers and callees of the selected Java member object. It allows you to quickly discover the call hierarchy within the code and to navigate through the calls.

To launch the Call Hierarchy view, first select a Java member object, and then use one of the following methods:

- Press Ctrl+Alt+H on Windows and Linux, or Control+Alt+H on Mac OS X.

- Right-click and choose **Open Call Hierarchy** from the context menu, as shown in Figure 4-12.

- In the top menu bar, choose **Window ➤ Show View ➤ Other… ➤ Call Hierarchy**.

Figure 4-12. *Selecting Open Call Hierarchy from the context menu*

The Call Hierarchy view also has its own menu. You can activate this menu by clicking the expansion arrow, as with the other views. This drop-down menu allows you to change the Call Hierarchy mode between caller and callee hierarchies. It also provides filtering capabilities, such as filtering by field access type while exploring field access call hierarchies.

As shown in Figure 4-13, the call hierarchy is displayed in a tree-like fashion on the left. The right side of the view is used to show the line number and the function that is called. When you click the plus icon on the left side of the tree items, the call hierarchy discovery continues one more step. The plus icon disappears when the last method in the call hierarchy has been reached.

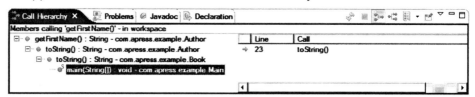

Figure 4-13. *Call Hierarchy view*

Markers

Markers are metadata that can be associated with Workbench resources. Markers are shown on the marker bar on the left border of the editor area. Eclipse supports different marker types. In this section, we will review three marker flavors: bookmarks, problems, and tasks.

Bookmarks View

Bookmarks provide a way to mark frequently used resources for easy access later. While working in a complex project, certain parts of the code, such as the main API, can be good candidates for bookmarks. You can add bookmarks for specific lines within a file or for the entire resource.

The Bookmarks view provides a list of these bookmarks in a tabular format, as shown in Figure 4-14.

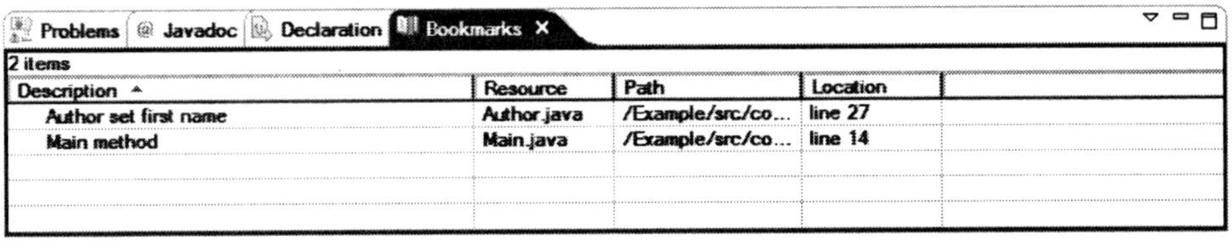

Problems	Javadoc	Declaration	Bookmarks ×			

2 items				
Description ▲	Resource	Path	Location	
Author set first name	Author.java	/Example/src/co...	line 27	
Main method	Main.java	/Example/src/co...	line 14	

Figure 4-14. *Bookmarks view*

If Bookmarks view is not visible, you can add it to the current perspective by choosing **Window ➤ Show View ➤ Other... ➤ Bookmarks**.

To add a new bookmark, right-click the marker bar in the editor area and choose **Add Bookmark...** from the context menu, as shown in Figure 4-15. A blue bookmark icon will appear in the marker bar on the selected line to indicate that the line is bookmarked. You can then manage bookmarks using the Bookmarks view.

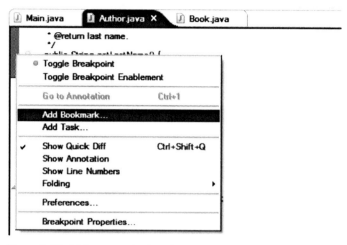

Figure 4-15. *Adding a new bookmark*

Problems View

The Problems view provides a central location for various Eclipse components to log problems, errors, and warnings. The Problems view presents this information in a tabular format, as shown in Figure 4-16.

Description ▲	Resource	Path	Location	Type	
⊟ ⊗ Errors (2 items)					
⌕ Type mismatch: cannot convert from int to	Author.java	/Example/src/co...	line 15	Java Problem	
⌕ Type mismatch: cannot convert from Strin	Book.java	/Example/src/co...	line 9	Java Problem	
⊟ ⚠ Warnings (1 item)					
⌕ The constructor Date(int, int, int) is depre	Author.java	/Example/src/co...	line 17	Java Problem	

Figure 4-16. *Problems view showing existing issues*

For example, during compile time, any error is first associated with the corresponding resource through a marker, and then reported to the user through the Problems view. Double-click the error message to quickly jump to the corresponding resource.

By default, the Problems view shows all problems and groups them based on their severity. Using the view menu (accessed through the window's expansion arrow), you can filter the list and change the grouping and sorting. When the problems have been addressed, they are automatically removed from the Problems view.

The Problems view also provides help for fixing the reported problems, through the Quick Fix functionality. To launch Quick Fix, press Ctrl+1 on Windows and Linux, or Command+1 on Mac OS X, or choose **Quick Fix** from the context menu of the selected problem item. Quick Fix provides a set of recommendations for fixing the problem, as shown in Figure 4-17.

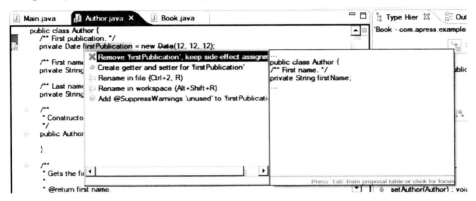

Figure 4-17. *Quick Fix provides recommendations for fixing a problem.*

Tasks View

The Tasks view allows you to associate tasks with Workbench resources. For example, a missing code segment or a known bug that needs to be addressed can be expressed by associating a task with relevant resources. The Tasks view presents this information in a tabular format, as shown in Figure 4-18.

	!	Description	Resource	Path	Location	Type
		FIXME: First and last name are required.	Author.java	/Example/src/co...	line 19	Java Task
		FIXME: No error checking for missing fields.	Book.java	/Example/src/co...	line 68	Java Task
		FIXME: Title must be checked for null	Book.java	/Example/src/co...	line 43	Java Task
		TODO: Check	Author.java	/Example/src/co...	line 69	Java Task
		TODO: Get books needs to be implemented	Author.java	/Example/src/co...	line 22	Java Task

Figure 4-18. *Tasks view*

Using the Tasks view's drop-down menu, you can organize this list. For example, you can reorder the list based on the task priorities or filter the list to show only a certain type of task.

As with most markers, a new task can be defined by right-clicking the marker bar on the corresponding line. You can also use certain keywords in the resources, as shown in Figure 4-19. The latter approach is much more frequently used by developers.

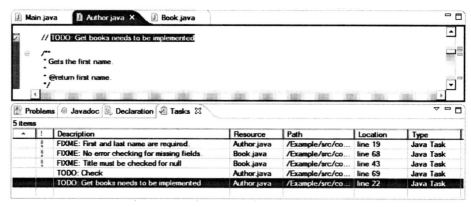

Figure 4-19. *Task automatically defined by TODO keyword*

The following are the most common keywords used to automatically define a task:

- TODO: This keyword is used to record any missing code part that needs to be implemented later. Developers mostly use TODO to record tasks that they are currently postponing and plan to address later.

- FIXME: This keyword is mostly used to record any known bugs in the code that need to be addressed.

When adding tasks to your resources, you are not limited to these keywords. Other keywords can be defined through the Task Tags Preferences dialog, as shown in Figure 4-20. To open this dialog, select **Window ➤ Preferences** on Windows and Linux, or **Eclipse ➤ Preferences** on Mac OS X, and navigate to Java, then Compiler, then Task Tags.

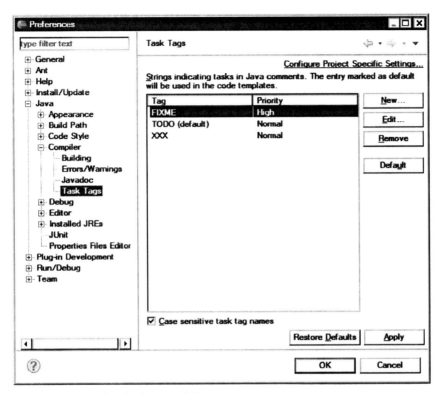

Figure 4-20. *Task Tags Preferences dialog*

Search

Effective searching is the key for easy navigation within a development environment. Eclipse provides multiple layers of search functionality that are specifically optimized for certain use cases.

The most basic search feature provided by Eclipse, also known as a file search, is searching the Workbench for a text string. To open the Search dialog, press Ctrl+H on Windows and Linux, or Control+H on Mac OS X, or choose **Search ▶ Search…** from the top menu.

As shown in Figure 4-21, the Search dialog provides extensive customization for searching. Although it is a very powerful feature, it is only optimized for searching text in generic files. Searching Java resources this way is not recommended, as there is already an optimal solution provided specifically for Java resources.

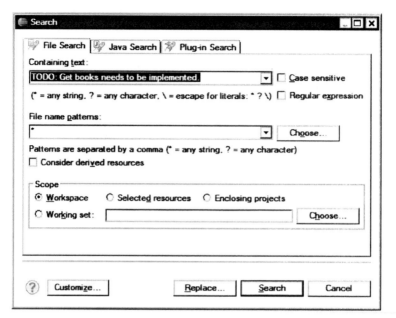

Figure 4-21. *Using the Search dialog for a file search*

A Java search is much faster than a file search for Java resources since it relies on the existing code indexes. You can launch a Java search by choosing **Search** ➤ **Java ...** from the top menu or by clicking the Java Search tab in the Search dialog. As shown in Figure 4-22, the Java Search tab provides additional parameters specific to Java that you can use to further customize a search.

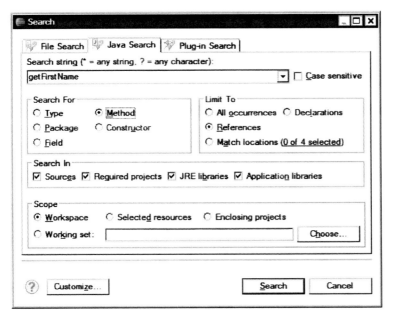

Figure 4-22. *Java Search tab of the Search dialog*

Search results are presented through the Search view, as shown in Figure 4-23. The Search view drop-down menu and toolbar provide further filtering capabilities to organize the search results based on user preferences.

Figure 4-23. *Search view*

The Search menu also provides some boilerplate searches, as shown in Figure 4-24. The currently selected Java resource can be used to quickly start a new search for references, decelerations, and implementors.

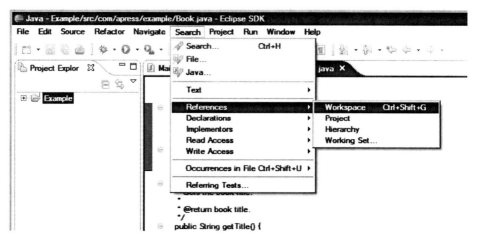

Figure 4-24. *Boilerplate searches*

Being able to navigate easily within the project definitely speeds up the coding process, but it is not enough alone. Developers still need to write a considerable amount of code while developing applications. In the next section, we will explore the advanced features that are offered by Eclipse for fast coding.

Fast Coding

In most software projects, the majority of developer's time does not go into developing the actual application logic. Developers spends considerable amount of time dealing with simple but labor intensive coding tasks, such as implementing getters and setters, or updating all references within the source after doing a code refactoring. Eclipse provides a set of advanced features, such as templates and code generators, to automate a portion of coding, and to reduce the amount of code that developers need to produce. In this section, we will review some these handy Eclipse features.

Templates

There are many coding patterns and code structures that we use every day while developing any type of application. Most of the time, we find ourselves copying and pasting code segments, and trying to adapt them to their new home by manipulating their parameter names. For example, logging is one of the must-haves for every project. While developing an application, developers often end up copying the logger initiation code many places.

Copy-and-paste functionality in most text editors certainly makes the task easy; however, it does require you to have immediate access to the original code segments in order to copy them first. So, developers may spend a majority of their time searching through previous projects in order to extract those precious code segments.

Eclipse provides a much more elegant solution to this problem through support for code templates. Code templates allow you to store frequently used code patterns and snippets within Eclipse. Eclipse handles the storage and indexing of these templates, and makes them easily available.

Eclipse supports multiple code template types. Users can define their own templates, as well as use predefined templates that come with plug-ins (which can be customized by users).

To get a better idea of the extent of template support in Eclipse, from the top menu bar, select **Window > Preferences** on Windows and Linux, or **Eclipse Preferences** on Mac OS X to launch the Eclipse Preferences dialog. Start typing **templates** to filter the extensive list of preferences to only templates, as shown in Figure 4-25.

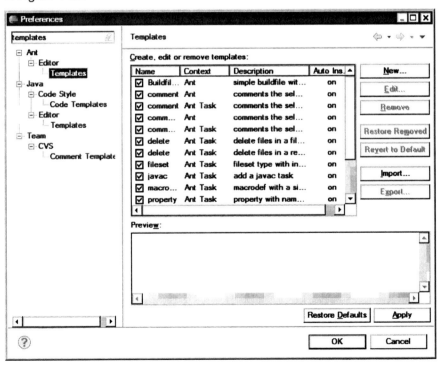

Figure 4-25. *Eclipse Preferences dialog filtered for templates*

As you may have noticed, two sets of templates are listed in the Java section of the Preferences dialog: Code Templates under Code Style and Templates under Editor. We'll look at both types in this section.

Code Templates

Code templates are mainly used during automatic code generation. The most basic code template is for the comment lines that are placed at the top of new files. In many companies, you will be required to include a copyright notice and a license at the top of every source file that you develop. To easily achieve this using a code template, select **Window > Preferences** on Windows and Linux, or **Eclipse > Preferences** on Mac OS X, and navigate to Java, then Code Style, then Code Templates. You will be presented with a list of available code templates, as shown in Figure 4-26.

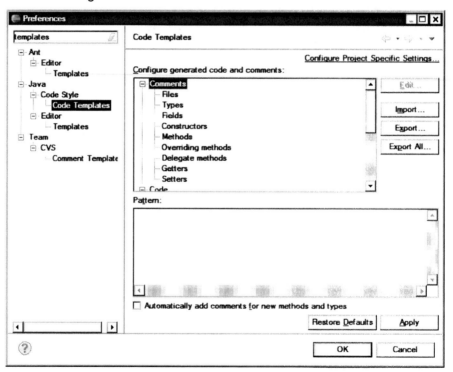

Figure 4-26. *Java code templates list*

Code templates are presented in a tree-like fashion under two main groups: Comments and Code. Click the triangle icon on the left side of the Comments group to expand the list of available comment code templates. The code template that we will modify for this example is the one named Files. After you select this template from the list, the bottom pane of the dialog will immediately show the current pattern for the selected code template, as shown in Figure 4-27.

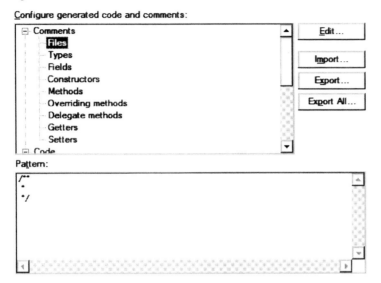

Figure 4-27. *File comment code template*

As you can see, currently it does not include any text, but only the comment decoration. In order to modify it, click the Edit button on the right. This will bring up the Edit Template dialog, as shown in Figure 4-28.

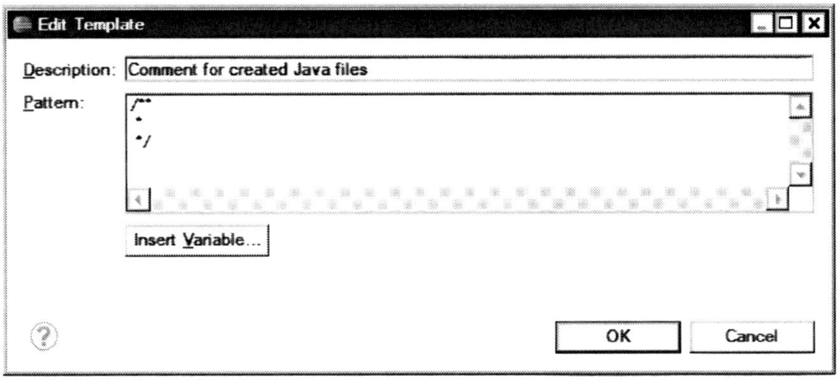

Figure 4-28. *Edit Template dialog*

You can now modify the file comment to say something like the following:

```
/**
 * Copyright © 2012 Apress Media LLC. All Rights Reserved.
 */
```

Code templates are all about reusability, and developers like to make them as generic as possible in order to avoid needing to keep them up to date. In our example, we have a hard-coded year, 2012, in the template. It would be better to have this copyright line reflect the current year, rather than always showing 2012. This can be achieved by adding a variable, which is easy to do with Eclipse's template support. To replace 2012 with the correct variable, click the Insert Variable... button below the Pattern text area. You will be presented with a list of available variables that can be used within the template, as shown in Figure 4-29.

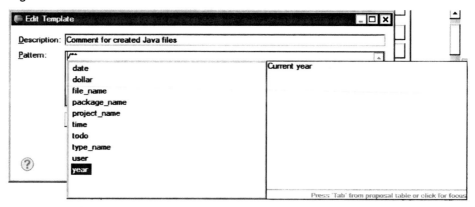

Figure 4-29. *Available variables for code templates*

For this example, choose year from the list of variables to replace 2012. Our file comment will now look like the following:

```
/**
 * Copyright © ${year} Apress Media LLC. All Rights Reserved.
 */
```

From now on, any new Java file that you add to your project will be generated with the copyright line in the file comment, as shown in Figure 4-30.

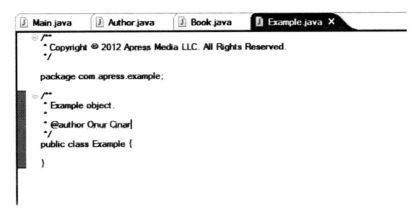

```
/**
 * Copyright © 2012 Apress Media LLC. All Rights Reserved.
 */

package com.apress.example;

/**
 * Example object.
 *
 * @author Onur Cinar
 */
public class Example {

}
```

Figure 4-30. *New Java file with the copyright in its file comment*

Editor Templates

Since the code templates can be consumed only through the code generators, Eclipse does not allow users to add new templates to that list. However, the second template type, editor templates, is primarily for users to define new templates and to use them while developing applications. Open the Eclipse Preferences dialog as described earlier, and navigate to Java, then Editor, then Templates, as shown in Figure 4-31.

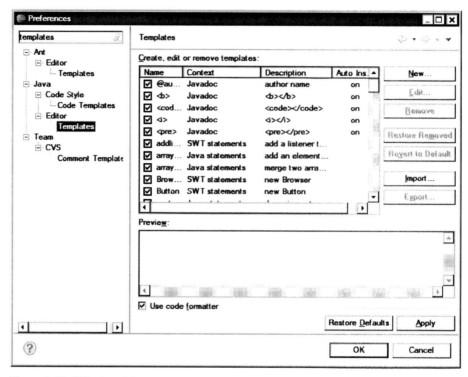

Figure 4-31. *Editor templates*

To define a new editor template, click the New button on the right. The New Template dialog will be launched, as shown in Figure 4-32.

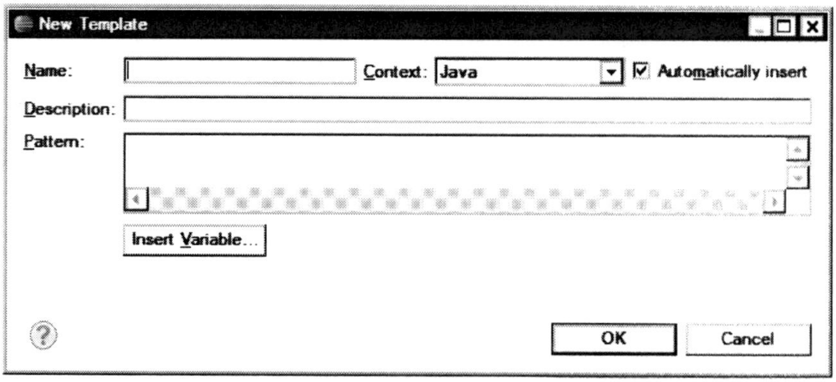

Figure 4-32. *New Template dialog for an editor template*

This dialog has two more fields than the Edit Template dialog for code templates: one for the name of the new template and another for the context. The name is primarily used to refer to this template while using it within the editor, and it is more like a keyword. The context is used by Eclipse to filter the templates based on the current context in order to offer only the applicable ones.

As an example, we will define a new editor template for the logger initiation code. Name the new template **Logger**, and select the Java context. We will start by copying an existing logger initialization line into the template's pattern editor.

```
private static final Logger logger = Logger.getLogger(Author.class.getName());
```

In order to make this editor template more generic, the reference to the class file should be converted to a variable. Click the Insert Variable… button, and you will be presented with a much larger list of variables than those available for code templates. Choose `enclosing_type` from the variables list to replace `Author` in the template. The new template will look like the following:

```
private static final Logger logger =
Logger.getLogger(${enclosing_type}.class.getName());
```

The `Logger` class is defined in the `java.util.logging` package, which is not part of the automatically imported set of Java packages. To make the editor template more generic, let's instruct Eclipse to import the `Logger` class while inserting the template into the code. To do this, select `import` from the list of variables, and add the parameter `java.util.logging.Logging`. As shown in Figure 4-33, the modified template will look like the following:

```
private static final Logger logger =
Logger.getLogger(${enclosing_type}.class.getName());
${:import(java.util.logging.Logger)}
```

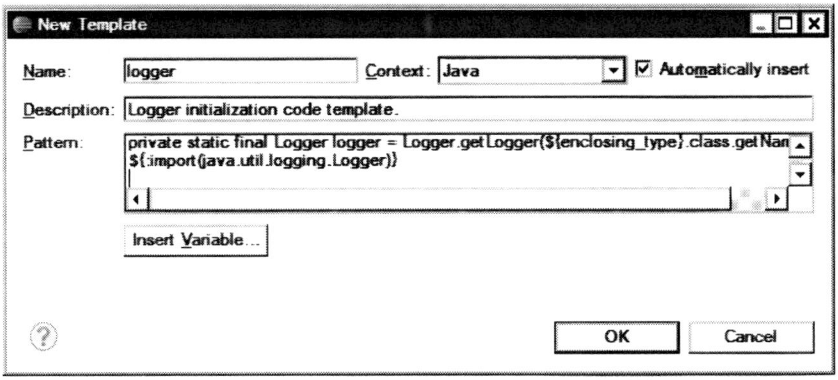

Figure 4-33. *Editor template fully defined in the dialog*

The editor template is now ready to be used. To insert it into the code, start typing **logger,** and then press Ctrl+spacebar on Windows and Linux, or Control+spacebar on Mac OS X to launch the Content Assist feature (discussed in the next section), as shown in Figure 4-34.

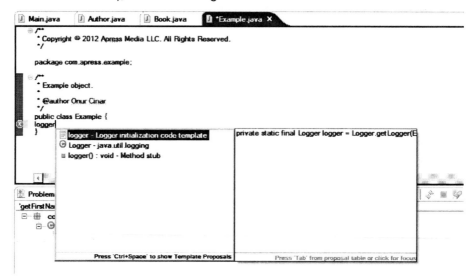

Figure 4-34. *Content Assist suggesting the editor template*

You will see a list of suggestions, including the editor template we defined in this example. Choose `logging` from the list in order to insert the logging initialization code template into the editor, as shown in Figure 4-35.

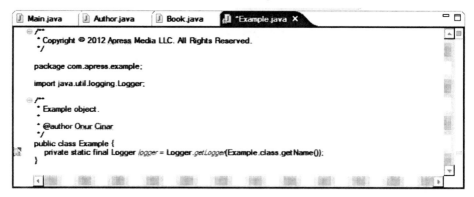

Figure 4-35. *Editor template inserted into the code*

Content Assist

Using a third-party API or working on a complex project will be difficult if you need to memorize and remember each and every type and method name. Most of the time, developers do recall the existence of a method, but not its full signature. Eclipse's Content Assist feature becomes really handy during those moments.

The easiest way to trigger Content Assist is through the dot character. For example, start typing **System.out.** and wait for a second. The dot character brings up Content Assist, which presents a list of suggestions to complete the current code line, as shown in Figure 4-36.

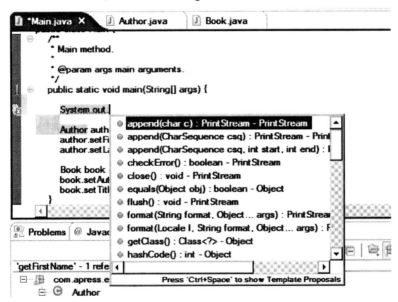

Figure 4-36. *Content Assist making suggestions to complete the line*

Content Assist prepares the list of the suggestions by using the first word on the left side of the cursor, and the list may be very long. In order to narrow down the suggestions, continue typing more characters, and Content Assist will filter the list accordingly. For our example, type **p**, and the list will now cover only suggestions starting with the letter *p*, as shown in Figure 4-37.

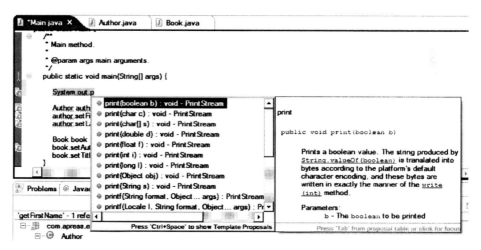

Figure 4-37. *Content Assist suggestions further filtered*

You can also navigate through the list of suggestions. When you select a suggestion, the proposed code will be automatically inserted into the line. If none of the suggestions is applicable, you can press the Esc key to close the Content Assist list.

Although the dot character automatically triggers Content Assist, it can also be manually launched by using the key combination Ctrl+spacebar on Windows and Linux, or Control+spacebar on Mac OS X at any time. Content Assist is a very powerful and handy tool for streamlining day-to-day Eclipse development.

Code Generators

To facilitate coding, Eclipse provides a set of code generators that automatically generate code for frequently used coding patterns. These code generator options are available through the Source menu on the top menu bar:

- **Override/Implement Methods:** Provides a list of methods from superclasses and implemented interfaces for overriding and implementing.

- **Generate Getters and Setters:** Generates getter and setter methods for selected fields.

- **Generate Delegate Methods:** Generates method delegates for fields in the current type.

- **Generate toString():** Generates the `toString()` method using content from selected fields and methods.

- **Generate hashCode() and equals():** Generates `hashCode()` and `equals()` methods based on the selected fields.

- **Generate Constructor Using Fields:** Adds a constructor that initializes selected fields.

- **Generate Constructors from Superclass:** Adds a constructor that is defined in the superclass of the current class.

The best example of Eclipse code generators is the getter and setter generator. In object-oriented programming, mutator methods are methods that are used to control changes to a variable. Methods like getters and setters are examples of mutator methods. Class variables are always declared as private, and getter and setter methods are public methods defined to manipulate those fields. In most development projects, getter and setter methods occupy a large portion of the source code, and developers may spend a considerable amount of time writing code for these simple but time-consuming methods.

Eclipse's getter and setter code generator provides an elegant solution to this problem. After defining the fields in a class, select **Source ➤ Generate Getters and Setters…** from the top menu bar to launch the Generate Getters and Setters dialog, as shown in Figure 4-38.

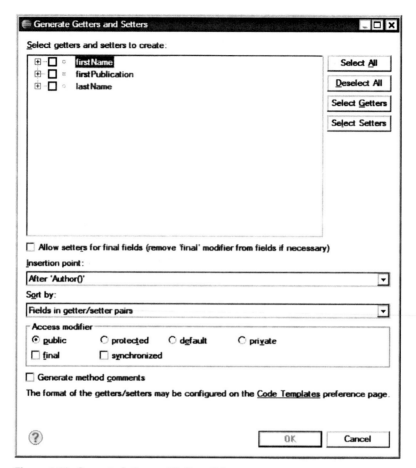

Figure 4-38. *Generate Getters and Setters dialog*

The Generate Getters and Setters dialog provides a list of the member fields in a tree-like fashion. The check box on the left side of each member field allows you to mark a field for getter and setter generation. To the left of the check box is a triangle icon to expand the selection to further show the individual methods that will be generated. By default, both the getter and setter are generated, unless you specify which mutator method to generate, as in the example in Figure 4-39.

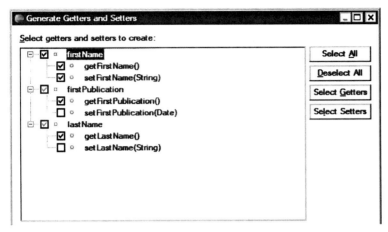

Figure 4-39. *Selecting individual methods to be generated*

The Generate Getters and Setters dialog also provides additional configurable parameters to specify the insertion point, sorting, and the access modifiers for the automatically generated methods.

Figure 4-40 shows automatically generated getters and setters. The format of the getters and setters is based on the Java code templates, and can be customized through the Eclipse Preferences dialog, by navigating to Java, then Code Style, then Code Templates, as discussed earlier in the chapter.

```
Main.java     Author.java X     Book.java

    public String getFirstName() {
        return firstName;
    }

    public void setFirstName(String firstName) {
        this.firstName = firstName;
    }

    public Date getFirstPublication() {
        return firstPublication;
    }

    public String getLastName() {
        return lastName;
    }

}
```

Figure 4-40. *Automatically generated getters and setters*

Refactoring

Refactoring refers to the process of transforming the code without changing its functionality. Refactoring is frequently done during the development cycle in order to improve the design and the efficiency of the code based on the new requirements.

Renaming is the simplest refactoring operation. However, it does require a considerable amount of manual work to adjust the code after the renaming. Every reference to the renamed object needs to be modified in order to be able use the code. Existing search-and-replace functionality is not applicable to this operation, since it may cause unintentional changes in other parts of the code. Due to the amount of manual operations required, this process is also prone to user error.

Eclipse provides a much more elegant solution to this problem. In order to rename a Java object, press Alt+Shift+R on Windows and Linux, or Alt+Command+R on Mac OS X, or choose **Refactor ➤ Rename** from the top menu bar. As shown in Figure 4-41, Eclipse will allow you to rename the object, and it will automatically refactor the application code accordingly.

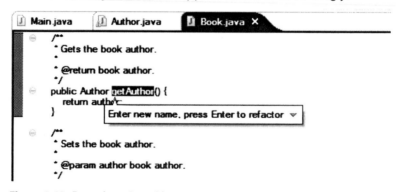

Figure 4-41. *Renaming a Java object*

Renaming is not the only refactoring operation supported by Eclipse, as you can see in the **Refactor** menu, shown in Figure 4-42.

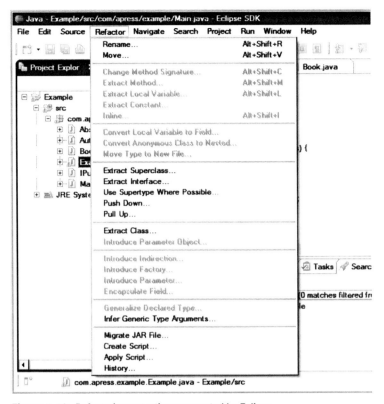

Figure 4-42. *Refactoring operations supported by Eclipse*

This menu provides easy access to many refactoring operations:

- **Rename:** Renames the selected Java object and corrects all references.

- **Move:** Moves the selected Java object and corrects all references.

- **Change Method Signature:** Changes parameter names and types, and updates all references accordingly.

- **Extract Method:** Extracts the currently selected code section as a new module, and replaces the selection with a reference to the newly defined method.

- **Extract Local Variable:** Extracts the currently selected variable as a new local variable, and replaces the selection with a reference to the newly defined local variable.

- **Extract Constant:** Extracts the currently selected expression as a new constant, and replaces the selection with a reference to the new constant.

- **Inline:** Inlines local variables, methods, or constants.

- **Convert Anonymous Class to Nested:** Converts the selected anonymous class to a member class.

- **Move Type to New File:** Moves the selected type to its own Java source file, and updates the references accordingly.

- **Convert Local Variable to Field:** Converts the selected local variable to a field, and updates the references and the initialization accordingly.

- **Extract Superclass:** Extracts a superclass from a set of siblings and changes the siblings to become a direct subclass of the newly defined superclass.

- **Extract Interface:** Extracts an interface with a set of selected methods, and makes the selected class implement this new interface.

- **Use Supertype Where Possible:** Replaces the occurrence of a type with its supertype when possible.

- **Push Down:** Moves methods between the superclass and a class.

- **Pull Up:** Moves methods between the class and its superclass.

- **Extract Class:** Extracts a set of fields as a new class, and replaces the references to these fields with the new class.

- **Introduce Parameter Object:** Replaces a set of parameters with a new class, and updates all callers of the method to pass an instance of this new class with the parameters.

- **Introduce Indirection:** Generates a static indirection method delegating to the selected method.

- **Introduce Factory:** Generates a new factory method for the selected type.

- **Introduce Parameter:** Replaces an expression with a reference to a new method parameter and updates all callers.

- **Encapsulate Field:** Replaces all references to a field with getters and setters.

- **Generalize Declared Type:** Allows the user to choose a supertype of the reference's current type if the reference can be safely changed to that supertype.

- **Infer Generic Type Arguments:** Replaces raw type occurrences of generic types with parameterized types where possible.

Some refactoring tasks may involve a combination of these refactoring operations. Eclipse keeps a history of the refactoring tasks, to allow you to undo specific refactoring steps. To view the refactoring history, choose **Refactor ➤ History** from the top menu bar.

Selected refactoring tasks can also be saved in to a script file for later use by choosing **Refactor ➤ Create Script…**. You can then choose **Refactor ➤ Apply Script…** to apply these refactoring steps again.

Scrapbook

The Scrapbook feature allows users to easily experiment with code snippets without dealing with the extra burden of writing full Java code. Scrapbook is like a code interpreter. It allows you to type only a piece of the code to experiment, and then it can quickly execute the code and show the result. Within the Scrapbook page, you can use classes defined in a project as well as the Java system classes.

To launch a Scrapbook page, select **File ➤ New ➤ Other… ➤ Java ➤ Java Run/Debug ➤ Scrapbook Page** from the top menu bar. An empty Scrapbook page will be added to the editor area, as shown in Figure 4-43.

Figure 4-43. *Scrapbook page*

Start typing the following example expression:

```
java.util.Date date = new java.util.Date();
date
```

Scrapbook provides the following three execution types:

- **Display**: Evaluates the expression and prints its value directly to the Scrapbook page.

- **Inspect**: Evaluates the expression and shows an inspection window with all the information the object provides.

- **Execute**: Evaluates the expression as regular Java code.

In order to use any of these execution types, first highlight the expression. Then start the display execution by pressing Ctrl+Shift+D on Windows and Linux, or Shift+Command+D on Mac OS X, or by choosing **Run > Display** from the top menu. The expression will be evaluated, and its value will be shown in the Scrapbook page, as shown in Figure 4-44.

Figure 4-44. *Scrapbook display*

Keep the expression highlighted, and start the inspect execution by pressing Ctrl+Shift+I on Windows and Linux, or Shift+Command+I on Mac OS X, or by choosing **Run > Inspect** from the top menu. The expression will be evaluated, and the Inspect window will appear at the top of the Scrapbook page, as shown in Figure 4-45.

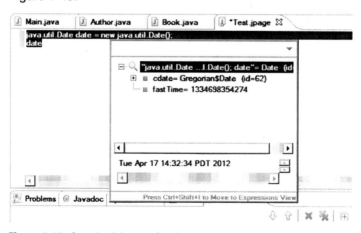

Figure 4-45. *Scrapbook Inspect function*

Change the expression to the following:

```
java.util.Date date = new java.util.Date();
System.out.println(date.toString());
```

Highlight the expression, and execute it by pressing Ctrl+U on Windows and Linux, or Command+U on Mac OS X, or by choosing the **Run ➤ Execute**. The expression will be executed like normal Java code, and the output will be displayed in the Console view, as shown in Figure 4-46.

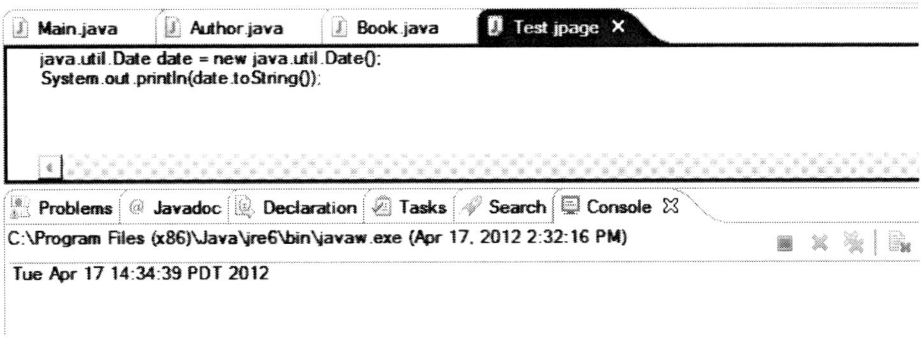

Figure 4-46. *Scrapbook Execute function*

Summary

In this chapter, we covered powerful Eclipse features that can boost the development cycle. We started the chapter by diving into the advanced navigation features offered by Eclipse, including views and the different types of markers to pinpoint code parts easily. We then looked at the Eclipse features for fast coding. These include code and editor templates, which can be employed to maintain code consistency, as well as code generators and refactoring functions that are provided by Eclipse to handle time-consuming development tasks. Later chapters will demonstrate these features in action.

Chapter

5

Chapter

Android Development Tools for Eclipse

In the previous four chapters, we have studied the Android framework and the Eclipse integrated development environment in great detail. In this chapter, we will be gluing these two worlds together using the Android Development Tools (ADT) plug-ins for Eclipse. We will start our journey by installing ADT and the Android Software Development Kit (SDK). We will then start exploring the views and tools they provide. In the next chapter, while developing our first Android project, we will start putting these views and tools into action.

Preparing Eclipse

Although Eclipse comes with the tools for Java development, Android-specific platform APIs and application packaging tools are required in order to develop Android applications using Eclipse.

Installing Android Development Tools

As explained in Chapter 3, the Eclipse platform is structured around the concept of plug-ins. ADT is a set of plug-ins for Android application development on the Eclipse platform.

ADT extends the capabilities of Eclipse integrated development environment to let application developers perform the following tasks:

- Quickly set up new Android projects

- Visually design advanced user interfaces

- Access and use Android framework components

- Debug, unit test, and release Android applications

ADT is free software that is provided under the open source Apache License. More information about the latest ADT version and the most current installation steps can be found at the ADT Plugin for Eclipse page (`http://developer.android.com/sdk/eclipse-adt.html`).

We will be using Eclipse's Install New Software wizard to install ADT. Launch the wizard by choosing **Help ➤ Install New Software** from the top menu bar, as shown in Figure 5-1.

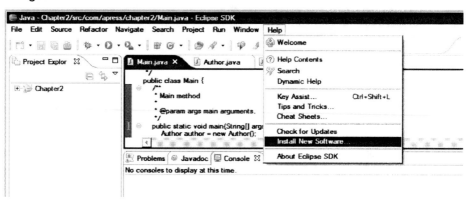

Figure 5-1. *Choosing to install new software*

The wizard will start and display a list of available plug-ins. Since ADT is not part of the official Eclipse software repository, you need to first add Android's Eclipse software repository as a new software site. To do this, click the Add button, as shown in Figure 5-2.

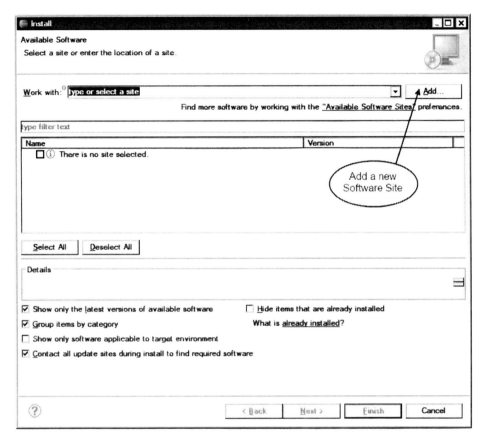

Figure 5-2. *Beginning to add new software*

The Add Repository dialog appears. In the Name field, enter a unique name to refer to this repository. In the Location field, enter the URL for Android's Eclipse software repository: `https://dl-ssl.google.com/android/eclipse/`, as shown in Figure 5-3.

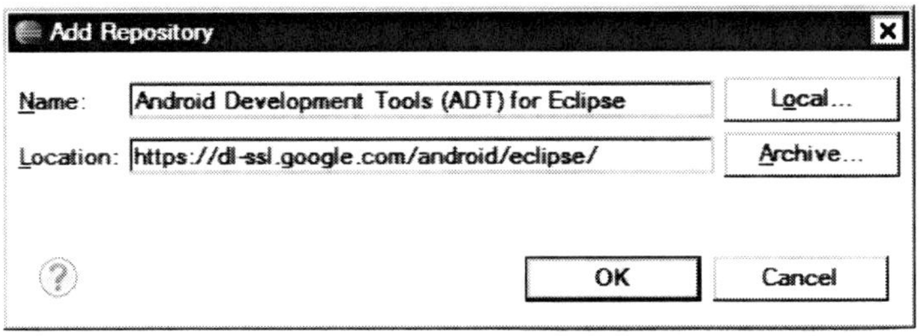

Figure 5-3. *Add Repository dialog completed with ADT information*

After you add the new software site, the Install New Software wizard will display a list of available ADT plug-ins, as shown in Figure 5-4. Each of these plug-ins is crucial for Android application development, and it is highly recommended that you install all of them. (We will discuss these plug-ins in the "Exploring ADT" section later in this chapter.) Click the Select All button to select all of the ADT plug-ins, and then click the Next button to move to the next step.

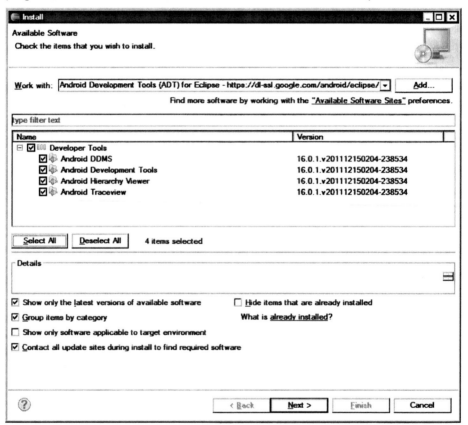

Figure 5-4. *Installing ADT developer tools*

Eclipse will go through the list of selected plug-ins to append any dependencies to the list, and then present the final download list for review. Click the Next button to move to the next step.

ADT also contains a set of other third-party components with different licensing terms. During the installation process, Eclipse presents each software license, and asks the user to accept the terms of the license agreements in order to continue with the installation. Review the license agreements, choose to accept their terms, and then click the Finish button to start the installation process. Eclipse will report the progress of the installation, as shown in Figure 5-5.

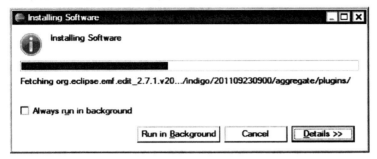

Figure 5-5. *ADT installation progress*

ADT plug-ins come within unsigned JAR files, which may trigger a security warning, as shown in Figure 5-6. Click the OK button to dismiss the warning and continue the installation. When the installation of ADT plug-ins is complete, Eclipse will need to restart in order to apply the changes.

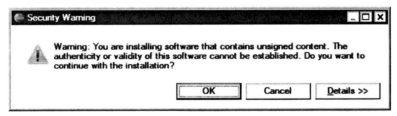

Figure 5-6. *Security warning due to unsigned ADT plug-ins*

Installing the Android SDK

ADT is a set of plug-ins to blend Android development tools into the Eclipse integrated development environment; it is not a substitute for the Android SDK.

The Android SDK is a comprehensive set of development tools, including Android platform Java libraries, an application packager, a debugger, an emulator, and extensive documentation. In order to do anything useful with ADT, the Android SDK needs to be installed on the machine. Upon restarting, ADT will welcome you with the SDK Configuration wizard, as shown in Figure 5-7.

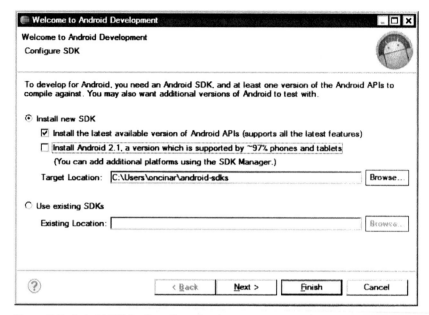

Figure 5-7. *Android SDK Configuration wizard*

The SDK Configuration wizard allows you to point ADT to an existing Android SDK (if it is previously installed), or to instruct ADT to download and install the Android SDK for you. Click the Finish button to move forward with the SDK configuration process. The SDK Configuration wizard will guide you through the process for installing the Android SDK to your host machine. Note the installation directory of the Android SDK, since you will need it to update the system Path variable, as described next.

Updating the Path

During Android SDK installation, the Path variable is not automatically added to the system. ADT does not require having the SDK binaries in the system Path variable, but to make these files easily accessible, it is strongly recommended that you add them.

Updating the Path on Microsoft Windows

Just as we did in Chapter 3 to add the JDK to the system Path variable, open the Control Panel and choose System to launch the System Properties dialog. Switch to the Advanced tab, and click the Environment Variables button. Select the Path variable from the System variables pane, and click the Edit button. Append ;*<sdk-dir>*\tools;*<sdk-dir>*\platform-tools to the Path variable value, replacing *<sdk-dir>* with the Android SDK installation directory, as shown in Figure 5-8. Click the OK button to save the changes.

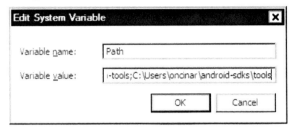

Figure 5-8. *Adding the Android SDK directories to the Windows system Path variable*

Updating the Path on Mac OS X and Linux

To append the Android SDK binary directories to your system Path variable, open a terminal window on Mac OS X, or a shell window on Linux, and enter the following command (replace *<sdk-dir>* with the Android SDK installation directory):

```
export PATH=$PATH:<sdk-dir>/tools:<sdk-dir>/platform-tools >> ~/.bashrc
```

Figure 5-9 shows the command in the terminal window.

Figure 5-9. *Adding the Android SDK directories to the Mac OS X system Path variable*

Installing Platform APIs

By default, the SDK Configuration wizard will install the latest version of the Android APIs; however, you can install different versions of Android APIs using the Android SDK Manager at any time. To launch the SDK Manager, choose **Window ➤ Android SDK Manager** from the top menu bar, as shown in Figure 5-10.

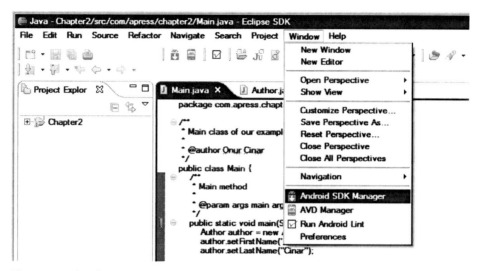

Figure 5-10. *Opening the Android SDK Manager*

As shown in Figure 5-11, the Android SDK Manager presents a list of Android SDK components, such as tools, APIs, and add-ons, that can be downloaded. The list is structured in a tree-like fashion. The first item in the list is Tools. These are the common and required components of the Android SDK. It is strongly recommended that you use the latest versions of the Tools components. The other components in the list are grouped under Android versions and API levels, and they are optional.

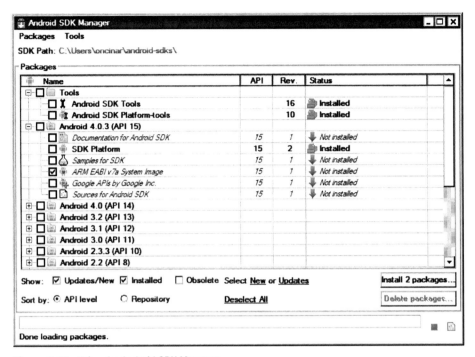

Figure 5-11. *Using the Android SDK Manager*

Click the plus sign next to these Android versions to see a list of available components. Depending on the selected version, you will be presented with a list of core components, as well as the available add-ons. Although this list changes based on the selected version, these are the most common components:

- **SDK Platform**: This is the core component that must be installed in order to develop applications for the selected Android version. The Android SDK Manager installs the SDK Platform under the `<sdk-dir>/platforms/android-<api-level>` directory, and the emulator system images under `<sdk-dir>/system-images/android-<api-level>` directory subfolders. The Android SDK makes these resources available to your application based on your application's target platform. Android developers are not expected to directly interact with these files.

- **Documentation for Android SDK:** This provides the offline version of the Android resources that are available at the `http://developer.android.com` website. The Android SDK Manager installs the documentation under the `<sdk-dir>/docs` directory if it is selected for installation. You can access the main page of the documentation by pointing your web browser to `file:///<sdk-dir>/docs/index.html`. For fast and offline access, you may consider installing this component.

- **Samples for SDK:** These provide example applications demonstrating the use of the Android APIs. The Android SDK Manager installs the sample applications under `<sdk-dir>/samples/android-<api-level>` directory subfolders. It is highly recommended that you install the sample applications because they are a great resource for learning about Android API features and experimenting with them.

- **Sources for Android SDK:** These provide the source code for the Android framework. The Android SDK Manager installs the source code under the `<sdk-dir>/sources/android-<api-level>` directory. These source files come in very handy while troubleshooting Android applications, since they allow developers to dive into the Android framework to quickly identify the root cause of many obscure problems.

- **Google APIs by Google Inc.:** This is not a part of the core components and is distributed as an add-on. The Android SDK Manager installs these APIs under the `<sdk-dir>/add-ons` directory. This add-on allows you to develop applications using Google's API and services, such as Google Maps. It also comes with an extended emulator system image that contains the Google system components that are not available in the default emulator system image.

As you may recall from the Chapter 1, the Android market is highly fragmented, and the newer versions of Android propagate very slowly. It is a common practice to build applications on the top of the most widely supported API level in order to cover a larger user base. At the time of this writing, the most widely used Android version is 2.3.3, which supports API level 10.

To install API level 10, click the plus sign next to Android 2.3.3 (API 10) in the list to expand it. Select the SDK Platform component and any other components that you would like to install, and click the Install Packages button. The Android SDK Manager will ask you to accept the licensing terms for the selected components. Choose Accept All, and then click the Install button to continue with the installation of the packages.

Certain components may require you to register on the producer's web site and provide download credentials. In those cases, the Android SDK Manager shows the corresponding dialogs to guide you through the process. The Android SDK Manager installs the selected components in their corresponding directories under the SDK directory. The location of the SDK directory is shown at the top of the Android SDK Manager dialog, labeled as "SDK Path" (see Figure 5-11).

Exploring ADT

ADT provides access to Android SDK components from within Eclipse. In this section, we will explore these components: the Android Virtual Device Manager, Dalvik Debug Monitor, Traceview, Hierarchy Viewer, and Android Lint.

Android Virtual Device Manager

The Android SDK comes with a full-featured emulator, a virtual device that runs on your machine. The Android emulator allows you to develop and test Android applications locally on your machine without using a physical device.

The Android emulator runs a full Android system stack, including the Linux kernel. It is a fully virtualized device that can mimic all of the hardware and software features of a real device. Each of these features can be customized by the user using the Android Virtual Device (AVD) Manager. To launch the AVD Manager, choose **Window ➤ AVD Manager** from the top menu bar, as shown in Figure 5-12.

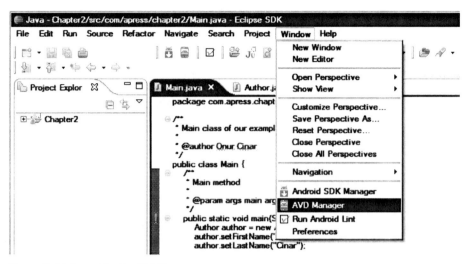

Figure 5-12. *Launching the AVD Manager*

The AVD Manager allows you to define multiple virtual device configurations. The AVD Manager dialog lists the previously defined configurations, as shown in Figure 5-13.

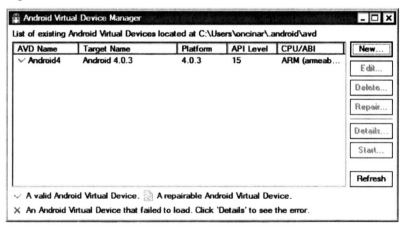

Figure 5-13. *Existing virtual devices listed in the AVD Manager dialog*

Configuring a New Virtual Device

To define a new virtual machine instance, click the New button on right side of the AVD Manager dialog. This opens the Create new Android Virtual Device (AVD) dialog, as shown in Figure 5-14.

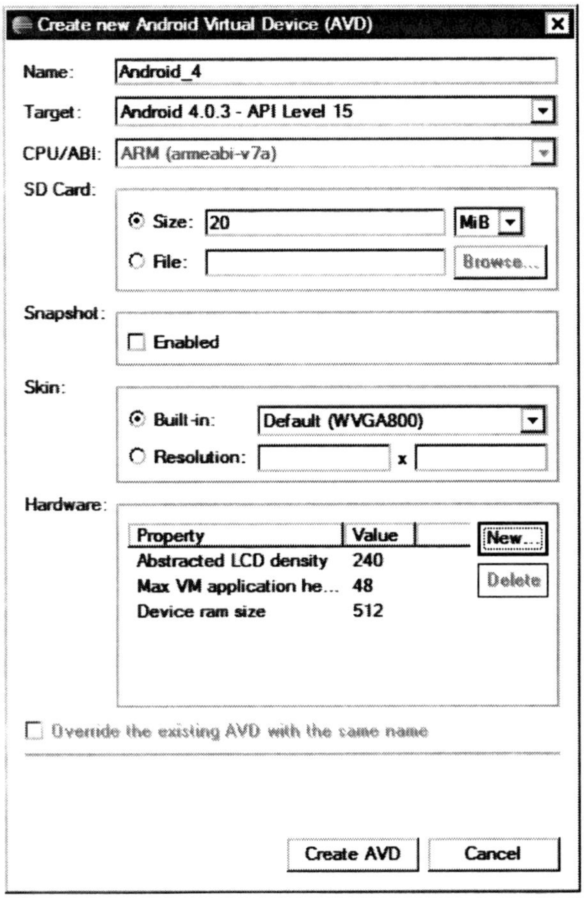

Create new Android Virtual Device (AVD)   [X]

Name:	Android_4
Target:	Android 4.0.3 - API Level 15 ▾
CPU/ABI:	ARM (armeabi-v7a) ▾

SD Card:
- ⊙ Size: 20   MiB ▾
- ○ File: _____ Browse...

Snapshot:
- ☐ Enabled

Skin:
- ⊙ Built-in: Default (WVGA800) ▾
- ○ Resolution: _____ x _____

Hardware:

Property	Value	
Abstracted LCD density	240	[New...]
Max VM application he...	48	[Delete]
Device ram size	512	

☐ Override the existing AVD with the same name

[Create AVD]   [Cancel]

Figure 5-14. *Configuring a new virtual device*

This dialog has the following fields:

- **Name**: This is the unique name for the new virtual device configuration.

- **Target**: This is the Android version number and the API level for the virtual device. The drop-down list shows only the Android versions that were installed using the Android SDK Manager. If the preferred version is not available, you will need to install it using the Android SDK Manager.

- **CPU/ABI**: This is machine architecture for the new virtual device. Currently, only ARM machine architecture is supported.

- **SD Card**: This is either the size of the SD card or the location of the existing disk image. This field can be empty if an SD card is not required for this virtual device configuration.

- **Snapshot**: This is to allow the persistence of the state of the virtual device between sessions.

- **Skin**: This is the skin and screen dimensions for the virtual device. The drop-down list is populated based on the installed versions and add-ons. Custom screen dimensions can also be defined.

- **Hardware**: This is the list of hardware features that the virtual device supports, such as a GPS and camera. You can enable features by clicking to the New button and selecting the individual items, as shown in Figure 5-15.

Figure 5-15. *Adding a hardware feature*

In the next chapters, we will be using the Android emulator. The following virtual machine configuration is recommended to execute the example code snippets in those chapters:

- The Name parameter should be set to **Android_10**.

- The Target parameter should be set to **Android 2.3.3 – API Level 10**. If this target is not available in the drop-down list, use the Android SDK Manager to download it.

      The SD Card size should be set to at least 128MB.

The other settings can be left as is.

After setting the parameters, click the Create AVD button to store the virtual device configuration.

Launching the Emulator

Virtual device configurations can be used to start emulator instances at any time. After selecting the virtual device configuration, click the Start button start a new emulator instance using the selected virtual device configuration. Before starting the emulator, the AVD Manager displays the Launch Options dialog, as shown in Figure 5-16.

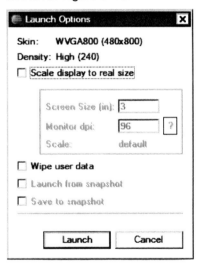

Figure 5-16. *Emulator Launch Options dialog*

The emulator screen may look too big depending on your screen size and resolution. Using the Launch Options dialog, check the "Scale display to real size" box, and set your monitor size and resolution to scale the emulator.

The Launch Options dialog also allows you to wipe the user data to bring the emulator to its initial state. If you set Snapshot to Enabled during the configuration, the Launch Options dialog also allows you to launch the emulator from the existing snapshot, and to decide whether the emulator state should be stored in the snapshot or discarded upon termination.

Click the Launch button in the Launch Options dialog to start the emulator, as shown in Figure 5-17. The Android emulator may take some time to start, depending on the CPU power of your host platform.

Figure 5-17. *Emulator instance*

Controlling the Emulator

The left pane of the emulator window shows the emulator display, and the right pane contains the soft keys. Touch events can be emulated using the mouse. Also, the key combinations listed in Table 5-1 can be used to control hardware features.

Table 5-1. *Emulator Control Shortcut Keys*

Key Combination	Description
Keypad 7, Ctrl+F11	Switches to previous layout orientation (portrait or landscape)
Keypad 9, Ctrl+F12	Switches to next layout orientation (portrait or landscape)
F8	Toggles cell networking
F9	Toggles code profiling
Alt+Enter	Toggles full-screen mode
F6	Toggles trackball

Android Console

The mouse- and keyboard-based control methods allow users to interact with the emulator and to do common tasks. However, directly controlling the hardware features, such as the network connectivity, is not possible through this method. The Android console provides an extensive interface that allows users to control the emulator and the hardware features. On a single machine, multiple emulator instances can run in parallel. Each emulator instance is automatically assigned a unique port number between 5554 and 5584. This number appears before the configuration name on the title bar of the emulator window (see in Figure 5-17).

The emulator listens on that port number to provide access to the Android console. A telnet application can be used to connect to that port to access the Android console. Telnet applications establish a TCP connection to the given port and allow the users to interact with the remote service. On Mac OS X and Linux platforms, a telnet application is provided by the operating system. For Windows systems, you can download a free telnet application, such as PuTTY (http://www.chiark.greenend.org.uk/~sgtatham/putty/download.html).

Using the telnet application based on your system, connect to the address localhost and the port number associated with the emulator instance. After you've connected to the Android console, the text-based interface allows you to control the emulator and the hardware features. By typing **help**, you can get a list the available commands, as shown in Figure 5-18.

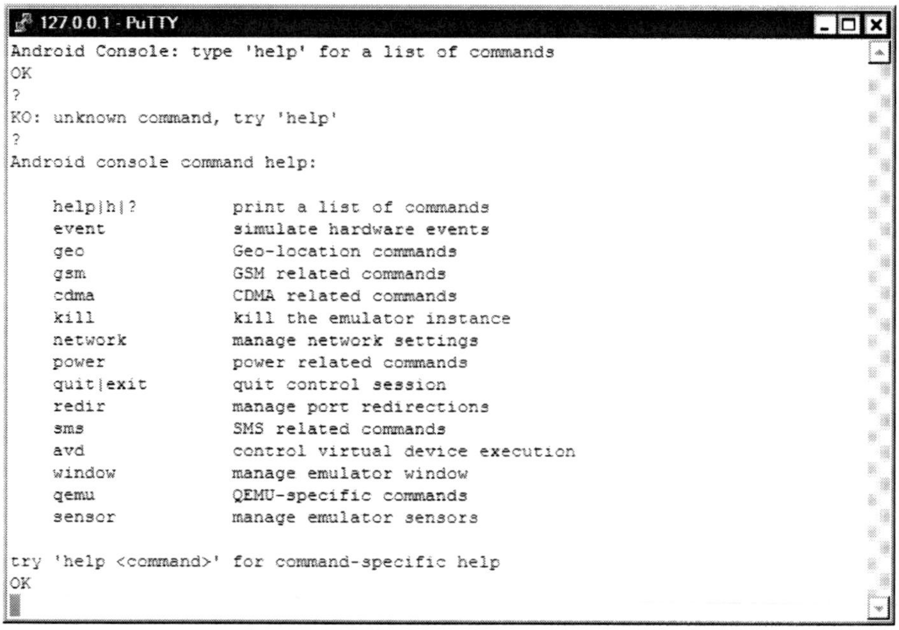

Figure 5-18. *Emulator control port list of commands*

Dalvik Debug Monitor Server

The Android SDK comes with a debugging tool called Dalvik Debug Monitor Server (DDMS). DDMS allows developers to monitor and interact with attached devices and emulators. It provides port-forwarding, screen capture, access to process and thread states, heap information, a file explorer, logs, and many other features.

DDMS also acts as a bridge between the Dalvik virtual machine running on the device or emulator, as well as the Eclipse debugger. It handles the lower-level communication setup to allow the Eclipse debugger to communicate with the Dalvik virtual machine. This allows developers to debug Android applications easily, as if they were plain Java applications running on the host machine.

Although DDMS comes as a stand-alone application with the Android SDK, it is broken down by ADT into multiple Eclipse views and provided as an Eclipse perspective combining these individual views. In this chapter, we will focus on the Eclipse perspective flavor of DDMS.

To launch the DDMS perspective, choose **Window** ➤ **Open Perspective** ➤ **Other …** from the top menu bar and select DDMS from the Open Perspective dialog. The

DDMS perspective is formed by multiple Android-specific views, as shown in Figure 5-19 and described in the following sections.

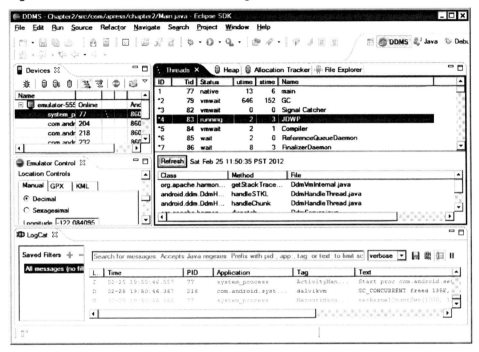

Figure 5-19. *DDMS perspective*

Devices View

The Devices view provides a list of attached devices and emulators. Each device can be expanded to show the list of running applications by clicking the plus sign on its left. The Devices view also provides a toolbar and drop-down menu to initiate common operations on the selected device or application, as shown in Figure 5-20.

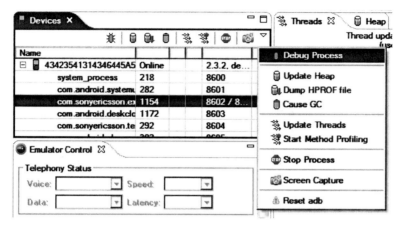

Figure 5-20. *Devices view drop-down menu*

The Devices view drop-down menu offers the following options:

- **Debug Process**: This option starts a debug session for the selected application.

- **Update Heap**: This option enables collecting heap information for the selected application.

- **Dump HPROF File**: This option dumps the heap of the selected application into an HPROF-formatted file for deeper memory investigation.

- **Cause GC**: This option triggers garbage collection for the selected application to free up unused memory.

- **Update Threads**: This option enables tracking thread status for the selected application.

- **Start Method Profiling**: This option enables collecting profiling data of method invocations from the selected application.

- **Stop Process**: This option stops the selected application process.

- **Screen Capture**: This option captures the device's current display into a file.

- **Reset adb**: This option resets the Android Debug Bridge (ADB) that is providing the connection between the host machine and the device.

Emulator Control View

If the selected device is an emulator, the Emulator Control view allows simulating voice and data networks and location status for debugging and testing purposes, as shown in Figure 5-21.

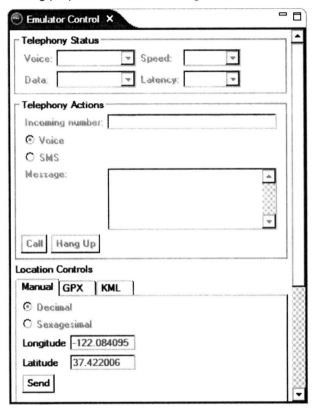

Figure 5-21. *Emulator Control view*

The Emulator Control view functionality is grouped into three sections:

  ▨ **Telephony Status**: This section allows changing the different aspects of a device's network status, such as the connection state, network speed, and latency.

  ▨ **Telephony Actions**: This section allows generating calls and SMS messages against the device in order to test the application's interaction with incoming voice calls and SMS messages.

      ■ **Location Controls**: This section allows setting a mock location for the device in order to test the application's interaction with location changes. The mock location can be specified as a fixed coordinate, or multiple locations can be injected into the device using the GPX- or KML-formatted coordinate files.

LogCat View

The LogCat view, shown in Figure 5-22, provides access to the log messages from the device. It presents the log messages in real time in a table-like fashion. The table is divided into multiple columns, including Level, Time, PID, Application, Tag, and Message.

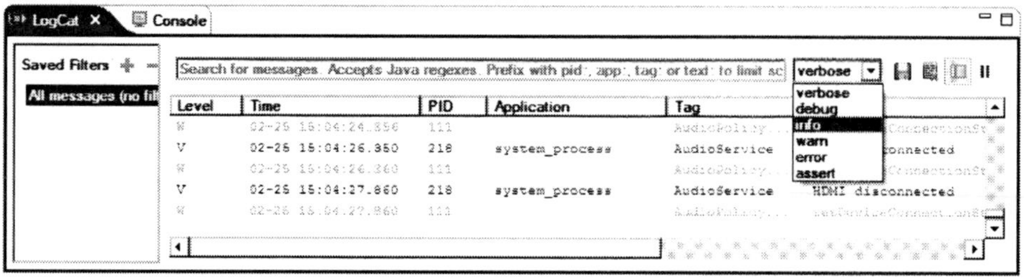

Figure 5-22. *LogCat view showing log messages*

The LogCat view allows filtering log messages by log level and also based on message filtering criteria. Commonly used log filters can also be stored and reused. You can save displayed log messages to a file using the LogCat view interface.

Threads View

The Threads view provides access to thread state and stack traces for the selected application. By default, thread tracking is not enabled. To access the thread information, select the application using the Devices view, and then click the Update Threads button. The Threads view presents the list of existing threads in a table format, as shown in Figure 5-23.

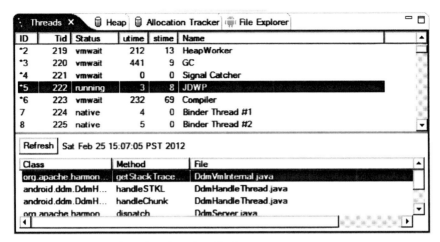

Figure 5-23. *Threads view of a selected application*

The Threads view columns provide the following information per thread:

- **ID**: This is the virtual machine assigned to the thread instance.
- **TID**: This is the thread ID assigned by the Linux operating system.
- **Status**: This is the current status of the thread, which can be any of the following states:
  - Running, when **executing code**
  - Sleeping, when **sleeping in a** `Thread.sleep()` **call**
  - Monitor, when **waiting for a monitor lock**
  - Waiting, when **waiting in an** `Object.wait()` **call**
  - Native, when **executing native code**
  - Vmwait, when **waiting on a virtual machine resource**
- **Utime**: This is the time spent running the user code in jiffies.
- **Stime**: This is the time spent running the system code in jiffies.
- **Name**: This is the name given to the thread by the application.

> **NOTE:** A **jiffy** is the unit of time for the duration of one tick of the system timer interrupt. On the Android system, a jiffy equals 4 milliseconds.

Heap View

The Heap view provides information about the amount of memory the selected application is using. It is a very important tool for investigating memory problems. It displays the list of heap allocations in a table format, as shown in Figure 5-24. This table shows the count, total size, and statistics about each heap allocation, grouped by the class type. The bottom pane of the Heap view contains a histogram chart demonstrating the allocation counts per allocation sizes.

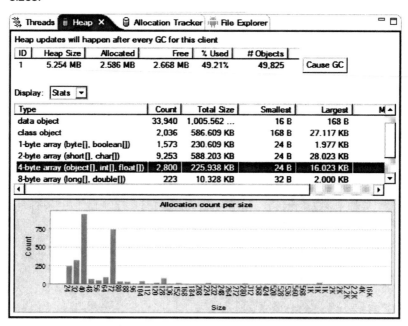

Figure 5-24. *Heap view*

By default, heap information is not collected from every application. To start collecting heap allocation information, select the application in the Devices view, and then click the Update Heap button. The Heap view will begin collecting heap allocation information from the application. Heap allocation information is collected when the virtual machine does garbage collection. To get a quick snapshot of the heap allocation, click the Cause GC button to trigger garbage collection.

Allocation Tracker View

The Allocation Tracker view allows tracking of the memory allocation of the selected application. It is a very useful tool for investigating memory problems in complex applications. This view provides the list of allocations in a table format, as shown in Figure 5-25. The columns show information about the allocation, including the allocated class type; allocation size; and in which class, method, and thread the allocation occurred.

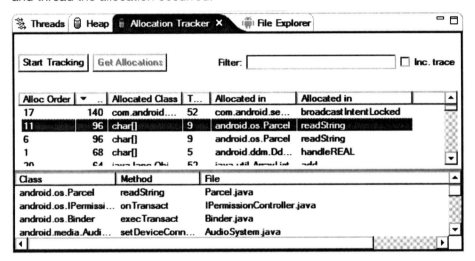

Figure 5-25. *Allocation Tracker view*

To start collecting allocation data from the selected application, click the Start Tracking button. Using the application, conduct any operations that are the subject of the memory investigation. During this process, you can get snapshots for the allocations by clicking the Get Allocations button. When you are finished with the investigation, stop the Allocation Tracker by clicking the Stop Tracking button.

File Explorer View

The File Explorer view allows users to interact with the file system on the selected device. As shown in Figure 5-26, it presents the file system of the devices in a combined tree and table format. You can expand directories by clicking the plus sign on their left. The list also shows the size, permissions, modification date, and time for each file and directory.

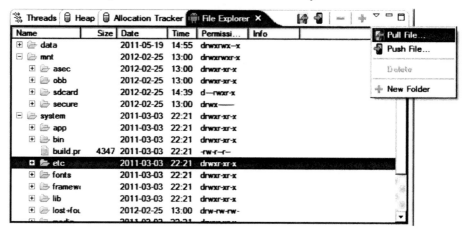

Figure 5-26. *File Explorer view listing files on the selected device*

The File Explorer view also provides file operations through its toolbar and its drop-down menu, which has the following options:

- **Pull File**: This option downloads a file from the device to the host machine.

- **Push File**: This option uploads a file from the host machine to the device.

- **Delete**: This option deletes the selected file from the device.

- **New Folder**: This option adds a new folder to the device.

These file operations run under a restricted user account, known as the shell user. For that reason, the operations that can be done on the device are limited by this user account's privileges. If an operation could not be completed due to restrictions, the File Explorer view will show an error dialog to inform the user.

Traceview

As the Heap and Allocation Tracker views allow you to analyze the memory consumption of their application, Traceview lets you analyze the breakdown of where CPU time has been spent during the execution of the application. Traceview comes with the Android SDK both as a stand-alone application and an Eclipse editor plug-in.

Traceview operates on recorded trace files. The Dalvik virtual machine does not generate these trace files by default. To create trace files, you can use the tracing methods provided through the `android.os.Debug` API, or you can enable tracing through DDMS by clicking the Start Method Profiling button in the Devices view. Traceview analyzes the trace file and presents the results, as shown in Figure 5-27.

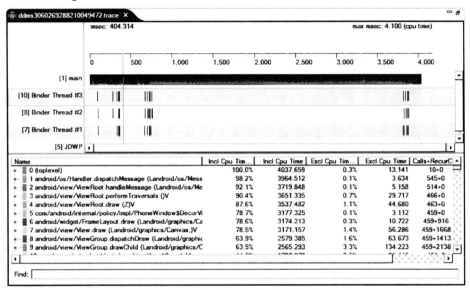

Figure 5-27. *Traceview analyzing a trace file*

Traceview has two panels:

    Timeline panel: The top panel shows each thread's execution in its own row, with time increasing to the right. Each method that was executed in this thread is color-coded and displayed as a thin line on the timeline.

    Profile panel: The bottom panel shows the detailed summary of time spent in each method. It shows both inclusive and exclusive times. Exclusive time is the time spent running the method itself. Inclusive time is the total time spent running the method and other methods that are called from this method. The Profile panel also shows the number of times the method is called. This panel provides extensive information for identifying methods that are consuming the most CPU time during the execution of the application.

Hierarchy Viewer

- An Android user interface is constructed on top of layout components that position its child views dynamically based on the available screen space. When these layouts and views are not properly structured, they can easily slow down the entire application, and it's hard to find these bottlenecks in a complex application.

- The Android SDK comes with a tool called Hierarchy Viewer, which allows you to debug and optimize user interfaces. It provides a visual representation of the layout and view hierarchy. It also determines the time it takes to measure, lay out, and draw a view. The bottlenecks are color-coded, which makes them easily visible.

- Hierarchy Viewer also provides the Pixel Perfect tool, which magnifies the user interfaces. This allows you to examine pixel properties of the actual display in order to make final touches.

Although Hierarchy Viewer comes as a stand-alone application with the Android SDK, it is broken down by ADT into multiple Eclipse views and provided as an Eclipse perspective that combines these individual views. In this chapter, we will focus on the Eclipse perspective flavor of Hierarchy Viewer.

To launch the Hierarchy Viewer perspective, choose **Window ➤ Open Perspective ➤ Other** ... from the top menu bar and select Hierarchy Viewer from the Open Perspective dialog. The Hierarchy Viewer perspective is formed by multiple Android-specific views, as shown in Figure 5-28 and described in the following sections.

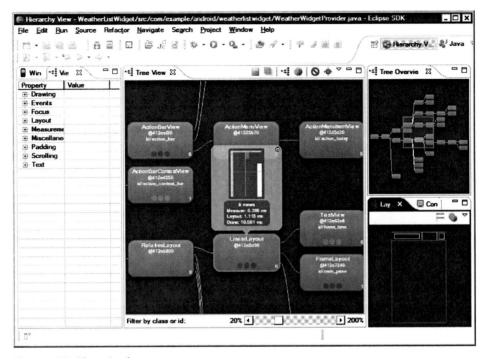

Figure 5-28. *Hierarchy view*

Windows View

The Windows view lists the attached devices and the emulators in a tree-like format. Each device can be expanded to show the active windows by clicking the plus sign on the left, as shown in Figure 5-29.

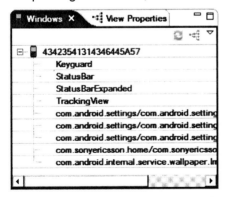

Figure 5-29. *Windows view showing the active windows*

A window needs to be selected in order to use Hierarchy Viewer. If your application is not visible on the list, click the Refresh button for the view to reload the active windows list.

Tree View

The Tree view shows the layout structure of the selected window in a tree-like fashion (see Figure 5-28). Each tree item is connected to its parent using lines, which makes it easier to visualize the view hierarchy.

Each view item shows its name and resource ID as its title. You can drag the content to navigate through the views. Below the title, the amounts of time spent in measure, layout, and draw steps are color-coded and shown as circles filled with green, yellow, or red. Red indicates that the view component is taking too much time in any of these steps. When you click a view item, the actual measurement for each of these steps is shown in milliseconds, as shown in Figure 5-30.

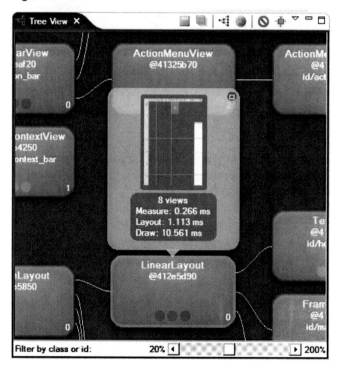

Figure 5-30. *Tree view showing view item details*

Tree Overview View

Depending on the size of the view hierarchy, showing all the views and components within the Tree view may not be possible. For navigation within the view hierarchy, the Tree Overview view provides a smaller map representing the entire Tree view window, as shown in Figure 5-31. The currently selected view is highlighted on the map.

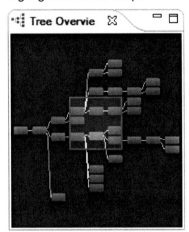

Figure 5-31. *Tree Overview view representing the entire Tree view as a map*

View Properties View

The View Properties view provides access to the properties of the selected view component. The View Properties view is displayed as a tab in the left pane. Using the View Properties view, you can examine all of the properties without needing to look at the application source code. To make the navigation easier, the properties are displayed in a tree format organized by the property category, as shown in Figure 5-32.

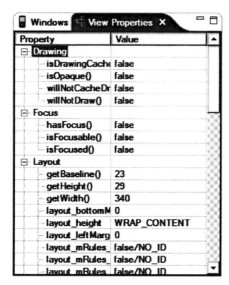

Figure 5-32. *View Properties view listing all of the properties of the active view*

Layout View

The Layout view provides a block representation of the entire window, as shown in Figure 5-33. When you select a view block, the corresponding view will be selected in both the Tree and View Properties views.

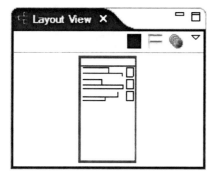

Figure 5-33. *Layout view showing the block representation*

The outline colors of the blocks also provide extra information regarding the views:

▨ Bold red represents the view that is currently selected in the Tree view.

- Light red represents the parent of the current selected view.

- White represents a visible view that is not a parent or child of the currently selected view.

Android Lint

Android Lint is a tool for scanning Android application projects for potential bugs and most common mistakes. It also finds any inconsistencies in layouts, resources, and the manifest file. It is a very powerful tool that should be employed during the development cycle in order to keep the application source code clean and robust.

The Android Lint tool can detect the following problems:

- Missing and unused translations

- Unused and inconsistent resources

- Typography suggestions for string resources

- Accessibility and internationalization problems such as hard-coded strings

- Layout performance problems

- Usability problems in layouts and input fields

- Icon and graphic problems, such as duplicate icons and wrong sizes

- Manifest errors

- Use of deprecated APIs

Android Lint is provided both as a stand-alone application, for quick integration into an existing build system, and an Eclipse plug-in that is integrated into the development environment. In this section, we will focus on the Lint Eclipse plug-in.

To start Android Lint, select a project and choose **Window ➤ Run Android Lint** from the top menu bar, as shown in Figure 5-34.

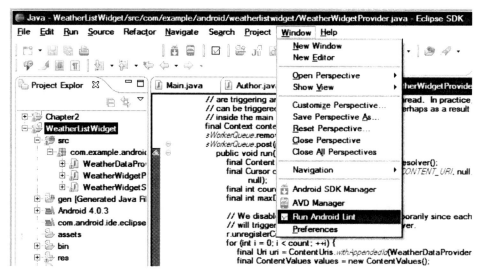

Figure 5-34. *Choosing to run Android Lint*

Android Lint goes through the project files, and presents its results through the Lint Warnings view, as shown in Figure 5-35.

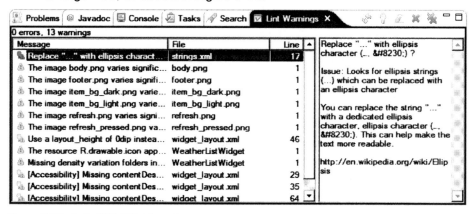

Figure 5-35. *Android Lint Warnings view*

The Lint warnings are listed in a table format. The columns show the Lint warning message and the associated file and line number. Selecting a warning item from the table shows a detailed description of the identified problem in the right pane.

Through its toolbar, the Lint Warnings view also allows you to initiate the following operations on the listed warnings:

- **Refresh**: This goes through the project files again and refreshes the list of Lint warnings.

- **Fix**: This fixes the warning automatically if a solution is known.

- **Ignore Type**: This ignores all of the warnings with the same type. For example, you can ignore all warnings related to image density.

- **Remove**: This removes the selected warning from the list.

- **Remove All**: This removes all warnings from the list.

Lint can also be configured through its Preferences dialog. Choose **Window ➤ Preferences** on Windows and Linux, or **Eclipse ➤ Preferences** on Mac OS X, from the top menu bar, and select Android, then Lint Error Checking from the Preferences category list to access the Lint properties. The Lint Preferences dialog provides a list of issues that can be detected through Lint. Using this list, you can change the severity levels associated with these issues, as shown in Figure 5-36. If an issue is not relevant to the project, its severity level can be set to Ignore in order to hide these issues from Lint warnings.

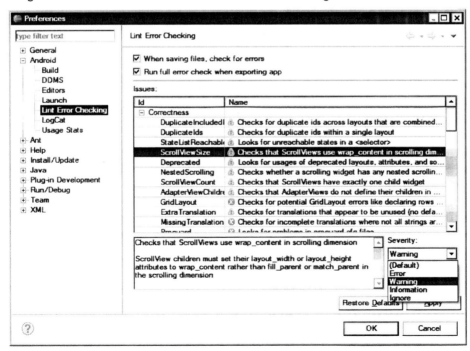

Figure 5-36. *Setting Lint preferences*

Releasing Applications

As discussed in earlier chapters, the Android platform requires each application to be signed by its author in order to be deployed on the Android platform. ADT provides a wizard to guide developers through the signing process.

During the development phase, the Android SDK transparently generated a debug key to sign the application automatically to streamline the process. But when the application is going to be released to the public, Android requires it to be signed with a release key.

Unlike other mobile platforms, Android does not rely on a certification authority to issue digital certificates to developers. Every Android developer can generate a key and sign an Android application on its host machine. When an application is installed on Android, its signature is used to check the authenticity of the application updates. If the application update is not signed with the same key, Android does not allow the new version to be deployed as an update. The ADT plug-in provides a set of wizards to generate keys and sign applications before public release.

To sign your application for release, using the Package Explorer, choose the application project, right-click it, and choose **Android Tools ➤ Export Signed Application Package...** from the context menu to launch the Export Android Application wizard, as shown in Figure 5-37.

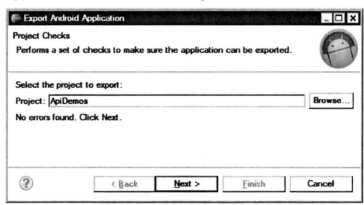

Figure 5-37. *Export Android Application wizard*

Confirm the project to be exported, and click the Next button to proceed. As shown in Figure 5-38, the wizard will ask for the location of the keystore to be used. If this is the first time you are signing an application, choose the Create new keystore radio button to generate a new one. Keystores hold one or more private keys. Using the Browse button, select the location and the file name for the keystore. Define a password to protect the keystore, and click the Next button to proceed.

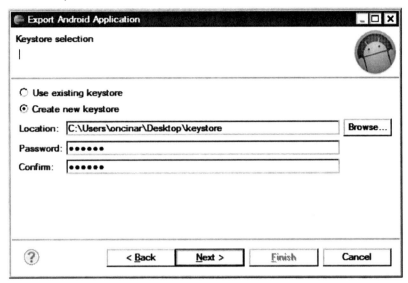

Figure 5-38. *Keystore selection for exporting a signed application*

If you choose to create a new keystore, the Export Android Application wizard presents a form to get enough information to properly produce a key, as shown in Figure 5-39. After you fill in the necessary information, click the Next button to proceed.

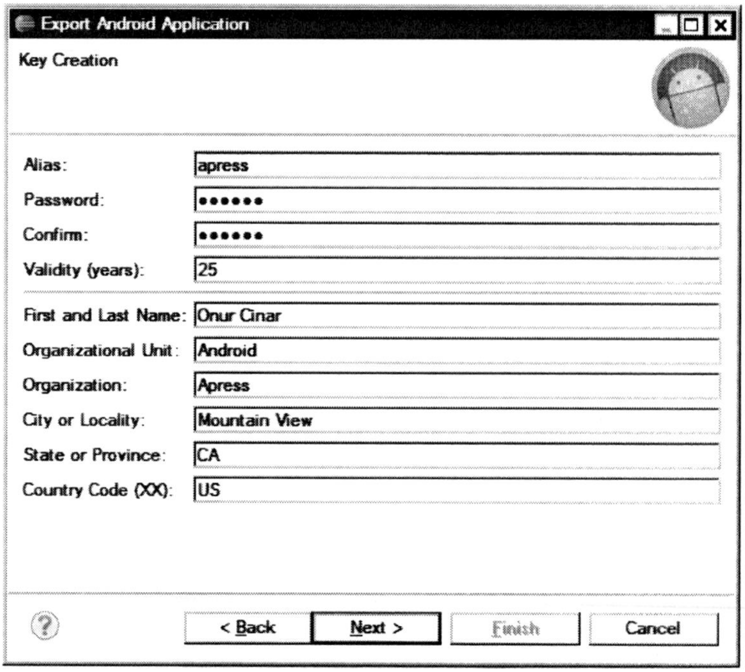

Figure 5-39. *Key creation information form*

If you already have a keystore that you are going to use, the wizard will ask you to select the key to be used from the given keystore, as shown in Figure 5-40.

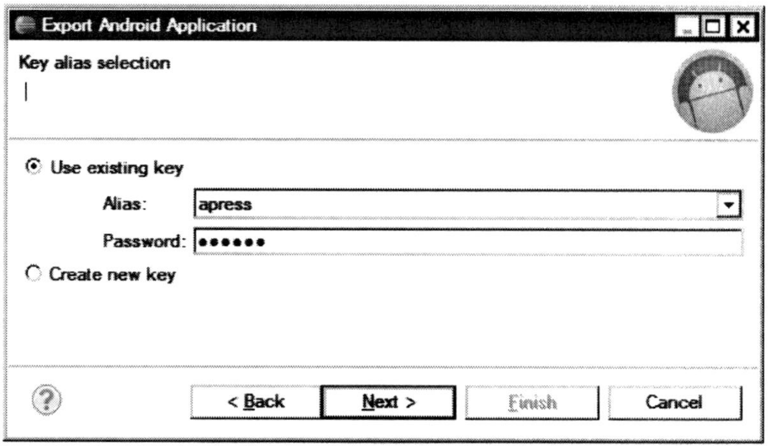

Figure 5-40. *Key selection by alias from the given keystore*

As the last step, the Export Android Application wizard will ask for the destination location for the signed APK file that will be released, as shown in Figure 5-41. Click the Browse button, and select the location and the file name. Then click the Finish button to start the process.

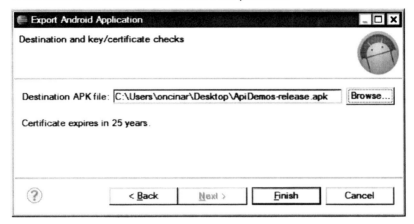

Figure 5-41. *Setting the destination for the signed APK file to be released*

The wizard will compile the Android application in release mode and sign it with the selected key. The signed APK file can be released to the public.

Summary

This chapter introduced the ADT plug-ins for Eclipse. We started our journey by installing ADT and the Android SDK. We then configured an Android virtual machine and explored its control interface. Next, we looked at DDMS, Traceview, Hierarchy Viewer, and Android Lint, exploring how to employ these tools during day-to-day Android development. Finally, we covered how to sign an Android application for release by using ADT.

Resources

The following resources are available for the topics covered in this chapter:

- Android Lint, `http://tools.android.com/tips/lint`

- Debugging and Profiling User Interfaces,
  `http://developer.android.com/guide/developing/debugging/debugging-ui.html`

- Dalvik Debug Monitor,
  `http://www.netmite.com/android/mydroid/dalvik/docs/debug mon.html`

- Android Tools Project, `http://tools.android.com/`

Chapter **6**

Project: Movie Player

In the previous chapter, we explored ADT for Eclipse. We reviewed the ADT views and tools, and how to involve them during day-to-day Android development. In this chapter, we will start putting all the tools and concepts that we have discussed in the previous chapters into action.

Our first Android project is a simple movie player application. Since the purpose of this experiment is to see Android development on Eclipse in action, we will not go too deeply into the Android framework APIs. In the next chapters, we will continue to build on this simple project.

An Overview of the Movie Player

Our movie player application will be a simple single activity application that will present a list of movie files, which are in the external storage. The list will show the thumbnail, name, and duration for each movie file. When you click a movie item in the list, the movie player application will rely on the Android platform to launch the corresponding video player activity to play the selected movie. Although this is a very simple project, it will allow us to experiment with most of the tools and concepts we have discussed in previous chapters.

We will start by using the New Android Project wizard to generate the skeleton project. Then we will use the editors provided by ADT to create the user interface. Through the manifest editor, we will modify the `AndroidManifest.xml` file based on our project's requirements. Using the layout editor, we will define the user interface layout for the movie list, as well as the layout for movie list items. We will employ the resource editor to properly define the string resources that we need in our user interface. While producing the necessary layout and resources, we will use Android Lint to validate the code in parallel. The application will rely on the media store content provider to fetch the list of movie files that are in external storage. The fetched information will be saved into movie objects that we will define in this chapter. We will also implement the movie list adapter to feed the information into the list view for presentation.

To play the selected movie files, we will rely on the Android platform by utilizing the startActivity method of the Activity class to launch the corresponding video player. While doing all of this, we will rely heavily on Eclipse's code templates, automatic code generators, and refactoring features to streamline the development process by letting Eclipse handle time-consuming operations.

Starting the MoviePlayer Project

To start our new Android project, choose File ➤ New ➤ Other from the top menu bar to open the New Project dialog, as shown in Figure 6-1.

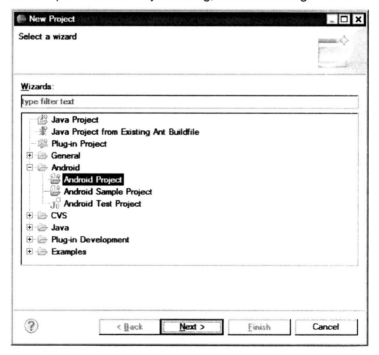

Figure 6-1. *Eclipse New Project dialog*

The New Project dialog is organized by project categories. Expand the Android project category, choose Android Project as the project type, and click the Next button. This launches the New Android Project wizard. As the first step, you supply the project name and its location. You can also choose whether to start with an empty project, build a project on top of an existing project, or start with an Android sample application, by selecting the corresponding radio button. For this example, name the project MoviePlayer, as shown in Figure 6-2, and then click the Next button.

Figure 6-2. *New Android Project wizard*

Next, the New Android Project wizard asks for the Android platform target for the new project, as shown in Figure 6-3. The list will show only the already installed SDKs. If your target platform is not in the list, you may need to download it using the Android SDK Manager. For this project, choose Android 2.3.3, API Level 10 as the target platform. This means that the new project will run on any Android device that supports API level 10 and above. Click the Next button to continue.

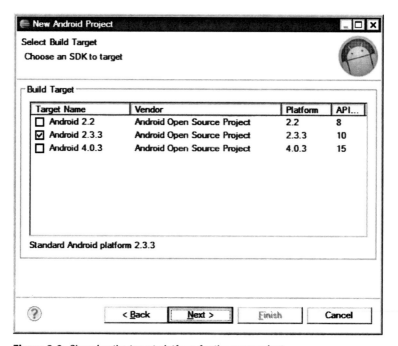

Figure 6-3. *Choosing the target platform for the new project*

Android applications are bundled as packages with a unique package name. The package naming concept and the naming convention are borrowed from the Java programming language. Package names are usually defined using a hierarchical naming pattern, with the levels of the hierarchy separated by dots. Although the Android application code may contain multiple packages, there should still be one main package for Android to refer to the application.

As the last step in defining a new project, the New Android Project wizard will ask for the application name and the unique package name. For our example, the package name is com.apress.movieplayer, as shown in Figure 6-4. Besides the package name, this dialog also asks for the minimum SDK. The minimum SDK identifies the minimum API level required in order to run this application on an Android device.

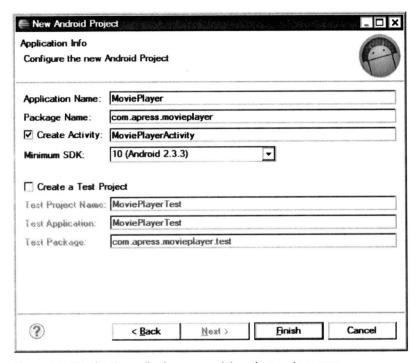

Figure 6-4. *Entering the application name and the unique package name*

As you can see in Figure 6-4, the New Android Project wizard can also generate most of the default components, such as the main activity and the unit test project, to provide enough skeleton code to make it faster to start a new project. Since our movie player application will need an activity to interact with the user, select the Create Activity option.

Click the Finish button. The New Android Project wizard will automatically generate the project layout as well as the required project files, as shown in Figure 6-5.

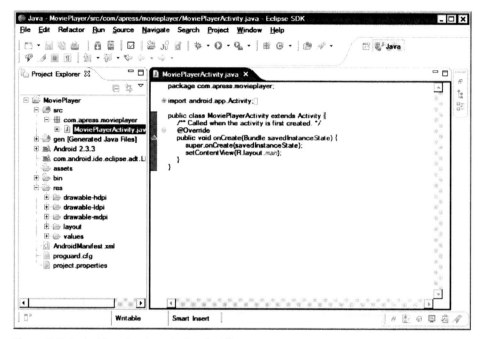

Figure 6-5. *Project layout and required project files*

The following project directories and files are created:

- `src`: This directory contains the Java source files. The application package is automatically generated in this directory by the New Android Project wizard.

- `gen`: This directory contains automatically generated project files, such as the R class for **resource index**. Users are not expected to modify the content of this directory. The content of this directory is regenerated each time the project is compiled.

- `assets`: This directory contains the application assets.

- `bin`: This directory contains the compiled class files and the installable Android package file for this application. Users are not expected to modify the content of this directory.

- res: This directory contains subdirectories for different types of application resources. The New Android Project wizard will automatically generate the layout, string resources, and icons for the main activity in the corresponding resource directories. Resources are organized as follows:

  - Animation resources are saved in the anim subdirectory.

  - Color resources are saved in the color subdirectory.

  - Image files are saved in corresponding drawable subdirectories depending on the target screen resolutions.

  - User interface resources are saved in the layout subdirectory.

  - Menu resources are saved in the menu subdirectory.

  - Other resources, such as string resources and user interface styles, are saved in the values subdirectory.

- AndroidManifest.xml: This is the application manifest file. The New Android Project wizard automatically generates this file with the content from the information collected through the wizard's dialogs.

- proguard.cfg: This is the ProGuard configuration file that is used by ProGuard while obfuscating the application package for release builds.

- project.properties: This is a properties file that is used by the Android SDK build system while compiling and packaging the application.

Using ADT Editors

ADT provides a variety of editors to manipulate project files. In the following sections, we will use these editors to customize the project skeleton based on our project requirements.

Manifest Editor

- Double-click the AndroidManifest.xml file to open it. ADT comes with a custom editor for manipulating the manifest files. Eclipse will detect the type of the file and open it with the manifest editor, as shown in Figure 6-6.

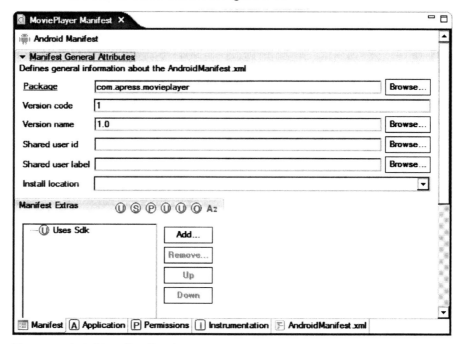

Figure 6-6. *Android manifest file editor*

The manifest editor provides a set of tabs to allow manipulating every aspect of the Android manifest file. Since the user interface provides all possible values, it makes editing manifest files easier and more robust. At any given time, you can switch to the XML tab (AndroidManifest.xml) to work with the XML source file as well.

Layout Editor

Android application user interfaces are defined using XML-based layout files. For complex user interfaces, maintaining these XML files becomes a very challenging task. ADT comes with a visual user interface editor plug-in for Eclipse, which allows you to design and maintain the layout XML files.

To see the layout editor in action, using the Project Explorer, navigate into the res directory, and then the layout directory, and choose the main.xml file. The main.xml file is the layout file for our main activity. Eclipse will automatically detect the type of this file and open it in the ADT's layout editor, as shown in Figure 6-7. The code generator has already populated this layout file with a "Hello World" message.

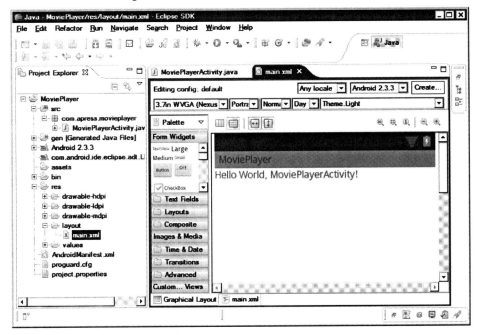

Figure 6-7. *Android visual layout editor*

The visual layout editor has three panes:

- The right pane displays the current layout as it will look on a real Android device.

- The top pane provides a set of drop-down menus to change the size and orientation of the display in order to see how the layout will adjust itself to these changes.

- The left pane contains a list of available widgets and layout components. You can drag-and-drop any view component from this pane to right pane to add a view component to the current layout.

Right-clicking a view component shows a list of available parameters, which you can change. Besides providing visual design capabilities, the editor also allows you to directly interact with the underlying XML-formatted layout code. To switch to the XML editing mode, select the `main.xml` tab at the bottom of the editor.

Now let's use the layout editor to change the layout of our movie player application.

Movie List Layout

We want to have our movie player application display movie files as a list. Switch to XML editor mode by selecting the `main.xml` tab, and the type the code in Listing 6-1.

Listing 6-1. *The main.xml File*

```xml
<?xml version="1.0" encoding="utf-8"?>
<LinearLayout xmlns:android="http://schemas.android.com/apk/res/android"
    android:layout_width="fill_parent"
    android:layout_height="fill_parent"
    android:orientation="vertical" >

    <ListView
        android:id="@+id/movieListView"
        android:layout_width="fill_parent"
        android:layout_height="fill_parent" >
    </ListView>
</LinearLayout>
```

This XML component contains only a single full-screen `android.widget.ListView`. Using the `android:id` attribute, we are assigning the ID `movieListView` to the `android.widget.ListView` component. Any view object may have an ID associated with it to uniquely identify it in the view hierarchy. IDs allow you to refer to view components in the application code. The at symbol (@) at the beginning of the ID string indicates that the XML parser should expand and identify it as an ID resource. The plus sign (+) that follows the at symbol indicates that this is a new resource name and must be added to the ID resources.

Now go back to the visual design mode to see the layout in action, as shown in Figure 6-8.

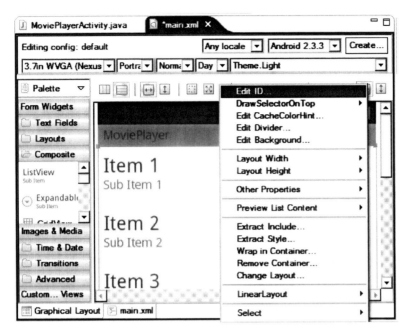

Figure 6-8. *ListView added to the layout*

Movie Item Layout

ListView, by default, allows you to quickly present the data as text items. However, for our movie player application, we would also like to show the movie thumbnail on the left in order to make it easier for the users to make selections.

To define this custom list item layout, choose **File ➤ New ➤ Other** from the top menu bar and select Android XML Layout File from the list, as shown in Figure 6-9.

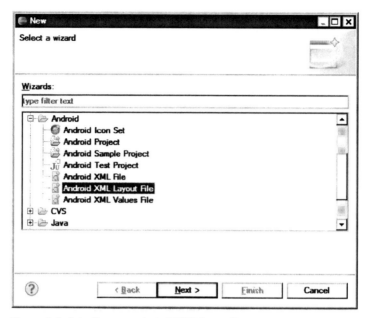

Figure 6-9. *Selecting a new Android XML layout file*

As the next step, the Android XML Layout File wizard will ask for the file name and the root element. The file name for this layout will be `movie_item.xml`. We would like the list items to have a thumbnail on the left, the movie title on the right, and the movie duration below the title. The way we were able to describe the layout strongly indicates that the `android.widget.RelativeLayout` is the right root element for the item layout. Select `RelativeLayout` from the list, as shown in Figure 6-10, and then click the Finish button.

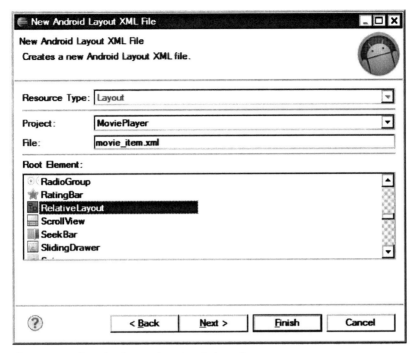

Figure 6-10. *Choosing the new layout root element*

In this layout, we are going to use an android.widget.ImageView view to show the movie thumbnail, and two android.widget.TextView views to show the movie title and the duration. Switch to the XML editor mode and type the XML code in Listing 6-2.

Listing 6-2. *The movie_item.xml File*

```xml
<?xml version="1.0" encoding="utf-8"?>
<RelativeLayout xmlns:android="http://schemas.android.com/apk/res/android"
    android:layout_width="match_parent"
    android:layout_height="match_parent">

    <ImageView
        android:id="@+id/thumbnail"
        android:layout_width="64dp"
        android:layout_height="64dp"
        android:layout_alignParentLeft="true"
        android:layout_alignParentTop="true"
        android:layout_marginRight="16dp"
        android:src="@drawable/ic_launcher" />
```

```
<TextView
    android:id="@+id/title"
    android:layout_width="wrap_content"
    android:layout_height="wrap_content"
    android:layout_alignTop="@+id/thumbnail"
    android:layout_toRightOf="@+id/thumbnail"
    android:text="Large Text"
    android:textAppearance="?android:attr/textAppearanceLarge" />

<TextView
    android:id="@+id/duration"
    android:layout_width="wrap_content"
    android:layout_height="wrap_content"
    android:layout_alignLeft="@+id/title"
    android:layout_below="@+id/title"
    android:text="Small Text"
    android:textAppearance="?android:attr/textAppearanceSmall" />

</RelativeLayout>
```

You can now switch to the visual editor mode to see the layout in action, as shown in Figure 6-11.

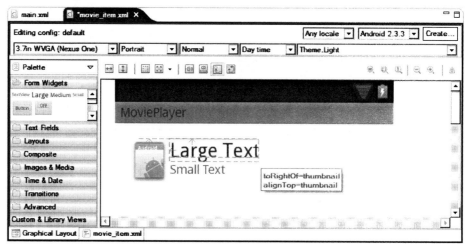

Figure 6-11: *Movie item added to the layout*

As you may have noticed, there is a tiny warning icon in the top-right corner of the visual layout editor. If you hover the mouse over this icon, you will see that Android Lint is warning you about possible issues with this layout. Clicking the warning icon brings up Android Lint's warning dialog, as shown in Figure 6-12.

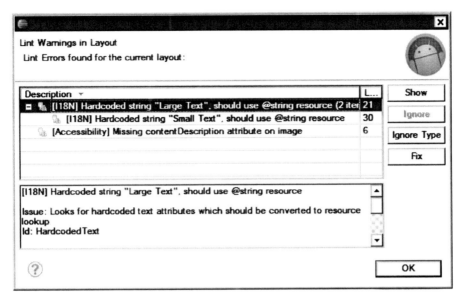

Figure 6-12. *Android Lint warning dialog showing layout problems*

For the first two errors, Android Lint is telling us that the strings we used in the XML layout file are hard-coded, and they should instead be in the string resources. Lint can automatically fix these errors for us, as described in Chapter 5.

Select the first issue that is related to the hard-coded "Large Text" string, and click the Fix button. Lint will show the Extract Android String dialog to confirm the proposed change, as shown in Figure 6-13. Click the OK button to proceed.

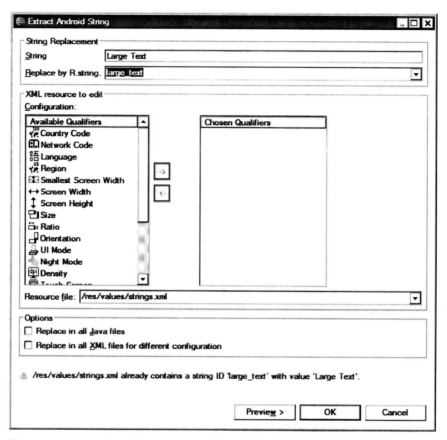

Figure 6-13. *Lint replacing the hard-coded string with a string reference*

Repeat the same procedure for the second error related to the "Small Text" string. Now the related portion of the layout XML file will look like the following:

```
<TextView
    android:id="@+id/title"
    android:layout_width="wrap_content"
    android:layout_height="wrap_content"
    android:layout_alignTop="@+id/thumbnail"
    android:layout_toRightOf="@+id/thumbnail"
    android:text="@string/large_text"
    android:textAppearance="?android:attr/textAppearanceLarge" />

<TextView
    android:id="@+id/duration"
    android:layout_width="wrap_content"
    android:layout_height="wrap_content"
```

```
        android:layout_alignLeft="@+id/title"
        android:layout_below="@+id/title"
        android:text="@string/small_text"
        android:textAppearance="?android:attr/textAppearanceSmall" />
```

For both errors, Lint defined a string resource, and replaced the value of
`android:text` attributes in the layout file with the corresponding string resource
ID. Not using any hard-coded strings in layout files is the proper way of defining
Android layouts.

Instead of having Lint fix the third error for us, let's fix it manually. In the layout
editor, define the `android:contentDescription` attribute for the thumbnail with
the string reference `thumbnail_description`. With this change, the `ImageView`
component will look like the following:

```
<ImageView
    android:id="@+id/thumbnail"
    android:layout_width="64dp"
    android:layout_height="64dp"
    android:layout_alignParentLeft="true"
    android:layout_alignParentTop="true"
    android:layout_marginRight="16dp"
    android:contentDescription="@string/thumbnail_description"
    android:src="@drawable/ic_launcher"  />
```

An error marker will be shown next to `thumbnail_description` since the string
resource is not yet defined. We will use the resource editor to define this string
resource.

Resource Editor

Android application string resources are stored in XML-formatted files. ADT
provides a custom editor for manipulating these resource files. Navigate to the
`res` directory, and then the `values` directory, and select the `strings.xml`
resource file. Eclipse will open the resource file within the custom editor, as
shown in Figure 6-14.

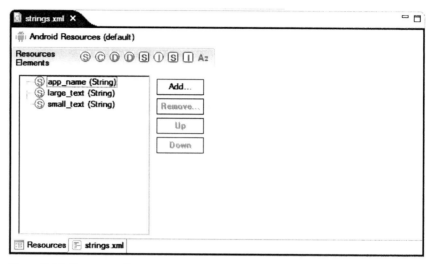

Figure 6-14. *Resource editor*

On the top pane of the editor, you will see a set of letters to filter the list of resources to contain only certain types of elements. By clicking the buttons on the right, you can manipulate the list of resources. At any time, by switching to the XML tab, you can directly interact with the resource XML source file.

To define the `thumbnail_description` string resource, click the Add button. In the dialog that appears, choose String as the resource type, as shown in Figure 6-15, and then click the OK button to proceed.

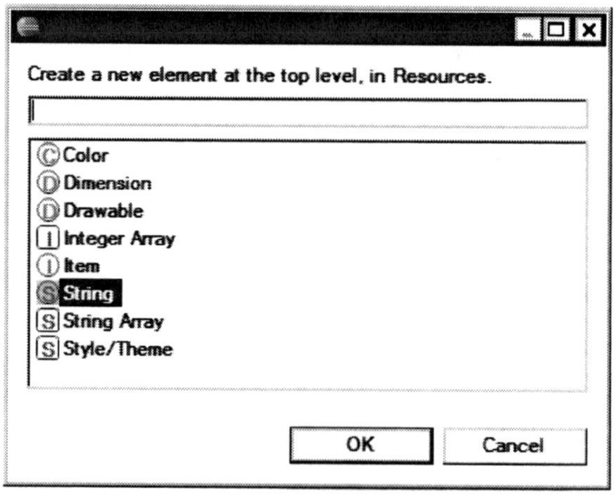

Figure 6-15. *Selecting the resource type*

Using the right pane, define the `thumbnail_description` string resource, as shown in Figure 6-16.

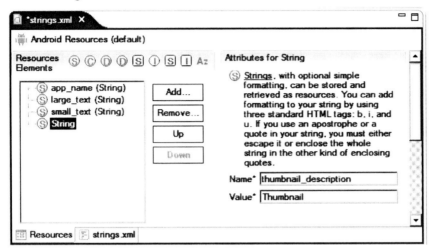

Figure 6-16. *Defining the string resource*

Defining the Classes

We have completed defining the user interface and the necessary resources. We will now start implementing the necessary model classes to hold the data that will be presented in the user interface.

Movie Class

For our movie player application, we will need a model class called `Movie` to store the information about each movie item. Choose **File ➤ New ➤ Class** from the top menu bar to define a new class. Eclipse will ask for the class name and its package. Set the class name field to `Movie`, and set the package name to `com.apress.movieplayer`. In the editor area, enter the Java code in Listing 6-3 (don't worry about the errors for now).

Listing 6-3. *The Movie.java File*

```
package com.apress.movieplayer;

/**
 * Movie file meta data.
 *
```

```
 * @author Onur Cinar
 */
class Movie {
    /** Movie title. */
    private final String title;

    /** Movie file. */
    private final String moviePath;

    /** MIME type. */
    private final String mimeType;

    /** Movie duration in ms. */
    private final long duration;

    /** Thumbnail file. */
    private final String thumbnailPath;

    /**
     * Constructor.
     *
     * @param mediaCursor
     *             media cursor.
     * @param thumbnailCursor
     *             thumbnail cursor.
     */
    public Movie(Cursor mediaCursor, Cursor thumbnailCursor) {
        title = mediaCursor.getString(mediaCursor
                .getColumnIndexOrThrow(MediaStore.Video.Media.TITLE));

        moviePath = mediaCursor.getString(mediaCursor
                .getColumnIndex(MediaStore.Video.Media.DATA));

        mimeType = mediaCursor.getString(mediaCursor
                .getColumnIndex(MediaStore.Video.Media.MIME_TYPE));

        duration = mediaCursor.getLong(mediaCursor
                .getColumnIndex(MediaStore.Video.Media.DURATION));

        if ((thumbnailCursor != null) && thumbnailCursor.moveToFirst()) {
            thumbnailPath = thumbnailCursor.getString(thumbnailCursor
                    .getColumnIndex(MediaStore.Video.Thumbnails.DATA));
        } else {
            thumbnailPath = null;
        }
    }
}
```

This defines a new Movie class with five member fields:

- Movie title

- Movie file URI

- MIME type of the movie file

- Duration in milliseconds

- Movie thumbnail URI

We will be getting the information from the `android.provider.MediaStore` content provider, which is a system content provider for providing information to the application regarding the media files on the device. While you're typing the code into the editor, you will start seeing error markers from Eclipse indicating errors in the code, as shown in Figure 6-17.

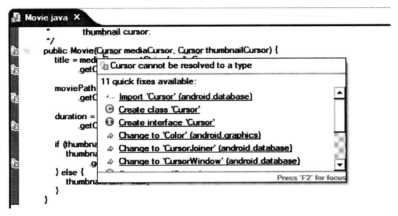

Figure 6-17. *Eclipse indicating errors in the code*

When you hover your mouse over the red underlined errors in the code, Eclipse will automatically display the Quick Fix view with recommendations for possible actions to fix the problem. In our application, the problem is that we haven't imported all of the referenced classes. You can use Quick Fix to fix them manually, or you can press Ctrl+O on Windows and Linux, or Command+O on Mac OS X, to organize and fix all of the imports.

In order to access the member fields, we will now need to define the getter and setter methods. As described in Chapter 4, we can have Eclipse automatically generate these getters and setters, as shown in Figure 6-18.

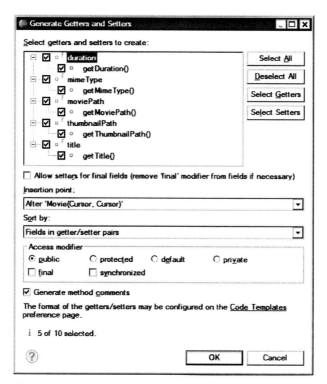

Figure 6-18. *Automatically generating getters and setters for the Movie class*

Now the source code for the Movie class will look like Listing 6-4.

Listing 6-4. *Movie.java after Generating the Getters and Setters*

```java
package com.apress.movieplayer;

import android.database.Cursor;
import android.provider.MediaStore;

/**
 * Movie file meta data.
 *
 * @author Onur Cinar
 */
class Movie {
    /** Movie title. */
    private final String title;

    /** Movie file. */
    private final String moviePath;
```

```java
/** MIME type. */
private final String mimeType;

/** Movie duration in ms. */
private final long duration;

/** Thumbnail file. */
private final String thumbnailPath;

/**
 * Constructor.
 *
 * @param mediaCursor
 *            media cursor.
 * @param thumbnailCursor
 *            thumbnail cursor.
 */
public Movie(Cursor mediaCursor, Cursor thumbnailCursor) {
    title = mediaCursor.getString(mediaCursor
            .getColumnIndexOrThrow(MediaStore.Video.Media.TITLE));

    moviePath = mediaCursor.getString(mediaCursor
            .getColumnIndex(MediaStore.Video.Media.DATA));

    mimeType = mediaCursor.getString(mediaCursor
            .getColumnIndex(MediaStore.Video.Media.MIME_TYPE));

    duration = mediaCursor.getLong(mediaCursor
            .getColumnIndex(MediaStore.Video.Media.DURATION));

    if (thumbnailCursor.moveToFirst()) {
        thumbnailPath = thumbnailCursor.getString(thumbnailCursor
                .getColumnIndex(MediaStore.Video.Thumbnails.DATA));
    } else {
        thumbnailPath = null;
    }
}

/**
 * Get the movie title.
 *
 * @return movie title.
 */
public String getTitle() {
    return title;
}

/**
 * Gets the movie path.
```

```java
 *
 * @return movie path.
 */
public String getMoviePath() {
    return moviePath;
}

/**
 * Gets the MIME type.
 *
 * @return MIME type.
 */
public String getMimeType() {
    return mimeType;
}

/**
 * Gets the movie duration.
 *
 * @return movie duration.
 */
public long getDuration() {
    return duration;
}

/**
 * Gets the thumbnail path.
 *
 * @return thumbnail path.
 */
public String getThumbnailPath() {
    return thumbnailPath;
}

/*
 * (non-Javadoc)
 *
 * @see java.lang.Object#toString()
 */
@Override
public String toString() {
    return "Movie [title=" + title + ", moviePath=" + moviePath
            + ", mimeType=" + mimeType + ", duration=" + duration
            + ", thumbnailPath=" + thumbnailPath + "]";
}
}
```

Movie List Adapter Class

The `android.widget.ListView` user interface component requires an adapter to consume its data. Although default adapters are provided by the Android framework, because of the custom item layouts, these default adapters are not usable in the movie player application.

To define a new adapter class, choose **File > New > Class** from the top menu bar. Name the new class file `MovieListAdapter`, and also set its superclass to `android.widget.BaseAdapter`, as shown in Figure 6-19.

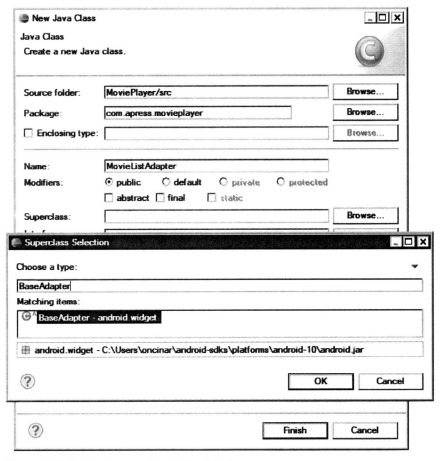

Figure 6-19. *Setting the superclass to BaseAdapter*

Eclipse will automatically generate the empty bodies for each of the abstract methods that needs to be implemented in the MovieListAdapter class. After implementing these methods, the MovieListAdapter code will look like Listing 6-5.

Listing 6-5. *The MovieListAdapter.java File*

```java
package com.apress.movieplayer;

import java.util.ArrayList;

import android.content.Context;
import android.net.Uri;
import android.view.LayoutInflater;
import android.view.View;
import android.view.ViewGroup;
import android.widget.BaseAdapter;
import android.widget.ImageView;
import android.widget.TextView;

/**
 * Movie list view adapter.
 *
 * @author Onur Cinar
 */
class MovieListAdapter extends BaseAdapter {
    /** Context instance. */
    private final Context context;

    /** Movie list. */
    private final ArrayList<Movie> movieList;

    /**
     * Constructor.
     *
     * @param context
     *              context instance.
     * @param movieList
     *              movie list.
     */
    public MovieListAdapter(Context context, ArrayList<Movie> movieList) {
        this.context = context;
        this.movieList = movieList;
    }

    /**
     * Gets the number of elements in movie list.
     *
     * @see BaseAdapter#getCount()
```

```java
 */
public int getCount() {
    return movieList.size();
}

/**
 * Gets the movie item at given position.
 *
 * @param poisition
 *            item position
 * @see BaseAdapter#getItem(int)
 */
public Object getItem(int position) {
    return movieList.get(position);
}

/**
 * Gets the movie id at given position.
 *
 * @param position
 *            item position
 * @return movie id
 * @see BaseAdapter#getItemId(int)
 */
public long getItemId(int position) {
    return position;
}

/**
 * Gets the item view for given position.
 *
 * @param position
 *            item position.
 * @param convertView
 *            existing view to use.
 * @param parent
 *            parent view.
 */
public View getView(int position, View convertView, ViewGroup parent) {
    // Check if convert view exists or inflate the layout
    if (convertView == null) {
        LayoutInflater layoutInflater = (LayoutInflater) context
                .getSystemService(Context.LAYOUT_INFLATER_SERVICE);
        convertView = layoutInflater.inflate(R.layout.movie_item, null);
    }

    // Get the movie at given position
    Movie movie = (Movie) getItem(position);

    // Set thumbnail
```

```java
        ImageView thumbnail = (ImageView) convertView
                .findViewById(R.id.thumbnail);

        if (movie.getThumbnailPath() != null) {
            thumbnail.setImageURI(Uri.parse(movie.getThumbnailPath()));
        } else {
            thumbnail.setImageResource(R.drawable.ic_launcher);
        }

        // Set title
        TextView title = (TextView) convertView.findViewById(R.id.title);
        title.setText(movie.getTitle());

        // Set duration
        TextView duration = (TextView) convertView.findViewById(R.id.duration);
        duration.setText(getDurationAsString(movie.getDuration()));

        return convertView;
    }

    /**
     * Gets the given duration as string.
     *
     * @param duration
     *            duration value.
     * @return duration string.
     */
    private static String getDurationAsString(long duration) {
        // Calculate milliseconds
        long milliseconds = duration % 1000;
        long seconds = duration / 1000;

        // Calculate seconds
        long minutes = seconds / 60;
        seconds %= 60;

        // Calculate hours and minutes
        long hours = minutes / 60;
        minutes %= 60;

        // Build the duration string
        String durationString = String.format("%1$02d:%2$02d:%3$02d.%4$03d",
                hours, minutes, seconds, milliseconds);

        return durationString;
    }
}
```

The `MovieListAdapter` constructor takes an array of `Movie` classes and feeds them as they are requested by `android.widget.ListView`. The `getView` method of `MovieListAdapter` populates our custom list item layout using the member fields of the `Movie` objects.

Activity Class

Now that we have satisfied all of the prerequisites, we can start writing the code for the activity class. `MoviePlayerActivity` will be providing the `android.widget.ListView` component to show the list of movies to the user. The movie information will be coming from the `android.provider.MediaStore` content provider.

Using the `managedQuery` method of the `Activity` class, we will first query `android.provider.MediaStore` for a set of movie information. For each movie, we will make a second query to `android.widget.MediaStore` to obtain the movie thumbnail. The results will later be stored in the `Movie` class instances, and they will be displayed in the list view. When you select a movie item, it will be played by the default video player based on its type. Enter the code in Listing 6-6 into the editor area for `MediaPlayerActivity`.

Listing 6-6. *The MediaPlayerActivity.java File*

```
package com.apress.movieplayer;

import java.util.ArrayList;

import android.app.Activity;
import android.content.Intent;
import android.database.Cursor;
import android.net.Uri;
import android.os.Bundle;
import android.provider.MediaStore;
import android.util.Log;
import android.view.View;
import android.widget.AdapterView;
import android.widget.AdapterView.OnItemClickListener;
import android.widget.ListView;

/**
 * Movie player.
 *
 * @author Onur Cinar
 */
public class MoviePlayerActivity extends Activity implements OnItemClickListener
{
    /** Log tag. */
    private static final String LOG_TAG = "MoviePlayer";
```

```java
/**
 * On create lifecycle method.
 *
 * @param savedInstanceState saved state.
 * @see Activity#onCreate(Bundle)
 */
@Override
public void onCreate(Bundle savedInstanceState) {
    super.onCreate(savedInstanceState);
    setContentView(R.layout.main);

    ArrayList<Movie> movieList = new ArrayList<Movie>();

    // Media columns to query
    String[] mediaColumns = { MediaStore.Video.Media._ID,
            MediaStore.Video.Media.TITLE, MediaStore.Video.Media.DURATION,
            MediaStore.Video.Media.DATA,
            MediaStore.Video.Media.MIME_TYPE };

    // Thumbnail columns to query
    String[] thumbnailColumns = { MediaStore.Video.Thumbnails.DATA };

    // Query external movie content for selected media columns
    Cursor mediaCursor = managedQuery(
            MediaStore.Video.Media.EXTERNAL_CONTENT_URI, mediaColumns,
            null, null, null);

    // Loop through media results
    if ((mediaCursor != null) && mediaCursor.moveToFirst()) {
        do {
            // Get the video id
            int id = mediaCursor.getInt(mediaCursor
                    .getColumnIndex(MediaStore.Video.Media._ID));

            // Get the thumbnail associated with the video
            Cursor thumbnailCursor = managedQuery(
                    MediaStore.Video.Thumbnails.EXTERNAL_CONTENT_URI,
                    thumbnailColumns, MediaStore.Video.Thumbnails.VIDEO_ID
                            + "=" + id, null, null);

            // New movie object from the data
            Movie movie = new Movie(mediaCursor, thumbnailCursor);
            Log.d(LOG_TAG, movie.toString());

            // Add to movie list
            movieList.add(movie);

        } while (mediaCursor.moveToNext());
    }
```

```
        // Define movie list adapter
        MovieListAdapter movieListAdapter = new MovieListAdapter(this,
movieList);

        // Set list view adapter to movie list adapter
        ListView movieListView = (ListView) findViewById(R.id.movieListView);
        movieListView.setAdapter(movieListAdapter);

        // Set  item click listener
        movieListView.setOnItemClickListener(this);
    }

    /**
     * On item click listener.
     */
    public void onItemClick(AdapterView<?> parent, View view, int position, long
id) {
        // Gets the selected movie
        Movie movie = (Movie) parent.getAdapter().getItem(position);

        // Plays the selected movie
        Intent intent = new Intent(Intent.ACTION_VIEW);
        intent.setDataAndType(Uri.parse(movie.getMoviePath()),
movie.getMimeType());
        startActivity(intent);
    }
}
```

Running the Application

Our sample application is now ready to try out. You can run it on an Android device or in the emulator. If you are going to run the movie player application in the Android emulator, make sure that the emulator is configured with the settings discussed in Chapter 5.

The movie player application requires a set of movie files to exist in the external storage, the SD card, in order to display anything. If you don't have any movie files, use the Camera application to record some sample movie files prior to starting the application.

When you're ready to test the application, choose **Run ➤ Run** from the top menu bar. Since this is the first time you are running this application, Eclipse will ask how you would like to run it, as shown in Figure 6-20.

> **CAUTION:** By default, certain Android devices are configured to act as a storage medium when they are attached to a host machine through USB. This may prevent the movie player application from accessing the SD card. Using the USB settings, change the USB operation mode to Charge Only to prevent the SD card from getting locked.

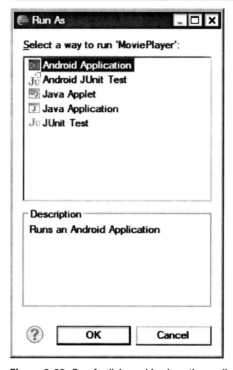

Figure 6-20. *Run As dialog asking how the application should run*

Select Android Application from the Run As dialog. If more than one device or emulator is currently attached, Eclipse will ask you to pick the target device on which to execute the application, as shown in Figure 6-21.

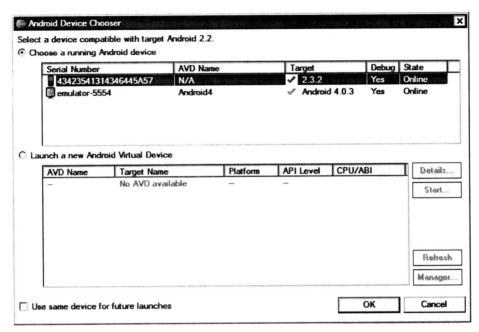

Figure 6-21. *Android Device Chooser dialog*

After you click OK in the dialog, the application will start on the selected Android device or emulator, as shown in Figure 6-22.

Figure 6-22. *Movie player application listing movies*

You can start the application again by choosing the movie player from the applications list on the device.

Summary

In this chapter, we started developing a movie player application to become familiar with the typical Android project development cycle. We put some of the core concepts and components covered in the previous chapters into action. We used the New Android Project wizard, manifest editor, layout editor, Android Lint, and resource editor. We also defined an Android activity and fetched data from a content provider. Throughout the chapter, we used Eclipse's code templates, code generators, and refactoring features to automate some of the development process. In the following chapters, we will extend this project to demonstrate other aspects of Android application development.

Android Native Development Using Eclipse

In the previous chapters, we have explored Android application development using Java. Android software development is not limited to using only Java technology. Android allows application developers to implement parts of their application using native-code languages such as C and C++ through the Android Native Development Kit (NDK).

In this chapter, we will start with an introduction to the Android NDK, and go through the steps to properly install it on major operating systems. We will briefly review the structure of the Android NDK and the components it provides. Then we will discuss how the NDK expects Android applications with native components to be structured.

In order to streamline the development experience, we will use the Sequoyah for Eclipse plug-in to integrate the Android NDK into the Eclipse platform.

After establishing the proper working environment for native development, we will start reviewing the tools for integrating native components provided through the JDK. We will focus on the Java Native Interface (JNI), the primary API used by native components to interact with the Java part of the application.

The Android Native Development Kit

The Android NDK is a companion tool set for the Android SDK, designed to allow developers to implement and embed performance-critical portions of their applications using native machine code. Although the Android framework is designed purely for Java-based applications, the NDK provides the necessary tools and components to develop parts of an Android application using machine code-generating programming languages like C, C++, and Assembly. Through the JNI technology, these native components run and are accessed seamlessly within the Java-based application while their implementations run as machine code, and are not interpreted by the Dalvik virtual machine.

When to Use Native Code?

Using native machine code does not always result in an automatic performance increase. Although the earlier versions of Java were known to be much slower than native code, the latest Java technology is highly optimized, and the speed difference is negligible in many cases. The JIT compilation feature of Java Virtual Machine allows the translation from the interpreted bytecode into machine code at application startup. The translated machine code is then used throughout the execution of the application, making the Java applications run as fast as their native counterparts.

Using native components in a Java application also increases the complexity of the overall application. In order to effectively execute side by side with the virtual machine, the native components are expected to be good neighbors and interact with their Java counterparts in a delicate way. If this interaction is not properly managed, the native components can result in hardly traceable instabilities within the application, and they can even take the entire application down by crashing the virtual machine.

Using native code in Android applications is definitely not a bad practice. In certain cases, it becomes highly beneficial because it can provide for reuse and improve the performance of some complex applications.

Applications rely on a set of modules and libraries to achieve their tasks. For example, the user interfaces contain graphics and icons to improve the user experience. These graphic resources are usually PNG or JPEG image files. These formats are not part of any programming language, so they are not directly consumable by the applications. Since developing the code necessary to deal with these formats is not an efficient use of time, applications rely on existing PNG or JPEG code libraries. Despite the popularity of Java, the code library ecosystem is still highly mandated by C/C++-based native code libraries.

Although most common libraries are already integrated with either Java or the Android framework, not everything is available out of the box.

The Android NDK allows application developers to easily integrate use of any native library with their Java-based Android applications. Without the NDK, these native libraries need to be rewritten in Java in order to be used by the Android applications. The Android NDK promotes reuse of non-Java based components within Android applications and facilitates the development process.

Regarding performance, as a platform-independent programming language, Java does not provide any mechanism for using the CPU-specific features for optimizing the code. Compared to desktop platforms, mobile device resources are highly scarce. For complex applications with high performance requirements, such as 3D games and multimedia applications, effectively using every possible CPU feature is key. ARM processors, such as ARM NEON and ARM VFPv3-D32, provide additional instruction sets in order to allow mobile applications to hardware-accelerate many performance-critical operations. The Android NDK allows development of application components as native code in order to use these CPU features.

What Is Provided by the NDK?

The Android NDK is a comprehensive set of APIs, cross-compilers, linkers, debuggers, build tools, documentation, and sample applications to allow development of native Android application components. It complements the Android SDK by providing native development features. The following are some of the native Android APIs it provides:

- C library
- Minimal standard C++ library
- Math library
- zlib compression library
- Android logging library
- Android pixel buffer library
- Android native application APIs
- OpenGL ES 3D graphics library
- OpenSL ES native audio library
- OpenMAX AL minimal support

Installing the Android NDK

The Android NDK is available for major operating systems. The installation packages are available from the Android NDK web site at `http://developer.android.com/sdk/ndk/index.html`. The following sections describe how to install the Android NDK on Microsoft Windows, Mac OS X, and Linux systems.

Installing the NDK on Microsoft Windows

The Android NDK was initially designed to work on UNIX-like systems. Some of the NDK components are shell scripts, and they are not directly executable on the Microsoft Windows operating system. Although the latest version of the Android NDK shows progress in making itself more independent and self-packaged, it still requires Cygwin to be installed on the host machine in order to fully operate. Cygwin is a UNIX-like environment and command-line interface for the Windows operating system. It comes with base UNIX applications, including a shell that allows running the Android NDK's build system.

At the time of writing, the latest version of the Android NDK for Windows is r7b, and it requires Cygwin 1.7 to be preinstalled on the host machine.

Installing Cygwin

To install Cygwin, navigate to `http://www.cygwin.com` and click Install Cygwin. The installation page will provide a link to the Cygwin installer, also known as the `setup.exe` application. Cygwin is not a single application; it is a large software distribution containing multiple applications. The Cygwin installer allows installing only the selected applications to the host machine.

When you run the Cygwin installer, you'll see the Cygwin Setup dialog, as shown in Figure 7-1.

Figure 7-1. *Running the Cygwin installer*

Click the Next button to move to the next step, where you will need to choose the download source, as shown in Figure 7-2.

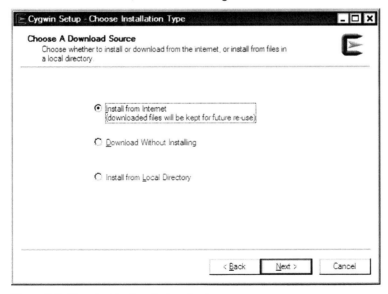

Figure 7-2. *Choosing the Cygwin download source*

Choose the Install from Internet option, and then click the Next button to instruct the Cygwin installer to download the packages from the network. In the next dialog, the installer will ask you to select the directory where you want to install Cygwin, as shown in Figure 7-3.

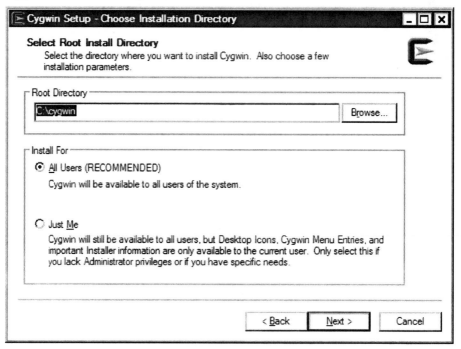

Figure 7-3. *Choosing the target directory for Cygwin*

By default, Cygwin will be installed under the C:\cygwin directory, which is the recommended location. Click the Next button to move to the next step.

The Cygwin installer first downloads the selected packages to the host machine, and then starts installing them as soon as everything is downloaded. The installer will ask for the location of this directory during the installation process, as shown in Figure 7-4.

Figure 7-4. *Selecting the local package directory*

Since the content of this directory will not be used after the installation, you can point it to a temporary location, such as the `Downloads` or `Temp` directory.

In the next step, the installer will ask for the connection type, as shown in Figure 7-5. Unless your network connection requires otherwise, choose Direct Connection, and then click the Next button to continue.

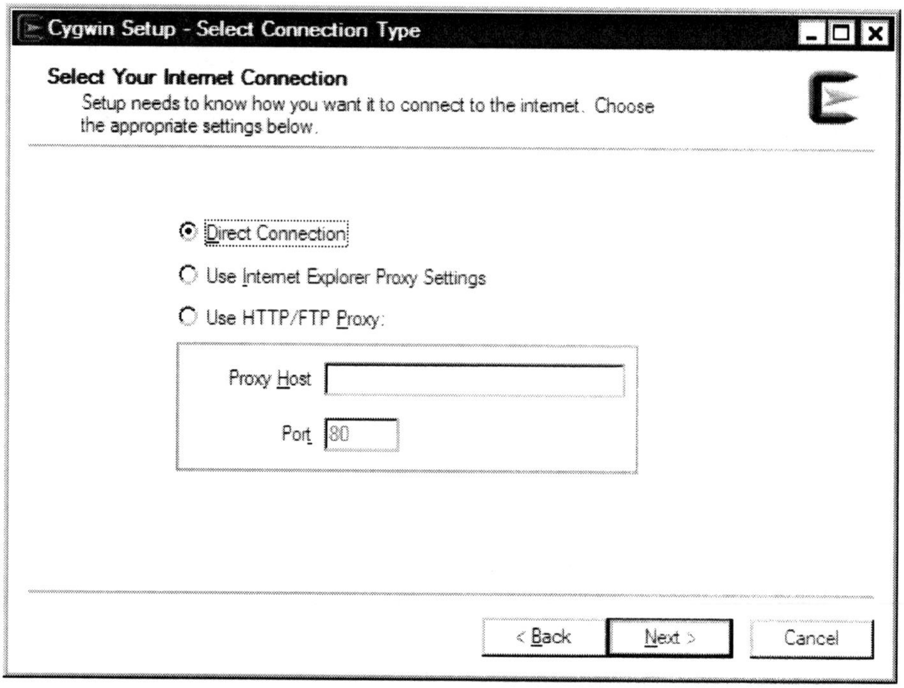

Figure 7-5. *Selecting the configuration type*

Cygwin is an open source project, and multiple organizations across the world donate their bandwidth by providing mirror sites for Cygwin packages. Depending on your geographical location, choose a download site from the list, as shown in Figure 7-6. Then click the Next button to proceed.

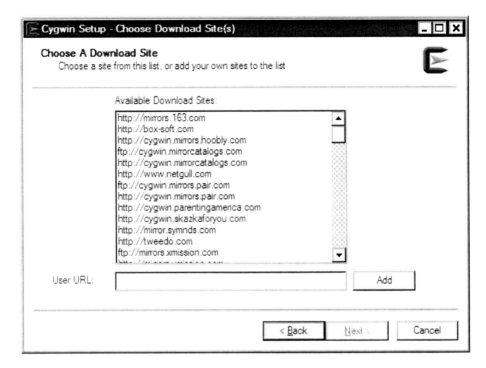

Figure 7-6. *Selecting a download site*

The installer will present you with a list of available applications in a tree format, as shown in Figure 7-7. The default selection is suitable for our purposes.

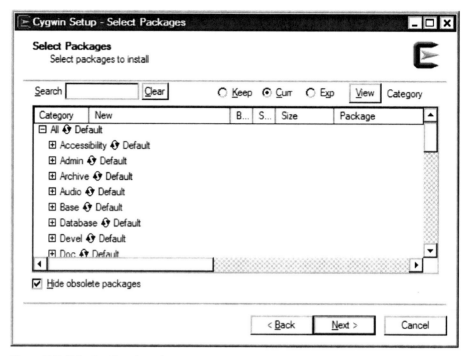

Figure 7-7. *Selecting Cygwin packages*

The Android NDK requires GNU Make 3.8.1 or later. To install GNU Make, type **make** in the Search field and press the Enter key. The installer will filter the list of applications accordingly. Expand the Devel section for development applications, and select the make application. Click the Next button, and the installation will start.

Installing the Android NDK

The Android NDK is provided as a compressed ZIP archive file for the Windows platform. Download the installation package from the Android NDK web site (http://developer.android.com/sdk/ndk/index.html). Then right-click it and choose **Extract All...** from the context menu. You'll see the Extract Compressed (Zipped) Folders dialog, as shown in Figure 7-8. Choose a destination directory, and then click the Extract button to install the Android NDK.

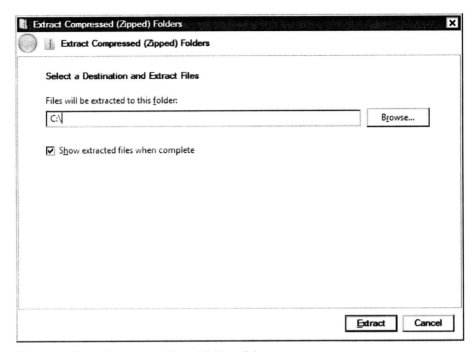

Figure 7-8. *Extract Compressed (Zipped) Folders dialog*

Updating the Path Variable

Adding both Cygwin and the Android NDK to the `Path` environment variable makes the Android NDK easily accessible. To modify the `Path` environment variable, go to the Control Panel and choose System, or select **Start ➤ Run**, and then type `sysdm.cpl`.

In the System Properties dialog, switch to the Advanced tab, and then click the Environment Variables button. In the System variables pane, click the Edit button. Edit the `Path` environment variable. Both the Android NDK and Cygwin binary directories should be appended to the `Path` variable, as shown in Figure 7-9. If you have used the default target directories during the installation process, you can append `;c:\cygwin\bin\;c:\android-ndk-r7b\` to the variable.

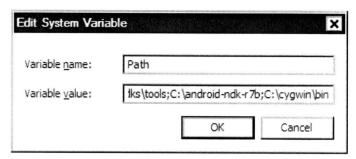

Figure 7-9. *Adding the Android NDK and Cygwin directories to the Path variable*

Installing the NDK on Mac OS X

The Android NDK is provided as a bzip2 compressed TAR file for the Mac OS X platform. Download the archive file from the Android NDK web site (`http://developer.android.com/sdk/ndk/index.html`). Then, inside the destination directory, execute `tar jxvf ~/Downloads/android-ndk-r7b-darwin-x86.tar.bz2` in a terminal window to extract the Android NDK files, as shown in Figure 7-10.

Figure 7-10. *Extracting the Android NDK files*

Adding the Android NDK directory to the `Path` variable makes it more accessible. To do this, execute `echo export PATH=\$PATH:$(pwd)/android-ndk-r7b >> ~/.bashrc` from the same directory where you extracted the Android NDK, as shown in Figure 7-11.

Figure 7-11. *Adding the Android NDK directory to the Path variable*

Installing the NDK on Linux

The Android NDK is provided as a bzip2 compressed TAR file for the Linux platform. Download the archive file from the Android NDK web site (`http://developer.android.com/sdk/ndk/index.html`). Then inside the destination directory, execute `tar jxvf android-ndk-r7b-linux-x86.tar.bz2` in a shell to extract the Android NDK files, as shown in Figure 7-12.

Figure 7-12. *Extracting Android NDK files*

Adding the Android NDK directory to the `Path` variable makes it more accessible. To do this, execute `echo export PATH=$PATH:$(pwd)/android-ndk-r7b >> ~/.bashrc` from the same directory where you extracted the Android NDK. as shown in Figure 7-13.

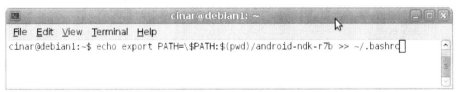

Figure 7-13. *Adding the Android NDK directory to the Path variable*

How the Android NDK Is Structured

During the installation process, all of the Android NDK components are installed under the target directory. The following are some of the important files and subdirectories:

- ndk-build: This shell script is the starting point of the Android NDK build system. It gets executed within the Android application directory, and it manages the build process for the native part of Android applications.

- ndk-gdb: This shell script allows debugging native components using the GNU Debugger. Upon starting, it sets up the communication between the device and the GNU Debugger.

- ndk-stack: This shell script is a helper to facilitate analyzing the stack traces that are produced when native components crash. It parses the given stack trace and maps the addresses to the source code file and line numbers. We will be experimenting with it later in this chapter.

- build: This directory contains the modules of the entire Android NDK build system. Developers are not expected to interact with these files directly.

- platforms: This directory contains header files and libraries for each Android target version. These files are used automatically by the Android NDK build system.

- samples: This directory contains sample applications to demonstrate the capabilities provided by the Android NDK. These sample projects are very useful for learning how to use the features that are provided by the Android NDK.

- sources: This directory contains add-on modules that developers can import into their existing Android NDK projects.

- toolchains: This directory contains cross-compilers for different target machine architectures that the Android NDK currently supports. The Android NDK build system uses the cross-compiler based on the selected target architecture.

How a Native Project Is Structured

Native components share the same project directory as the Java-based Android applications. Here is a list of the important files and directories:

- jni: This subdirectory holds the C/C++ header and source files for the native components.

- jni/Android.mk: This is the build file that describes the native project. It contains the list of source files to compile and the libraries to link. It is imported into the main Makefile during the build process. The content looks like the following:

```
# Stores the current directory
LOCAL_PATH := $(call my-dir)

# Clears the build variables
include $(CLEAR_VARS)

# Native components get compiled into modules
LOCAL_MODULE := hello-jni

# Native code source files
LOCAL_SRC_FILES := hello-jni.c
LOCAL_SRC_FILES += test1.c test2.c

# Builds a shared library for this module
include $(BUILD_SHARED_LIBRARY)
```

- jni/Application.mk: This is an optional global build file that specifies which native modules will be built and the list of common configuration flags for all application modules. The content looks like the following:

```
# Defines which modules to build; otherwise
# all modules are built
APP_MODULES := hello-jni

# Alters the optimization level for building
# either in release or debug mode
APP_OPTIM := release

# Defines which target machine architectures
# to build for
APP_ABI := armeabi armeabi-v7a

# Compiler flags for all modules
APP_CFLAGS := -I/opt/module
```

▒ `libs`: This subdirectory is generated as a result of the build process. It is divided into one or more subdirectories, depending on the target machine architecture. These subdirectories hold the compiled shared libraries that contain the native components. The `libs` subdirectory is created automatically when the Android SDK packages the application into an installable APK file.

▒ `obj`: This subdirectory is generated as a result of the build process. It contains compiled object files for each source file and also the debug versions of the shared libraries.

Sequoyah for Eclipse

The ADT plug-in for Eclipse handles only the Java part of Android applications. It does not automatically handle the native components, and relies on the Android developer to manually compile them in advance. The Sequoyah plug-in for Eclipse streamlines this process.

Sequoyah is an open source Eclipse plug-in project that aims to provide a complete mobile development environment based on the Eclipse platform. Sequoyah inherits components from many other Eclipse projects, such as Tools for Mobile Linux (TmL), Mobile Tools for Java (MTJ), and Pulsar, in order to provide a complete environment. The most notable feature of Sequoyah is its ability to add Android native code support to existing Android projects.

Installing Sequoyah

Sequoyah is available through the Eclipse plug-ins repository. Start Eclipse and choose **Help ➤ Install New Software…** from the top menu bar to launch the installation wizard. For the Work with field, choose the Indigo repository. Type **Sequoyah** into the filter text field below the Work with field, and Eclipse will filter the list of available plug-ins. Expand the Mobile and Device Development category and select Sequoyah Android Native Code Support, as shown in Figure 7-14. Click the Next button to proceed.

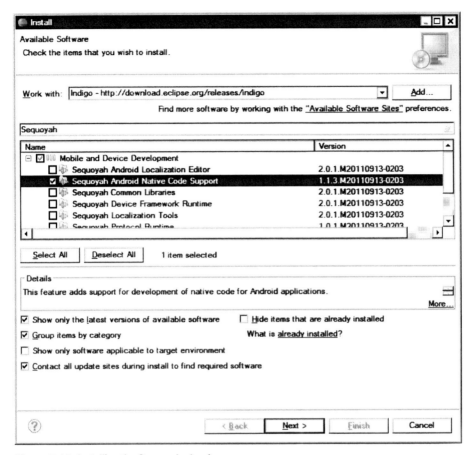

Figure 7-14. *Installing the Sequoyah plug-in*

The Sequoyah plug-in depends on C/C++ Development Tools (CDT) to function. CDT provides a fully functional C/C++ integrated development environment based on the Eclipse platform. The installation wizard will present the list of dependencies, as shown in Figure 7-15. Click the Next button to proceed with the installation.

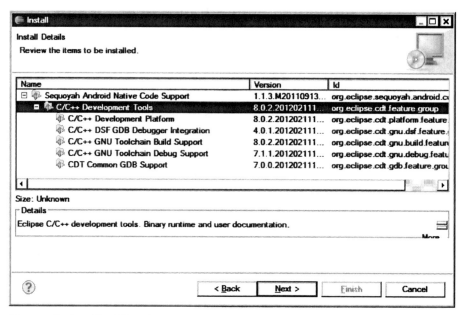

Figure 7-15. *Installing C/C++ Development Tools*

Eclipse will present the license agreement for the selected plug-ins. Accept the license agreements and click the Finish button to start the installation. You'll need to restart Eclipse after the installation completes.

Configuring Sequoyah

Sequoyah needs to know the location for the Android NDK installation in order to function. Launch the Preferences dialog by choosing **Window** ➤ **Preferences** on Windows and Linux, or **Eclipse** ➤ **Preferences** on Mac OS X. In the Preferences dialog, expand the Android category, and choose Native Development. Click the Browse button and choose the NDK location, as shown in Figure 7-16.

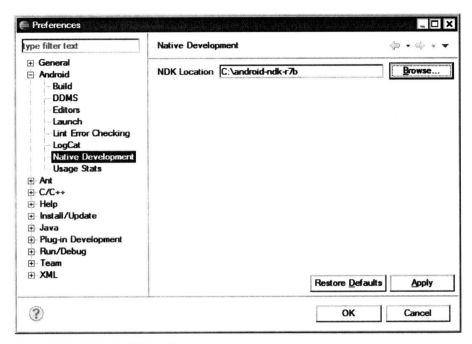

Figure 7-16. *Setting the NDK location*

Adding Native Code Support

To validate the Sequoyah configuration, we will build an Android NDK sample application through Eclipse. We'll use Hello JNI, a sample Android NDK application that loads a string from a native method implemented in a shared library and displays it in the application's user interface.

Launch the New Android Project wizard by choosing **File ➤ New ➤ Android Project** from the top menu bar. Name the project `HelloJni`, and choose the "Create project from existing source" option. Then click the Browse button and choose `<NDK Directory>\samples\hello-jni` as the location, as shown in Figure 7-17. Click the Next button to proceed.

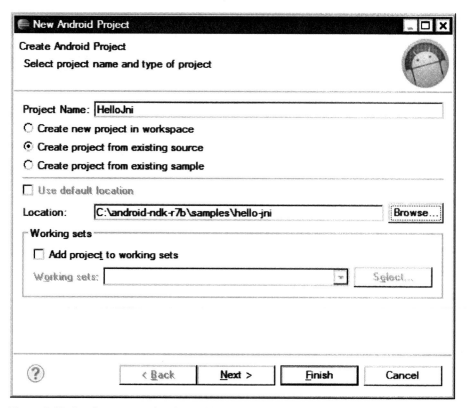

Figure 7-17. *Starting a new project for the NDK sample application*

The New Android Project wizard will ask for the target Android version. The Android NDK supports Android versions 1.5 and later. Since Android 2.3.3 is our preferred platform, choose Android 2.3.3 as the SDK target for the new project, and click the Finish button to add the sample Android project to Eclipse.

Upon importing the project, you may see an error message saying "Unable to resolve target 'android-8'." This is due to a bug with the current version of the ADT plug-in. Since ADT version 14, the project properties file has been renamed from `default.properties` to `project.properties`. When the project is imported though Eclipse, the ADT plug-in generates the `project.properties` file, but keeps the `default.properties` file as well, confusing the build system. Using the Package Explorer, open both the `default.properties` and `project.properties` files, and copy the value of the target property from the `default.properties` file to the `project.properties` file. Using the Package Explorer, right-click the `default.properties` file and choose **Delete** from the context menu.

Although the sample project contains the native code, ADT will not be able to build it. You need to first add native code support to the project to allow Sequoyah to build the native code as a part of the Android application build process. Right-click the project and choose **Android Tools ➤ Add Native Support** from the context menu, as shown in Figure 7-18.

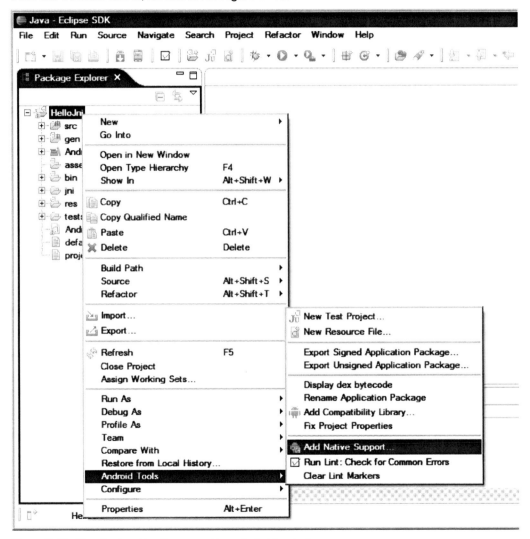

Figure 7-18. *Choosing to add native support to an Android project*

Eclipse displays the Add Android Native Support dialog, as shown in Figure 7-19. The most important field in this dialog is the name for the shared object library that will be generated after the native code is compiled. The Android NDK packages the native code in shared libraries that are loaded by the Java application during runtime. Although the dialog has only one field for the shared library, an Android application can have multiple shared libraries defined. We'll revisit the internals of the Android NDK build system later in this chapter. Click the Finish button to add native support to the project.

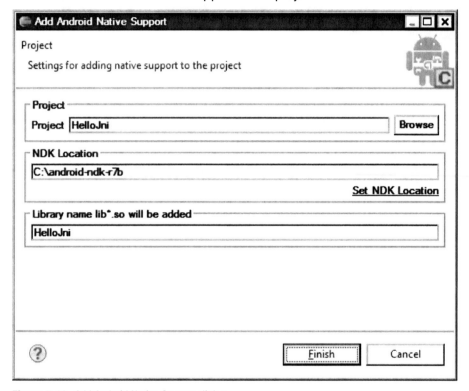

Figure 7-19. *Add Android Native Support dialog*

Building with Native Components

The process of building Android applications with native components is the same process as building a plain Java-based Android application. Sequoyah injects the necessary build steps into the flow automatically. As soon as the Android application is compiled, the Console view will display log messages related to the Android NDK, as shown in Figure 7-20. In case of an error, these messages are parsed automatically and presented to the developer through the Problems view.

Figure 7-20. *Console view showing Android NDK log messages*

At this stage, you can run the application on a device or with the emulator.

Our build environment is now ready for native development. In the following sections, we will explore some of the Java tools that can facilitate native development.

Java Tools

Two Java tools are commonly used for native development: `javah` and `javap`. These tools are part of the JDK, and they are provided as command-line executables. In this section, we will explore their functions, and we will integrate them into Eclipse in order to streamline their use during the development process.

First, we need to define a variable that will allow us to point to the Android framework JAR file while defining the external tool. In Eclipse, choose **Window ➤ Preferences** on Windows and Linux, or **Eclipse ➤ Preferences** on Mac OS X, to open the Preferences dialog. To filter the list, type **String Substitution**, as shown in Figure 7-21.

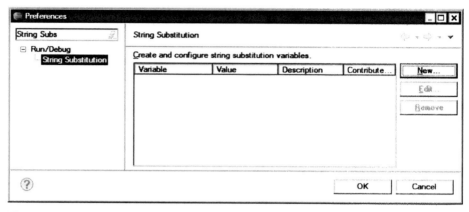

Figure 7-21. *Setting string substitutions*

Click the New button to define a new variable. In the New String Substitution Variable dialog, set the variable name to android_jar. For the Value setting, use the Browse button to navigate to the platforms subdirectory in the Android SDK (not the NDK) installation directory. The list of directories depends on the platforms you have installed. Select the highest platform. Prepend \android.jar to the value if you are running on a Windows host machine, or /android.jar for Mac OS X and Linux systems, as shown in Figure 7-22. Click the OK button to close the dialog.

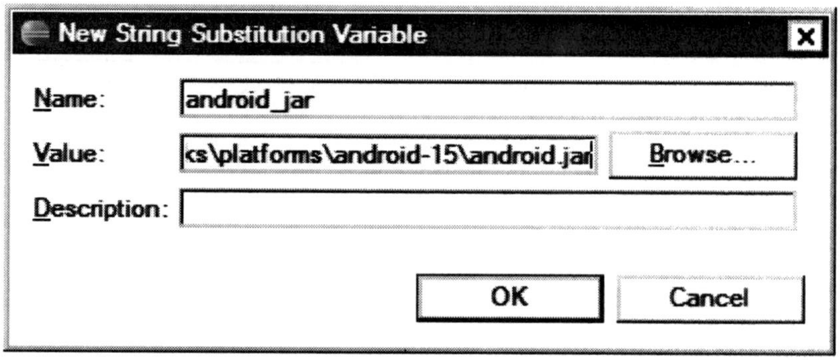

Figure 7-22. *Adding a string substitution variable*

We are now ready to start integrating the javah and javap tools with the Eclipse integrated development environment.

C Header and Stub File Generator: javah

The `javah` tool generates C header and source files that are required to implement native methods. It takes the compiled class files and parses them for native methods, and generates the necessary header and source files. Although this can be achieved without using the `javah` tool, it makes the process more robust and much easier. It is one of the most frequently used tools during native development.

In order to streamline the use of `javah`, we will define a new external tool using Eclipse. Choose **Run ➤ External Tools ➤ External Tool Configurations…** from the top menu bar. In the External Tools Configurations dialog, select Program, and then click the New launch configuration button. Fill in the tool information as follows and shown in Figure 7-23:

- **Name:** Set the name to `javah`.

- **Location:** Set the location to `${system_path:javah}`, so Eclipse can extract the full path to the `javah` tool by using the system path.

- **Working Directory:** Set the working directory to `${project_loc}`, which is the project's root directory.

- **Arguments:** Set the arguments to `-verbose -jni -classpath "${project_loc}/bin/classes;${android_jar}" -d "${project_loc}/jni" ${java_type_name}`. On Mac OS X and Linux systems, separate the classpaths with a colon rather than a semicolon.

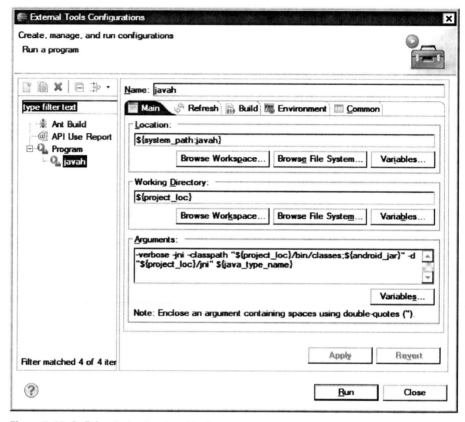

Figure 7-23. *Defining the javah external tool*

Click Apply to save the external tool definition.

To use the `javah` external tool, select a class file with native methods, and choose **Run ➤ External Tools ➤ javah** from the top menu bar. Eclipse will first build the project to make sure that the class files are up to date. The `javah` tool will then generate the C header file in the `jni` subdirectory. If you prefer to have `javah` generate stub C source files as well, change the external tool definition, and append `-stub` to the arguments.

Java Class File Disassembler: javap

The `javap` tool disassembles the given compiled class file for the requested information. It is frequently used during native development to extract proper field and method signatures easily.

As with `javah`, we will define a new external tool for `javap` using Eclipse. Choose **Run ➤ External Tools ➤ External Tool Configurations** from the top menu bar. In the External Tools Configurations dialog, select Program and click the New launch configuration button. Fill in the tool information as follows and shown in Figure 7-24:

- **Name:** Set the name to `javap`.

- **Location:** Set the location to `${system_path:javap}`, so Eclipse can extract the full path to the `javap` tool by using the system path.

- **Working Directory:** Set the working directory to `${project_loc}`, which is the project's root directory.

- **Arguments:** Set the arguments to `-classpath "${project_loc}/bin/classes;${android_jar}" -p -s ${java_type_name}`. On Mac OS X, and Linux systems, replace the semicolon with a colon character to separate the classpaths.

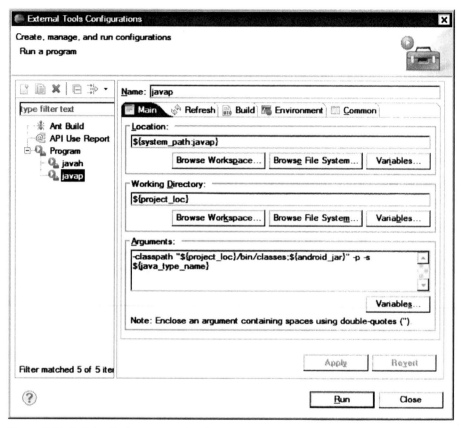

Figure 7-24. *Defining the javap external tool*

To use the `javap` external tool, select a class file with native methods, and choose **Run ➤ External Tools ➤ javap** from the top menu bar. Eclipse will first build the project to make sure that the class files are up to date. The `javap` tool will then parse the compiled Java class, and output the field and method signatures to the Console view, as shown in Figure 7-25.

Figure 7-25. *Some javap output showing field and method signatures*

Both of these Java tools help developers by automatically generating the stub code for native files, as well as the field and method signatures. In the next section, we will start exploring the JNI, which we will use while coding the actual implementations of these stub functions.

The Java Native Interface

The JNI is a powerful feature of the Java programming language. It allows certain methods of Java classes to be implemented natively, and still be called and used as ordinary Java methods. The Android NDK provides platform-specific features, and relies on JNI technology to glue the native code to the Java application.

A Simple JNI Example

Before going into the details of JNI technology, we'll walk through a JNI example application. We will start with a simple Hello World application.

```
public class HelloWorldActivity extends Activity {
    @Override
    public void onCreate(Bundle savedInstanceState) {
        super.onCreate(savedInstanceState);

        TextView textView = new TextView(this);
        textView.setText(sayHelloWorld());
        setContentView(textView);
    }
```

```
private String sayHelloWorld() {
    return "Hello World!";
}
}
```

The `HelloWorldActivity` class contains a single method, `sayHelloWorld`, which returns the "Hello World!" message when called. For this example, we will implement the `sayHelloWorld` method natively using C/C++. To do this, we need to first remove the method's body, and then add the `native` keyword to the method's signature.

```
private native String sayHelloWorld();
```

The `native` keyword indicates that the method is implemented natively. Although the virtual machine now knows that the method is implemented natively, it still does not know where to find the implementation.

As mentioned earlier, native methods are compiled into a shared library. This shared library needs to be loaded first for the virtual machine to find the native method implementations. The `java.lang.System` class provides the `loadLibrary` method for Java applications to load shared libraries during runtime. Assuming that the native method is compiled into a shared library called `libHelloWorld.so`, the following method call should be added to the code.

```
static {
    System.loadLibrary("HelloWorld");
}
```

The `loadLibrary` method is called within the `static` context, because we would like to have it loaded only once during the virtual machine's lifetime. After making this change, the Java part of the sample application is now complete.

```
public class HelloWorldActivity extends Activity {
    @Override
    public void onCreate(Bundle savedInstanceState) {
        super.onCreate(savedInstanceState);

        TextView textView = new TextView(this);
        textView.setText(sayHelloWorld());
        setContentView(textView);
    }

    private native String sayHelloWorld();

    static {
        System.loadLibrary("HelloWorld");
    }
}
```

In order to start writing the C/C++ code, we first need to generate the function signature for the sayHelloWorld method. We will be using the javah tool introduced earlier in the chapter to generate the C/C++ header and source files. Calling the javah tool produces the header file com_apress_HelloWorldActivity.h with the following content.

```
/* DO NOT EDIT THIS FILE - it is machine generated */
#include <jni.h>
/* Header for class com_apress_HelloWorldActivity */

#ifndef _Included_com_apress_HelloWorldActivity
#define _Included_com_apress_HelloWorldActivity
#ifdef __cplusplus
extern "C" {
#endif
/*
 * Class:     com_apress_HelloWorldActivity
 * Method:    sayHelloWorld
 * Signature: ()Ljava/lang/String;
 */
JNIEXPORT jstring JNICALL Java_com_apress_HelloWorldActivity_sayHelloWorld
  (JNIEnv *, jobject);

#ifdef __cplusplus
}
#endif
#endif
```

The header file first includes the jni.h header file This header file contains definitions of JNI data types and functions.

The header file also maps the HelloWorldActivity class's sayHelloWorld method to the Java_com_apress_HelloWorldActivity_sayHelloWorld native function. This explicit function naming allows the virtual machine to automatically find native functions in loaded shared libraries. Although the Java method sayHelloWorld does not take any parameters, the native function takes two parameters. The first parameter, JNIEnv, is an interface pointer that points to a function table of available JNI functions. The second parameter is a Java object reference to the HelloWorldActivity class instance. The JNIEnv interface pointer is always provided with each native function call. The second parameter can either be an object reference for member methods or a class reference for static methods.

Using the automatically generated header file, we will provide the native implementation in a C/C++ source file.

```
#include "com_apress_HelloWorldActivity.h"
```

```
jstring Java_com_apress_HelloWorldActivity_sayHelloWorld(JNIEnv* pEnv, jobject
thiz) {
    return (*env)->NewStringUTF(env, "Hello World!");
}
```

As seen in the code, we cannot directly return the C string "Hello World!" as is, since Java will not know how to handle it. Using the `NewStringUTF` function from the `JNIEnv` interface, the C string is converted into a Java `String` reference.

After the C/C++ source code is compiled into a shared library, the application will be ready. We will not go into the details of the compilation, since this will be handled automatically by the Android NDK through Eclipse.

Data Types

There are two kinds of data types in Java:

- Primitive types such as `boolean`, `byte`, `char`, `short`, `int`, `long`, `float`, and `double`
- Reference types such as `String`, arrays, and other classes

Let's take a closer look at each of these data types.

Primitive Types

Primitive types are directly mapped to C/C++ equivalents. The JNI uses type definitions to make this mapping transparent to developers. For example, the Java `int` type is mapped to `jint` in the `jni.h` header file, as follows:

```
typedef    int    jint;    /* signed 32 bits */
```

Table 7-1 shows the primitive type mapping and the type sizes.

Table 7-1. *Java Primitive Type Mapping*

Java Type	Native Type	Size
Boolean	jboolean	Unsigned 8 bits
Byte	jbyte	Signed 8 bits
Char	jchar	Unsigned 16 bits
Short	jshort	Signed 16 bits

Java Type	Native Type	Size
Int	Jint	Signed 32 bits
Long	jlong	Signed 64 bits
Float	jfloat	32 bits
Double	jdouble	64 bits

Reference Types

Reference types are handled differently by the JNI. They are passed as opaque references to native methods. Native code can interact and manipulate the reference types only through the set of functions provided by the JNIEnv interface. Their internal data structure is not exposed directly to native code. The reference type mapping is shown in Table 7-2.

Table 7-2. *Java Reference Type Mapping*

Java Type	Native Type
java.lang.Class	jclass
java.lang.Throwable	jthrowable
java.lang.String	jstring
Other objects	jobject
java.lang.Object[]	jobjectArray
boolean[]	jbooleanArray
byte[]	jbyteArray
char[]	jcharArray
short[]	jshortArray
int[]	jintArray
long[]	jlongArray

Java Type	Native Type
float[]	jfloatArray
double[]	jdoubleArray
Other arrays	jarray

String Operations

Java strings are handled by the JNI as reference types. Java strings are not directly convertible to native C strings. JNI provides the necessary functions to convert between Java and native strings. These functions can handle both Unicode and UTF-8 encoded strings. In case of a memory overflow, these functions return NULL to inform the native code that an exception has been thrown in the virtual machine and the native code should not continue.

```
const jbyte* str;
str = (*env)->GetStringUTFChars(env, javaString, NULL);
if (0 != str) {
    printf("Java string: %s", str);
}
```

Strings obtained though the JNI functions need to be properly released after the native code is finished using them, or memory leaks will occur. The correct release function to use depends on the function used to obtain the string.

```
(*env)->ReleaseStringUTFChars(env, javaString, str);
```

New string instances can also be constructed from the native code using the new string functions.

```
jstring javaString;
javaString = (*env)->NewStringUTF(env, "Hello World!");
```

Array Operations

Java arrays are handled by the JNI as reference types. The JNI provides the necessary functions to access and manipulate Java arrays. Two types of array functions are provided: Get<*Type*>ArrayRegion and Get<*Type*>ArrayElements.

The Get<*Type*>ArrayRegion function copies the given primitive Java array to the given C array.

```
jint nativeArray[10];
(*env)->GetIntArrayRegion(env, javaArray, 0, 10, nativeArray);
```

The Get<*Type*>ArrayElements function allows the native code to get a direct pointer to array elements, but it does require the native code to release these pointers when it finishes.

```
jint* nativeDirectArray;
nativeDirectArray = (*env)->GetIntArrayElements(env, javaArray, NULL);
if (0 != nativeDirectArray) {

    (*env)->ReleaseIntArrayElements(env, javaArray, nativeDirectArray, 0);
}
```

New array instances can also be constructed from the native code using the New<*Type*>Array function.

```
jintArray javaArray;
javaArray = (*env)->NewIntArray(env, 10);
if (0 != javaArray) {
    (*env)->SetIntArrayRegion(env, javaArray, 0, 10, nativeArray);
}
```

Accessing Fields

Java has two types of fields: instance fields and static fields. Each instance of a class owns its copy of the instance fields, whereas all instances of the a class share the same static fields.

The JNI provides functions to access both field types. The following is an example of a Java class with one static and one instance field:

```
public class JavaClass {
    /** Instance field */
    private String instanceField = "Instance Field";

    /** Static field */
    private static String staticField = "Static Field";

    /**
     * Access fields native method.
     */
    private native void accessFields();

    ...
}
```

The accessFields method is a native method, which will have the following signature for this example:

```
void Java_com_apress_JavaClass_accessFields(JNIEnv* env, jobject instance) {
```

The JNIEnv interface pointer and the object instance are provided by the virtual machine to the native function when it is called. The JNI provides access to both types of fields through field IDs. You can obtain field IDs through the class object for the given instance. The class object is obtained through the GetObjectClass function.

```
jclass clazz;
…
clazz = (*env)->GetObjectClass(env, instance);
```

Depending on the field type, there are two functions to obtain the field ID from the class: GetFieldId function for instance fields and GetStaticFieldId for static fields. Both functions return the field ID as a jfieldID type.

```
jfieldID instanceFieldId;
jfieldID staticFieldId;
…
instanceFieldId = (*env)->GetFieldID(env, clazz, "instanceField",
"Ljava/lang/String;");

staticFieldId = (*env)->GetStaticFieldID(env, clazz, "staticField",
"Ljava/lang/String;");
```

The last parameter of both functions takes the field descriptor that represents the field type in Java. In the example code, "Ljava/lang/String" indicates that the field type is a String.

The JNI follows a specific format for the field descriptor. The easiest way to extract the field descriptor from an existing class file is through the javap tool introduced earlier in the chapter. The output from javap will show the signatures for each field and method in the class file.

```
public class com.apress.JavaClass {
  private static java.lang.String staticField;
    Signature: Ljava/lang/String;
  private java.lang.String instanceField;
    Signature: Ljava/lang/String;
  static {};
    Signature: ()V

  public com.apress.JavaClass();
    Signature: ()V

  private native void accessFields();
    Signature: ()V
}
```

After you obtain the field ID, you can get the actual field through the
Get<*Type*>Field function for instance fields, or the GetStatic<*Type*>Field
function for static fields.

```
jstring instanceField;
jstring staticField;
…
instanceField = (*env)->GetObjectField(env, instance, instanceFieldId);
staticField = (*env)->GetStaticObjectField(env, clazz, staticFieldId);
```

In case of a memory overflow, both of these functions can return NULL, and the
native code should not continue to execute. The field IDs can be cached in
order to improve application performance.

Calling Methods

As with fields, there are two types of methods in Java: instance methods and
static methods. The JNI provides functions to access both types. The following
is a Java class that contains one static method and one instance method.

```
public class JavaClass {
    /**
     * Instance method.
     */
    private String instanceMethod() {
        return "Instance Method";
    }

    /**
     * Static method.
     */
    private static String staticMethod() {
        return "Static Method";
    }

    /**
     * Access methods native method.
     */
    private native void accessMethods();

    ...
}
```

The accessMethods method is a native method that will have the following
signature for this example:

```
void Java_com_apress_JavaClass_accessMethods(JNIEnv* env, jobject
instance) {
```

The JNIEnv interface pointer and the object instance are provided by the virtual machine to the native function when it is called. The JNI provides access to both types of methods through method IDs.

You can obtain method IDs through the class object for the given instance. Use the GetMethodID function to obtain the method ID of an instance method or the GetStaticMethodID function to get the method ID of a static field. Both functions return the method ID as a jmethodID type.

```
jmethodID instanceMethodId;
jmethodID staticMethodId;
…
instanceMethodId = (*env)->GetMethodID(env, clazz, "instanceMethod",
"()Ljava/lang/String;");
staticMethodId = (*env)->GetStaticMethodID(env, clazz, "staticMethod",
"()Ljava/lang/String;");
```

As with the field functions, the last parameter of both functions takes the method descriptor that represents the method signature in Java. Method signatures can be obtained through the javap tool. The output from javap will show the signatures for each field and method in the class file.

```
public class com.apress.JavaClass {
  public com.apress.JavaClass();
    Signature: ()V

  private java.lang.String instanceMethod();
    Signature: ()Ljava/lang/String;

  private static java.lang.String staticMethod();
    Signature: ()Ljava/lang/String;

  private native void accessMethods();
    Signature: ()V
}
```

Using the method ID, you can call the actual method through the Call<*Type*>Method function for instance methods or the CallStatic<*Type*>Field function for static methods.

```
jstring instanceMethodResult;
jstring staticMethodResult;
…
instanceMethodResult = (*env)->CallStringMethod(env, instance,
instanceMethodId);
staticMethodResult = (*env)->CallStaticStringMethod(env, clazz, staticMethodId);
```

In case of a memory overflow, both of these functions can return NULL, and the native code should not continue executing. The method IDs can be cached in order to improve application performance.

Exception Handling

Exception handling is an important aspect of the Java programming language. Exceptions behave differently in the JNI than they do in Java.

When an exception is thrown in a virtual machine, the control is transferred automatically to the nearest `try/catch` statement that matches the exception type. The virtual machine then clears the exception and executes the exception handler. In contrast, the JNI requires developers to explicitly implement the exception handling flow after an exception has occurred.

The `JNIEnv` interface provides a set of functions related to exceptions. To see these functions in action, we will use the following Java class as an example.

```
public class JavaClass {
    /**
     * Throwing method.
     */
    private void throwingMethod() throws NullPointerException {
        throw new NullPointerException("Null pointer");
    }

    /**
     * Access methods native method.
     */
    private native void accessMethods();
}
```

The `accessMethods` native method needs to explicitly do the exception handling while calling the `throwingMethod` method. The JNI provides the `ExceptionOccurred` function to query the virtual machine if there is pending exception. The exception handler needs to explicitly clear the exception using the `ExceptionClear` function after it finishes with it.

```
jthrowable ex;
…
(*env)->CallVoidMethod(env, instance, throwingMethodId);
ex = (*env)->ExceptionOccurred(env);
if (0 != ex) {
    (*env)->ExceptionClear(env);

    /* Exception handler. */
}
```

The JNI allows the native code to throw exceptions as well. Since exceptions are Java classes, the exception class should be obtained first using the `FindClass` function, and the `ThrowNew` function can be used to initiate and throw the new exception.

```
jclass clazz;
...
clazz = (*env)->FindClass(env, "java/lang/NullPointerException");
if (0 != clazz) {
    (*env)->ThrowNew(env, clazz, "Exception message.");
}
```

Local and Global References

References play an important role in Java programming. The virtual machine manages the lifetime of class instances by tracking their references and garbage-collecting the ones that are no longer referenced. Since native code is not a managed environment, the JNI provides a set of functions to allow native code to explicitly manage the object references and lifetimes. The JNI supports three type kinds of references: local references, global references, and weak global references, as described in the following sections.

Local References

Most JNI functions return local references. Local references cannot be cached and reused in subsequent invocations since their lifetime is limited to the native method. Local references are freed once the native function returns. For example, the `FindClass` function returns a local reference; it is freed automatically when the native method returns. Native code can also be freed explicitly through the `DeleteLocalRef` function.

```
jclass clazz;
...
clazz = (*env)->FindClass(env, "java/lang/String");
...
(*env)->DeleteLocalRef(env, clazz);
...
```

This becomes really handy while doing multiple memory-intensive operations within a single method invocation.

Global and Weak Global References

Global references remain valid across subsequent invocations of the native methods until they are explicitly freed by the native code. Global references can be initiated from local references through the `NewGlobalRef` function.

```
jclass localClazz;
jclass globalClazz;
...
```

```
localClazz = (*env)->FindClass(env, "java/lang/String");
globalClazz = (*env)->NewGlobalRef(env, localClazz);
…
(*env)->DeleteLocalRef(env, localClazz);
```

When a global reference is no longer needed by the native code, you can free it at any time through the DeleteGlobalRef function:

```
(*env)->DeleteGlobalRef(env, globalClazz);
```

Another flavor of global references is the weak global reference. Like global references, weak global references remain valid across subsequent invocations of the native methods. Unlike global references, weak global references do not prevent the underlying object from being garbage-collected. Weak global references can be initiated using the NewWeakGlobalRef function.

```
jclass weakGlobalClazz;
…
weakGlobalClazz = (*env)->NewWeakGlobalRef(env, localClazz);
```

To determine if the weak global reference is still pointing to a live class instance, you can use the IsSameObject function:

```
if (JNI_FALSE == (*env)->IsSameObject(env, weakGlobalClazz, NULL)) {
    /* Object is still live and can be used. */
} else {
    /* Object is garbage collected and cannot be used. */
}
```

Weak global references can be freed at any time using the DeleteWeakGlobalRef function.

```
(*env)->DeleteWeakGlobalRef(env, weakGlobalClazz);
```

Threading

The virtual machine supports running native code as a part of the multithreaded environment. There are certain constraints of JNI technology to keep in mind while developing native components:

- Local references are valid only during the execution of the native method and in the thread context that is executing the native method. Local references cannot be shared among multiple threads. Only global references can be shared by multiple threads.

- The JNIEnv interface pointer that is passed into each native method call is also valid in the thread associated with the method call. It cannot be cached and used by other threads.

Synchronization

Synchronization is an important aspect of multithreaded programming. Similar to Java's synchronized blocks, JNI's monitors allow the native code to synchronize using Java objects. The virtual machine guarantees that the thread that acquired the monitor executes safely, while the other threads wait until the monitored object becomes available. The synchronized block in a Java application looks like the following:

```
synchronized(obj) {
    /* Synchronized thread-safe code block. */
}
```

The same can be achieved using the JNI's monitor methods:

```
if (JNI_OK == (*env)->MonitorEnter(env, obj)) {
    /* Error handling. */
}

/* Synchronized thread-safe code block. */

if (JNI_OK == (*env)->MonitorExit(env, obj)) {
    /* Error handling. */
}
```

The call to the MonitorEnter function should be matched with a call to MonitorExit in order to prevent deadlocks in the code.

Native Threads

As noted earlier in the chapter, the JNI is mostly used for integrating native libraries and modules into Java applications. These native components may already be using native threads in order to execute certain tasks in parallel. Since those native threads are not known to the virtual machine, they cannot directly communicate with the Java components. Native threads should be attached to the virtual machine first in order to interact with the remaining portion of the application.

The JNI provides the AttachCurrentThread function to allow native code to attach native threads to the virtual machine.

```
JavaVM* cachedJvm;
...
JNIEnv* env;
...
/* Attach the current thread to virtual machine. */
(*cachedJvm)->AttachCurrentThread(cachedJvm, &env, NULL);

/* Thread can communicate with the Java application using the JNIEnv interface.
*/

/* Detach the current thread from virtual machine. */
(*cachedJvm)->DetachCurrentThread(cachedJvm);
```

Troubleshooting

Native code running on a device is much harder to troubleshoot than Java code. In this section, we will review the Android NDK tools that can be used to ease the troubleshooting process.

Logging from Native Code

The easiest way of troubleshooting native code is to properly log the application state and events. The Android NDK provides support for two types of logging mechanisms: Android-specific logging and console logging.

Android-Specific Logging

The NDK provides two Android-specific logging functions to allow native components to log messages in the Android system log: `__android_log_print` and `__android_log_write`. These messages can then be viewed through the LogCat view in DDMS. To use these logging functions, the `android/log.h` header file should be included in the source file.

```
#include <android/log.h>
```

The native component can log messages to the system log at any time by calling these functions.

```
__android_log_write(ANDROID_LOG_INFO, "NativeCode", "Info message.");
```

Besides the header file, the logging library should also be linked while building the shared library. This requires updating the jni/**Android.mk** file.

```
LOCAL_LDLIBS := -llog
```

The application will log the messages into the Android system log, and these messages will appear in the LogCat view.

Console Logging

When integrating existing libraries and modules into an Android application project, changing their logging mechanism to Android-specific logging may not be possible. Most logging mechanisms either log messages to a file or directly to the console.

The console file descriptors, `stdout` and `stderr`, are not visible by default on the Android platform. To redirect these log messages to the Android system log, open a command prompt on Windows, or a terminal window on Linux and Mac OS X, and execute the following commands:

```
$ adb shell stop
$ adb shell setprop log.redirect-stdio true
$ adb shell start
```

The system retains this setting until the device reboots. If you want to make these settings the default, add them to the `/data/local.prop` file on the device or emulator.

Debugging Native Code

Native components can be debugged using the GNU Debugger (GDB). The Android NDK provides a shell script, called `ndk-gdb`, to set up the communication between the application and GDB.

GDB provides an extensive debugging environment in text mode. In this section, we will glue `ndk-gdb` to the Eclipse platform in order to streamline the debugging process.

Before setting up an `ndk-gdb` debug session, the application itself should be defined as debuggable in its `AndroidManifest.xml` file. To do this, using the Package Explorer, open the `AndroidManifest.xml` file, and in the manifest editor, switch to the Application tab. The manifest editor provides a form-based interface for manipulating the Android manifest file. Using the drop-down menu, set the Debuggable attribute to true, as shown in Figure 7-26.

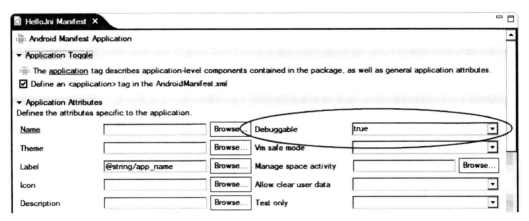

Figure 7-26. *Setting the Debuggable attribute in the AndroidManifest.xml file*

After you make this change, rebuild the application and deploy it again to the target device or the emulator. The `ndk-gdb` tool expects the application to already be deployed on the platform. You can start the application through Eclipse to have it deployed automatically, or you can rely on the `adb` command-line tool to install the APK file manually.

Text Mode Debugging Using ndk-gdb

To configure Eclipse to invoke the `ndk-gdb` tool directly from the integrated development environment, from Eclipse, choose Run   External Tools   External Tool Configurations from the top menu bar. In the External Tools Configuration dialog, select Program and click the New launch configuration button. Fill in the tool information as follows and shown in Figure 7-27:

- **Name:** Set the name to `ndk-gdb`.

- **Location:** On Windows-based host machines, set the location to `c:\cygwin\bin\bash.exe`. On Mac OS X- and Linux-based host machines, set the location to `/bin/bash`.

- **Working Directory:** Set the working directory to `${project_loc}`, which is the project's root directory.

■ **Arguments:** If you are using a Windows host machine, set the
arguments to `-c "/cygdrive/c/android-ndk-r7b/ndk-gdb --
start"`. By default, the `ndk-gdb` tool tries to attach to an
existing running instance of the application. The `--start`
argument explicitly launches the application prior to
establishing the debug session. It will launch the first
launchable activity in the application package. To launch a
specific activity, add the `--launch=<name>` argument as well.

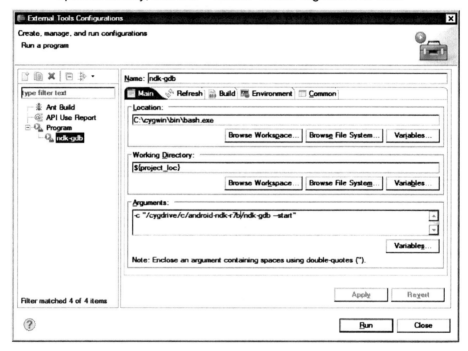

Figure 7-27. *Defining the ndk-gdb external tool*

Click the Apply button to save the external tool definition.

Before you use the `ndk-gdb` external tool, make sure that the application is set to
debuggable and properly deployed to the target device, as described earlier.

To run `ndk-gdb`, select the project using the Package Explorer, and then select
Run ➤ External Tools ➤ ndk-gdb. The `ndk-gdb` tool will be launched in the Console
view. It does a set of checks to make sure that the debug session can be
established properly. If you have any problems using `ndk-gdb`, append `--
verbose` to the list of arguments to turn on detailed logging, which will help with
troubleshooting.

For more information about ndk-gdb, including the other command-line arguments that it supports, execute ndk-gdb with the --help argument. You can also refer to the NDK-GDB.html documentation file in the NDK's doc directory.

Graphical Mode Debugging Using Eclipse

Text mode debugging is the officially supported method of debugging native components in Android applications. However, you can set up graphical mode debugging by tweaking certain Android NDK files based on the Android NDK version R7. Since this is not an official way of debugging native Android applications, these steps may change with the new releases of Android NDK, but the general flow should be the same.

Graphical mode debugging requires a set of files that should be pregenerated using the text mode ndk-gdb tool. Before running graphical mode debugging for the first time for an application, execute the ndk-gdb external tool as described in the previous section. As discussed, make sure that the application is debuggable and properly deployed to the device. After you run the ndk-gdb tool, it will generate a set of files that are necessary to define the graphical debugging configuration. We will modify these files slightly and use them to establish a debug session using Eclipse.

Since Eclipse will be using its internal GDB debugger client, we need prevent ndk-gdb from starting in the client session. Go into the Android NDK installation directory and make a copy of the ndk-gdb script, naming it ndk-gdb-eclipse. Open the ndk-gdb-eclipse script, and remove the last line:

```
$GDBCLIENT -x `native_path $GDBSETUP`
```

The ndk-gdb tool also prepares a configuration setup script called gdb.setup under obj/local/<*target architecture*> in the project directory. We need to modify this script file, but since it will be overwritten by ndk-build during the build process, we will modify a copy of it instead. Make a copy of the script file and name it gdb-eclipse.setup. Right-click gdb-eclipse.setup and choose **Open With ➤ Text Editor** to open the file in Eclipse. Remove the last line:

```
target remote :5039
```

Following the same steps described in the preceding section, define a new external tool configuration for the ndk-gdb-eclipse script. Start Eclipse, and choose **Run ➤ Debug Configurations** from the top menu bar. In the Debug Configurations dialog, select the C/C++ application, and click the New icon to define a new debug configuration. As shown in Figure 7-28, fill in the tool information as follows:

■ **C/C++ Application:** Using the Browse button, navigate to the obj/local/<target architecture> directory under the project directory and select the app_process application. If the app_process application is not there, you will need to first run the default ndk-gdb session in order to generate it.

■ **Process Launcher:** Click the Select other… link at the bottom of the dialog, choose the "User configuration specific settings" option, and choose Standard Create Process Launcher.

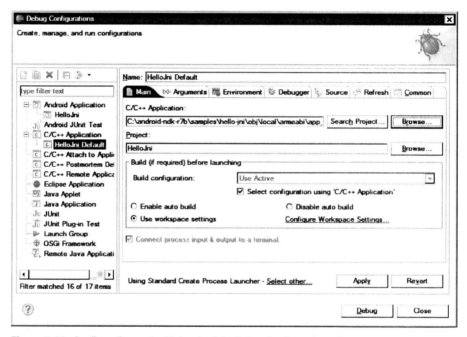

Figure 7-28. *Configuration on the Main tab of the Debug Configurations dialog*

Select the Debugger tab, and fill in the debugger information as follows and shown in Figure 7-29:

■ **Debugger:** Select gdbserver as the debugger.

■ **Stop on startup at:** This can be checked and set to your main native function, or to JNI_OnLoad if it is implemented.

- **GDB debugger:** Using the Browse button, navigate into the `toolchains` subdirectory in the Android NDK directory. Depending on your target machine architecture, find the corresponding **gdb.exe** flavor. On the Windows platform, it is located at `<NDK Directory>\toolchains\arm-linux-androideabi-4.4.3\prebuilt\windows\bin\arm-linux-androideabi-gdb.exe`.

- **GDB command file:** Using the Browse button, select the `gdb-eclipse.setup` file that you generated earlier.

- **GDB command set:** On Windows-based host machines, choose Cygwin from the drop-down menu. On other platforms, keep this setting as Standard.

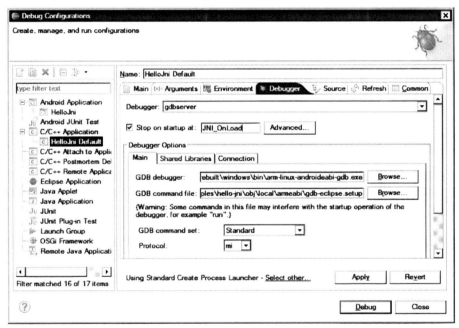

Figure 7-29. *Configuration on the Debugger tab of the Debug Configurations dialog*

Select the Connection tab within the Debugger tab, and fill in the information as follows and shown in Figure 7-30:

- **Type:** Select TCP as the connection type.

■ **Host name or IP address:** Set this to `localhost`, since the Android Debug Bridge (ADB) will be doing the forwarding between the device and the host machine.

■ **Port number:** Set thie port number to 5039.

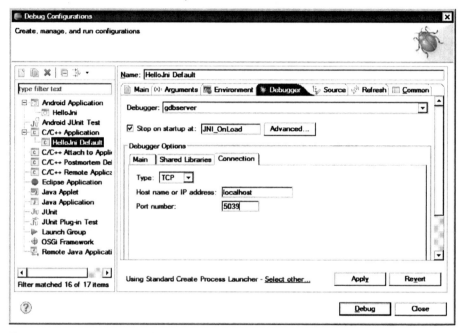

Figure 7-30. *Debugger connection configuration*

Eclipse is now ready to debug the native components. To successfully establish the debug session, follow these steps:

1. Launch your Android emulator instance or connect your Android device to your host machine.

2. Put a breakpoint into the `com.example.hellojni.HelloJni` Java class, after the `loadLibrary` call, by introducing a dummy call, such as `System.out.println()`; and enabling the breakpoint on the dummy call. This will stop the Java debugger immediately after the shared library is loaded.

3. Start a Java debug session.

4. When the debugger reaches the breakpoint, select the project, and then launch the `ndk-gdb-eclipse` external tool that you defined earlier by choosing **Run ➤ External Tools ➤ ndk-gdb-eclipse**.

5. When the `ndk-gdb-eclipse` tool establishes the connection to GDB, select the C/C++ debug session that you defined earlier.

6. Eclipse will ask to switch to Debug perspective. You can now start debugging the native components.

As noted at the beginning of this section, since this graphical debugging setup is not officially supported by the Android NDK, it may not work exactly the same way with later versions of the NDK.

Analyzing the Stack Traces

If a native component crashes, a stack trace is logged into the system logs. This stack trace can be accessed through the LogCat view, as shown in Figure 7-31.

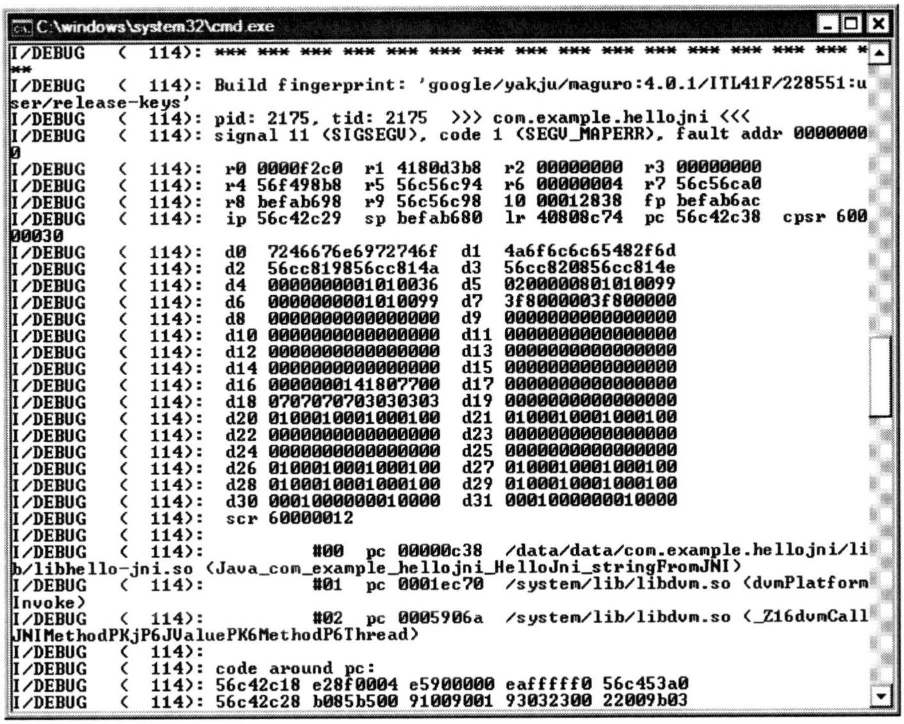

```
C:\windows\system32\cmd.exe
I/DEBUG   ( 114): *** *** *** *** *** *** *** *** *** *** *** *** *** *** *** *
**
I/DEBUG   ( 114): Build fingerprint: 'google/yakju/maguro:4.0.1/ITL41F/228551:u
ser/release-keys'
I/DEBUG   ( 114): pid: 2175, tid: 2175  >>> com.example.hellojni <<<
I/DEBUG   ( 114): signal 11 (SIGSEGV), code 1 (SEGV_MAPERR), fault addr 0000000
0
I/DEBUG   ( 114):  r0 0000f2c0  r1 4180d3b8  r2 00000000  r3 00000000
I/DEBUG   ( 114):  r4 56f498b8  r5 56c56c94  r6 00000004  r7 56c56ca0
I/DEBUG   ( 114):  r8 befab698  r9 56c56c98  10 00012838  fp befab6ac
I/DEBUG   ( 114):  ip 56c42c29  sp befab680  lr 40808c74  pc 56c42c38  cpsr 600
00030
I/DEBUG   ( 114):  d0  7246676e6972746f  d1  4a6f6c6c65482f6d
I/DEBUG   ( 114):  d2  56cc819856cc814a  d3  56cc820856cc814e
I/DEBUG   ( 114):  d4  0000000001010036  d5  0200000801010099
I/DEBUG   ( 114):  d6  0000000001010099  d7  3f8000003f800000
I/DEBUG   ( 114):  d8  0000000000000000  d9  0000000000000000
I/DEBUG   ( 114):  d10 0000000000000000  d11 0000000000000000
I/DEBUG   ( 114):  d12 0000000000000000  d13 0000000000000000
I/DEBUG   ( 114):  d14 0000000000000000  d15 0000000000000000
I/DEBUG   ( 114):  d16 0000000141807700  d17 0000000000000000
I/DEBUG   ( 114):  d18 0707070703030303  d19 0000000000000000
I/DEBUG   ( 114):  d20 0100010001000100  d21 0100010001000100
I/DEBUG   ( 114):  d22 0000000000000000  d23 0000000000000000
I/DEBUG   ( 114):  d24 0000000000000000  d25 0000000000000000
I/DEBUG   ( 114):  d26 0100010001000100  d27 0100010001000100
I/DEBUG   ( 114):  d28 0100010001000100  d29 0100010001000100
I/DEBUG   ( 114):  d30 0001000000010000  d31 0001000000010000
I/DEBUG   ( 114):  scr 60000012
I/DEBUG   ( 114):
I/DEBUG   ( 114):          #00  pc 00000c38  /data/data/com.example.hellojni/li
b/libhello-jni.so (Java_com_example_hellojni_HelloJni_stringFromJNI)
I/DEBUG   ( 114):          #01  pc 0001ec70  /system/lib/libdvm.so (dvmPlatform
Invoke)
I/DEBUG   ( 114):          #02  pc 0005906a  /system/lib/libdvm.so (_Z16dvmCall
JNIMethodPKjP6JValuePK6MethodP6Thread)
I/DEBUG   ( 114):
I/DEBUG   ( 114): code around pc:
I/DEBUG   ( 114): 56c42c18 e28f0004 e5900000 eaffff0 56c453a0
I/DEBUG   ( 114): 56c42c28 b085b500 91009001 93032300 22009b03
```

Figure 7-31. *LogCat view showing a stack trace*

The following lines show the stack trace with function names and addresses.

```
I/DEBUG  ( 114):          #00  pc 00000c38
/data/data/com.example.hellojni/lib/libhello-jni.so
(Java_com_example_hellojni_HelloJni_stringFromJNI)
I/DEBUG  ( 114):          #01  pc 0001ec70  /system/lib/libdvm.so
(dvmPlatformInvoke)
I/DEBUG  ( 114):          #02  pc 0005906a  /system/lib/libdvm.so (_Z16dvmCall
JNIMethodPKjP6JValuePK6MethodP6Thread)
```

As seen in the stack trace, the native code crashed at address 00000c38 in the
Java_com_example_hellojni_HelloJni_stringFromJNI function. This information
may not be enough while troubleshooting complex native components. The
Android NDK comes with the ndk-stack tool to decode the stack trace into file
names and line numbers. From the project directory, you can call the ndk-stack
tool on the command line as follows:

```
adb logcat | ndk-stack -sym obj\local\armeabi
```

The tool parses the log lines for crash dumps, and decodes the stack traces to
show the file names and line numbers. As shown in Figure 7-32, the address
00000c38 was translated in the file hello-jni.c and at line number 31.

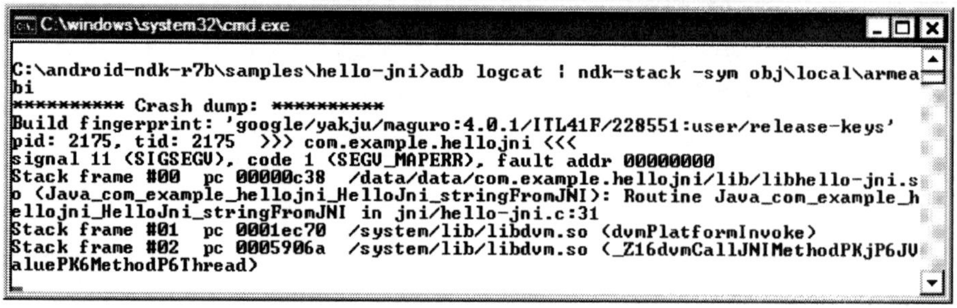

Figure 7-32. *Stack trace decoded by the ndk-stack tool*

The ndk-stack tool can also be used directly from the Eclipse platform, as an
external tool, in order to streamline the troubleshooting process. Once again,
from Eclipse, choose **Run   External Tools   External Tool Configurations...** from the
top menu bar. In the External Tools Configurations dialog, select Program and
click the New launch configuration button. Complete the external tool
information as follows and shown in Figure 7-33:

▪ **Name:** Name the new external tool configuration ndk-stack.

▪ **Location:** On Windows, use ${system_path:cmd} as the
location. On Linux and Mac OS X, use ${system_path:bash}
as the location.

- **Working Directory:** On all platforms, the working directory is
  ${project_loc}.

- **Arguments:** On Windows, enter the arguments /C "adb
  logcat –d | ndk-stack –sym obj\local\armeabi". On Linux
  and Mac OS X, enter -C "adb logcat –d | ndk-stack –sym
  obj/local/armeabi" as the arguments.

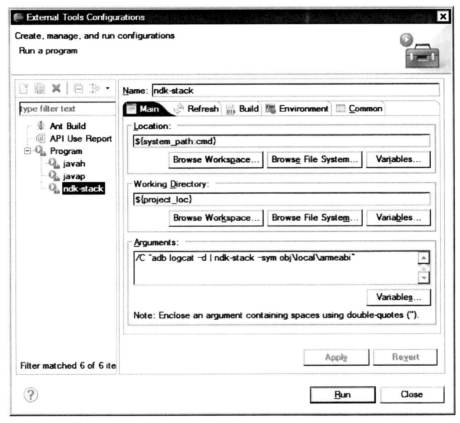

Figure 7-33. *Defining the ndk-stack external tool*

To prevent Eclipse from rebuilding the application every time the tool is
launched, go to the Build tab and uncheck Build before launch.

Now you can use the ndk-stack tool. After an application crashes, choose Run ➤
External Tools ➤ ndk-stack. The tool will be executed, and the output will be
displayed in the Console view, as shown in Figure 7-34.

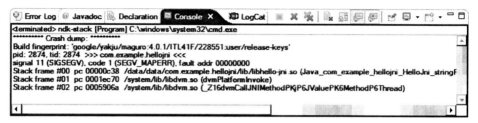

Figure 7-34. *The ndk-stack output displayed in the Console view*

Summary

In this chapter, we explored the Android NDK, including its purpose and the features it provides. We went through the Android NDK installation process on most popular host platforms. We glued the Android NDK to the Eclipse platform through Sequoyah plug-ins. Then we looked at the core of the Android NDK, the JNI technology, and discussed the important aspects of developing hybrid applications. We also touched on the most common troubleshooting tasks and how they can be streamlined through the Eclipse platform.

Resources

The following resources are available for the topics covered in this chapter:

- Sequoyah Project, `http://www.eclipse.org/sequoyah/`

- Android Debug Bridge (ADB), `http://developer.android.com/guide/developing/tools/adb.html`

- *Java Native Interface: Programmer's Guide and Specification*, `http://java.sun.com/docs/books/jni/`

Chapter

8

Project: Extending Movie Player for AVI Movies

In Chapter 6, we developed a movie player application on Android. The application obtains the names of existing movie files through the content provider, and presents them to the user in a list format. After the user selects a movie, the application indirectly launches the default video player activity to play the movie.

Since our movie player is relying on the default video player, it can play only the video formats that are supported by the Android platform. In this chapter, we will expand the movie player application to support Audio Video Interleave (AVI) movie files. AVI is more of a container format that can wrap many different media types. For the sake of simplicity, our AVI player will support only AVI files with uncompressed video in RGB565 color space.

Handling Dependencies

Although the AVI format is not too complicated, supporting it does require a considerable amount of effort to be implemented from scratch in Java. A quick web search for AVI libraries comes up with a list of open source solutions, mostly implemented in C/C++. To take advantage of these existing libraries, the Android NDK is the right tool.

The AVI implementation that we will be using throughout this project is AVILib. It comes as a component of a larger open source project called Transcode.

To download Transcode, navigate to `http://tcforge.berlios.de/` using your browser, and follow the Downloads link. At the time of this writing, the latest version of Transcode is 1.1.5. Transcode comes as a bzip2 compressed TAR archive file. To extract its content, open Cygwin if you are on a Windows-based platform, or a terminal window on Mac OS and Linux, go to the directory where you downloaded Transcode, and enter `tar jxvf transcode-1.1.5.tar.bz2`.

As shown in Figure 8-1, Transcode comes with a lot of other components, AVILib is provided in its own directory called `avilib`.

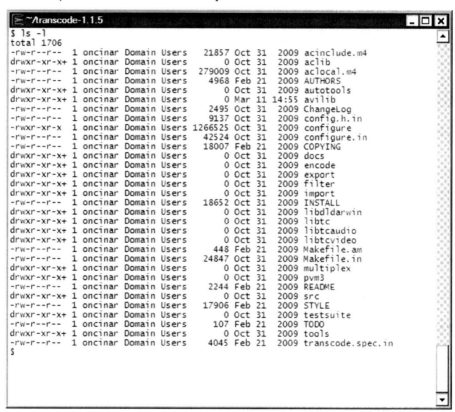

Figure 8-1. *Contents of the Transcode library*

For more information about Transcode, visit the Transcode Forge web site, at `http://tcforge.berlios.de/`.

Adding Native Support

Before we start integrating AVILib into our existing `MoviePlayer` project, we need to first add native support to it. Right-click the `MoviePlayer` project and choose **Android Tools ➤ Add Native Support…** from the context menu to launch the Add Native Support dialog. Click the Finish button to use the default parameters. Sequoyah (which we installed in the previous chapter) will modify the project configuration, and it also will include a set of boilerplate files, as shown in Figure 8-2.

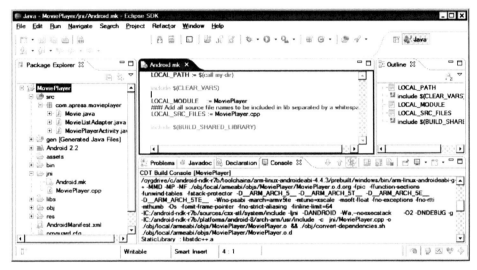

Figure 8-2. *Adding native support to MoviePlayer*

Integrating AVILib

The latest version of the Android NDK comes with support for modules. This allows third-party modules to be deployed on a central location, from which other platforms can quickly pull them into their build process. You can read more about it in the `IMPORT-MODULE.html` file included with the Android NDK documentation. For the sake of simplicity, we will include the AVILib library directly in our project.

Adding AVILib to the Project

Copy the `avilib` directory from Transcode into the `MoviePlayer` project's `jni` directory as a subdirectory, as shown in Figure 8-3.

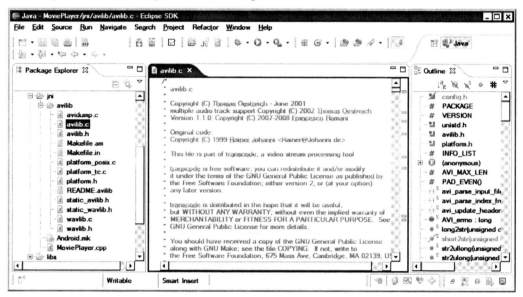

Figure 8-3. *Copying the AVILib directory into the jni directory*

Using Eclipse, open the `platform.h` header file from the `jni` directory, and remove the following `include` statement from the file:

```
#include "config.h"
```

We removed this line because we are not going to use the `Makefile` that came with AVILib; instead, we will use the Android NDK's build system.

Modifying the Android.mk File

The Android NDK requires that the AVILib module and its source files are defined in the `Android.mk` file in order to compile it. Using Eclipse, open the `Android.mk` file. The first line, `LOCAL_PATH := $(call my-dir)`, sets the current work directory for the Android NDK project, and it needs to be the first command in the `Android.mk` file. Immediately after this line, we will start to define a new module for AVILib.

```
#
# AVILib
#
include $(CLEAR_VARS)
```

The `include $(CLEAR_VARS)` line allows the Android NDK to clear the module-specific variables first in order to prevent any conflict. Every module in the `Android.mk` file has a name. This name is used while referring to this specific module from other modules or from the `Application.mk` file.

```
# Module name is avilib
LOCAL_MODULE := avilib
```

The source files for AVILib are in the subdirectory named `avilib`. We need only two source files in order to compile the AVILib.

```
# Source files
LOCAL_SRC_FILES := avilib/avilib.c avilib/platform_posix.c
```

As you can see, the `avilib/` prefix is repeated, since all source files are under the `avilib` subdirectory. The `Android.mk` file is actually a `Makefile` with a lot of Android-specific macros. The `Android.mk` file is processed by the GNU Make tool, and it supports all functions provided through GNU Make. We can break the line into two lines by using GNU Make's `addprefix` function.

```
# Temporary variable to hold list of source files
MY_SRC_FILES := avilib.c platform_posix.c

# Prefix them with the sub-directory name
LOCAL_SRC_FILES := $(addprefix avilib/, $(MY_SRC_FILES))
```

The first line contains only the source file names. The second line sets the `LOCAL_SRC_FILES` by prefixing the source file names with `avilib/`.

```
# Export the includes directory for dependent modules
LOCAL_EXPORT_C_INCLUDES := $(LOCAL_PATH)/avilib
```

Modules usually have their include path hierarchy; for example, AVILib header files are in the `avilib` subdirectory. Modules can also depend on other modules with other include paths, and keeping track of the combined include path may become a time-consuming task. The Android NDK provides the `LOCAL_EXPORT_C_INCLUDES` variable to allow modules to export their include path to their dependents. Dependent modules automatically inherit the include path, and no manual processing is required.

```
# Build it as static library
include $(BUILD_STATIC_LIBRARY)
```

We will finalize the module definition by telling the Android NDK that we would like to build AVILib as a static library. AVILib does not need to be a shared library, since we will not be exposing any functions directly to Java from AVILib. Listing 8-1 shows how the `Android.mk` file looks now.

Listing 8-1. *The jni/Android.mk File*

```
LOCAL_PATH := $(call my-dir)

#
# AVILib
#
include $(CLEAR_VARS)

# Module name is avilib
LOCAL_MODULE := avilib

# Temporary variable to hold list of source files
MY_SRC_FILES := avilib.c platform_posix.c

# Prefix them with the sub-directory name
LOCAL_SRC_FILES := $(addprefix avilib/, $(MY_SRC_FILES))

# Export the includes directory for dependent modules
LOCAL_EXPORT_C_INCLUDES := $(LOCAL_PATH)/avilib

# Build it as static library
include $(BUILD_STATIC_LIBRARY)

#
# Movie Player
#
include $(CLEAR_VARS)

# Module name
LOCAL_MODULE := MoviePlayer

# Source files
LOCAL_SRC_FILES := MoviePlayer.cpp

# Build as shared library
include $(BUILD_SHARED_LIBRARY)
```

To make sure that we can now build AVILib, choose **Project ➤ Build Project** from the top menu bar to build the **MoviePlayer** project. If everything goes well, you will see the "Build Finished" message, as shown in *Figure 8-4*.

Figure 8-4. *Console view showing that the build is finished*

Implementing the AVI Player

We will now start implementing the AVI player class. The AVI player class will rely on AVILib to properly read the AVI video files, and it will rely on Android APIs to render the video frames as they are read. Due to its dependencies, the AVI player class will be a hybrid class with one part in Java and the other part in native space. We'll start by defining the tip of the iceberg, the Java portion of the AVI player.

The Java Part

The Java part of the AVI player will take the name of the AVI video file and hand it over to AVILib through its native methods. As the frames start coming, it will set up an Android surface to render these frames.

To start implementing the Java part of the AVI player, select the `com.apress.movieplayer` Java package through the Project Explorer, choose **File ➤ New ➤ Class** from the top menu bar, and name the new class as `AviPlayer`. Listing 8-2 shows the content of the `AviPlayer` class file.

Listing 8-2. *The AviPlayer.java File*

```java
package com.apress.movieplayer;

import android.graphics.Bitmap;
import android.util.Log;
import android.view.SurfaceHolder;

/**
 * AVI player.
```

```java
 *
 * @author Onur Cinar
 */
class AviPlayer implements Runnable {
    /** Log tag. */
    private static final String LOG_TAG = "AviPlayer";

    /** Surface holder. */
    private SurfaceHolder surfaceHolder;

    /** Movie file. */
    private String movieFile;

    /** Playing flag. */
    private boolean isPlaying;

    /** Thread instance. */
    private Thread thread;

    /**
     * Sets the surface holder.
     *
     * @param surfaceHolder
     *            surface holder.
     */
    public void setSurfaceHolder(SurfaceHolder surfaceHolder) {
        this.surfaceHolder = surfaceHolder;
    }

    /**
     * Sets the movie file.
     *
     * @param movieFile
     *            movie file.
     */
    public void setMovieFile(String movieFile) {
        this.movieFile = movieFile;
    }

    /**
     * Start playing.
     */
    public synchronized void play() {
        if (thread == null) {
            isPlaying = true;

            thread = new Thread(this);
            thread.start();
        }
    }
```

```java
/**
 * Stop playing.
 */
public synchronized void stop() {
    isPlaying = false;
}

/**
 * Runs in its thread.
 */
public void run() {
    try {
        render(surfaceHolder, movieFile);
    } catch (Exception e) {
        Log.e(LOG_TAG, "render", e);
    }

    thread = null;
}

/**
 * New bitmap using given width and height.
 *
 * @param width
 *            bitmap width.
 * @param height
 *            bitmap height.
 * @return bitmap instance.
 */
private static Bitmap newBitmap(int width, int height) {
    return Bitmap.createBitmap(width, height, Bitmap.Config.RGB_565);
}

/**
 * Renders the frames from the AVI file.
 *
 * @param surfaceHolder surface holder.
 * @param movieFile movie file.
 * @throws Exception
 */
private native void render(SurfaceHolder surfaceHolder, String movieFile)
        throws Exception;

/** Loads the native library. */
static {
    System.loadLibrary("MoviePlayer");
}
}
```

The `AviPlayer` class is very simple player implementation. It provides setter methods to define the movie file and an `android.view.Surface` instance to render the frames. There are two methods, `play` and `stop`, to control the player. Since the AVI movie file can take a long time to play, the AVI player has its own thread for doing the rendering tasks. As you can see in the code, the Java portion does not contain any code related to handling AVI files. The native render method will take care of processing and rendering the AVI movie file.

The Native Part

The native part of the AVI player will act as a bridge between the AVILib module and the Java part of the AVI player. The native part will get the AVI video file name from the Java part, and it will start reading it through the AVILib module. As the frames are read, it hands them over to the Java part for rendering.

To start implementing the native portion of the player, we will need to generate the C header file for AVI player. As in the previous chapter, we will use the `javah` tool for this task. Select the `AviPlayer` class, and start `javah` from the external tools menu, as shown in Figure 8-5.

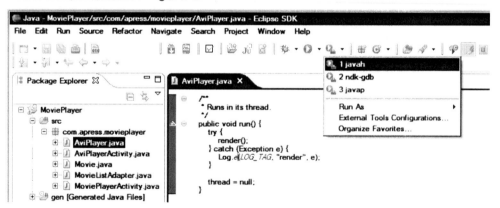

Figure 8-5. *Using javah to generate the header file*

The tool will process the AVI player class and generate the `com_apress_movieplayer_AviPlayer.h` C header file in the `jni` subdirectory. Listing 8-3 shows the content of the header file.

Listing 8-3. *The com_apress_movieplayer_AviPlayer.h File*

```
/* DO NOT EDIT THIS FILE - it is machine generated */
#include <jni.h>
/* Header for class com_apress_movieplayer_AviPlayer */
```

```
#ifndef _Included_com_apress_movieplayer_AviPlayer
#define _Included_com_apress_movieplayer_AviPlayer
#ifdef __cplusplus
extern "C" {
#endif
/*
 * Class:     com_apress_movieplayer_AviPlayer
 * Method:    render
 * Signature: (Landroid/view/SurfaceHolder;Ljava/lang/String;)V
 */
JNIEXPORT void JNICALL Java_com_apress_movieplayer_AviPlayer_render
  (JNIEnv *, jobject, jobject, jstring);

#ifdef __cplusplus
}
#endif
#endif
```

Based on the generated header file, we will now need to implement the
`Java_com_apress_movieplayer_AviPlayer_render` function. Select the `jni`
directory, and choose **File ➤ New ➤ Other… ➤ C/C++ ➤ Source File** from the top
menu bar. Name the C source file as `com_apress_movieplayer_AviPlayer.c`.

As shown in Listing 8-4, the first part of the C source file simply includes the
necessary libraries. We will be using the Android NDK's bitmap library for
drawing the AVI frames, and its log library for extensively logging the operations,
in order to make this example easier to follow. As you may have noticed, there is
a set of macros for different levels of logging. These macros make the Android
NDK's logging mechanism easier to use and add more logging information to
aid in troubleshooting.

Listing 8-4. *The com_apress_movieplayer_AviPlayer.c File*

```
#include "com_apress_movieplayer_AviPlayer.h"

#include <limits.h>
#include <android/bitmap.h>
#include <android/log.h>

#include <avilib.h>

#define LOG_TAG "AviPlayer"

#define LOG_PRINT(level,fmt,...) \
        __android_log_print(level, LOG_TAG, "%s: " fmt, __PRETTY_FUNCTION__, \
##__VA_ARGS__)

#define LOG_DEBUG(fmt,...) \
        LOG_PRINT(ANDROID_LOG_DEBUG, fmt, ##__VA_ARGS__)
```

```
#define LOG_WARNING(fmt,...) \
        LOG_PRINT(ANDROID_LOG_WARN, fmt, ##__VA_ARGS__)

#define LOG_ERROR(fmt,...) \
        LOG_PRINT(ANDROID_LOG_ERROR, fmt, ##__VA_ARGS__)

#define LOG_INFO(fmt,...) \
        LOG_PRINT(ANDROID_LOG_INFO, fmt, ##__VA_ARGS__)
```

Listing 8-5 provides a struct for caching and sharing the frequently used method and field IDs, as well as objects like the surface holder and the bitmap, between the native functions.

Listing 8-5. *The avi_player struct*

```
/**
 * AVI player instance fields.
 */
typedef struct avi_player {
    JNIEnv* env;
    jobject obj;
    jclass clazz;

    /* SurfaceHolder */
    jmethodID lockCanvasMethodId;
    jmethodID unlockCanvasAndPostMethodId;

    /* Canvas */
    jmethodID drawBitmapMethodId;

    jfieldID isPlayingFieldId;
    jobject surfaceHolder;
    jobject bitmap;

} avi_player_t;
```

Defining the Bitmap Helper Function

The newBitmap function, shown in Listing 8-6, is a helper function that calls the static newBitmap function in Java to generate a bitmap with the given dimensions. It uses some of the JNI functions and error handling operations discussed in the previous chapter.

Listing 8-6. *The newBitmap Function*

```
/**
 * Calls the new bitmap method with the given width and height.
 *
```

```
 * @param p avi player.
 * @param width bitmap width.
 * @param height bitmap height.
 * @return bitmap instance.
 */
jobject newBitmap(avi_player_t* p, int width, int height) {
    jobject bitmap = 0;
    jmethodID newBitmapMethodId = 0;

    LOG_DEBUG("BEGIN p=%p width=%d height=%d", p, width, height);

    newBitmapMethodId = (*p->env)->GetStaticMethodID(p->env, p->clazz,
            "newBitmap", "(II)Landroid/graphics/Bitmap;");
    if (0 == newBitmapMethodId) {
        LOG_ERROR("Unable to find newBitmap method");
        goto exit;
    }

    bitmap = (*p->env)->CallStaticObjectMethod(p->env, p->clazz,
            newBitmapMethodId, width, height);

exit:
    LOG_DEBUG("END bitmap=%p", bitmap);
    return bitmap;
}
```

Caching the AVI Player IDs and References

The newBitmap function (Listing 8-6) looks up the Java method by using the
signature (II)Landroid/graphics/Bitmap;. As discussed in the previous
chapter, to quickly find these signatures, we can use the javap tool. Select the
AviPlayer Java class, and choose to use the javap external tool. After
processing the Java class file, javap will output the following:

```
Compiled from "AviPlayer.java"
class com.apress.movieplayer.AviPlayer implements java.lang.Runnable {
  private static final java.lang.String LOG_TAG;
    Signature: Ljava/lang/String;
  private android.view.SurfaceHolder surfaceHolder;
    Signature: Landroid/view/SurfaceHolder;
  private java.lang.String movieFile;
    Signature: Ljava/lang/String;
  private boolean isPlaying;
    Signature: Z
  private java.lang.Thread thread;
    Signature: Ljava/lang/Thread;
  static {};
    Signature: ()V
```

```
com.apress.movieplayer.AviPlayer();
  Signature: ()V

public void setSurfaceHolder(android.view.SurfaceHolder);
  Signature: (Landroid/view/SurfaceHolder;)V

public void setMovieFile(java.lang.String);
  Signature: (Ljava/lang/String;)V

public synchronized void play();
  Signature: ()V

public synchronized void stop();
  Signature: ()V

public void run();
  Signature: ()V

private static android.graphics.Bitmap newBitmap(int, int);
  Signature: (II)Landroid/graphics/Bitmap;

private native void render(android.view.SurfaceHolder, java.lang.String)
throws java.lang.Exception;
  Signature: (Landroid/view/SurfaceHolder;Ljava/lang/String;)V
}
```

By looking at the output, we can easily extract the signatures for the member
fields and methods. In order to speed up the access, these field and method IDs
can be cached. Listing 8-7 provides a code segment for caching the class
reference for AviPlayer, as well as the field ID for the isPlaying member field.

Listing 8-7. *The cacheAviPlayer Function*

```
/**

 * Caches the AVI player.
 *
 * @param p avi player.
 * @return result code.
 */
int cacheAviPlayer(avi_player_t* p) {
    int result = 0;
    jclass clazz = 0;
    jfieldID isPlayingFieldId = 0;

    /* Get object class instance. */
    clazz = (*p->env)->GetObjectClass(p->env, p->obj);
    if (0 == clazz) {
        LOG_ERROR("Unable to get class");
```

```
        goto exit;
    }

    /* Get is playing field id. */
    isPlayingFieldId = (*p->env)->GetFieldID(p->env, clazz, "isPlaying", "Z");
    if (0 == isPlayingFieldId) {
        LOG_ERROR("Unable to get isPlaying field id");
        (*p->env)->DeleteLocalRef(p->env, clazz);
        goto exit;
    }

    result = 1;

    p->clazz = clazz;
    p->isPlayingFieldId = isPlayingFieldId;

exit:
    return result;
}
```

The isPlaying member field's value will be used to control the lifetime of the player later in the code.

Caching the Surface Holder IDs and References

The Android framework allows the user interface (UI) to be modified only in the UI thread. Movie files usually take a long time to play, and they involve many UI operations throughout the playback. Doing these operations directly in the UI thread is not a good practice.

The Android framework provides surface objects to allow applications to draw to the UI from a non-UI thread. Surfaces are the best tools for media applications. The surface objects are accessible to Android applications through the SurfaceHolder object. The SurfaceHolder object provides two main methods, lockCanvas and unlockCanvasAndPost, to allow applications to manipulate the surface objects. Since we are implementing a movie player application, these methods will be called extensively throughout the playback. Listing 8-8 shows the cacheSurfaceHolderMethods function to cache the method IDs for these frequently used methods.

Listing 8-8. *The cacheSurfaceHolderMethods Function*

```
/**
 * Cache surface holder method ids.
 *
 * @param p avi player.
 * @return result code.
```

```
*/
int cacheSurfaceHolderMethods(avi_player_t* p) {
    int result = 0;

    jclass surfaceHolderClazz = 0;
    jmethodID lockCanvasMethodId = 0;
    jmethodID unlockCanvasAndPostMethodId = 0;

    surfaceHolderClazz = (*p->env)->FindClass(p->env,
            "android/view/SurfaceHolder");
    if (0 == surfaceHolderClazz) {
        LOG_ERROR("Unable to find surfaceHolder class");
        goto exit;
    }

    lockCanvasMethodId = (*p->env)->GetMethodID(p->env, surfaceHolderClazz,
            "lockCanvas", "()Landroid/graphics/Canvas;");
    if (0 == lockCanvasMethodId) {
        LOG_ERROR("Unable to find lockCanvas method");
        goto exit;
    }

    unlockCanvasAndPostMethodId = (*p->env)->GetMethodID(p->env,
            surfaceHolderClazz, "unlockCanvasAndPost",
            "(Landroid/graphics/Canvas;)V");
    if (0 == unlockCanvasAndPostMethodId) {
        LOG_ERROR("Unable to find unlockCanvasAndPost method");
        goto exit;
    }

    p->lockCanvasMethodId = lockCanvasMethodId;
    p->unlockCanvasAndPostMethodId = unlockCanvasAndPostMethodId;

    result = 1;

exit:
    return result;
}
```

Caching Canvas IDs and References

The SurfaceHolder object provides a canvas to paint on. The AVI player code
will convert each AVI frame into a bitmap object, and that object will be drawn
on the canvas. This operation will also occur many times during the playback.
The cacheCanvasMethods function, shown in Listing 8-9, caches the method ID
for the drawBitmap method of the Canvas class.

Listing 8-9. *The cacheCanvasMethods Function*

```
/**
 * Cache canvas method ids.
 *
 * @param p avi player.
 * @return result code
 */
int cacheCanvasMethods(avi_player_t* p) {
    int result = 0;

    jclass canvasClazz = 0;
    jmethodID drawBitmapMethodId = 0;

    canvasClazz = (*p->env)->FindClass(p->env, "android/graphics/Canvas");
    if (0 == canvasClazz) {
        LOG_ERROR("Unable to find canvas class");
        goto exit;
    }

    drawBitmapMethodId = (*p->env)->GetMethodID(p->env, canvasClazz,
            "drawBitmap",
            "(Landroid/graphics/Bitmap;FFLandroid/graphics/Paint;)V");
    if (0 == drawBitmapMethodId) {
        LOG_ERROR("Unable to get drawBitmap method");
        goto exit;
    }

    p->drawBitmapMethodId = drawBitmapMethodId;

    result = 1;

exit:
    return result;
}
```

Drawing the Bitmap to the Canvas

The drawBitmap native function, shown in Listing 8-10, uses the previously cached method IDs to paint the given bitmap objects to the surface object. As you may have noticed, at the end of the function, the local reference to the Canvas object is deleted. Since JNI functions return local references that are valid throughout the lifetime of the native method call, the Canvas object will not be cleaned up automatically until the playback ends. Since the drawBitmap function will be called many times during the playback, it can quickly fill the memory with Canvas instances that are no longer used. To prevent that, the function deletes its local reference to the Canvas object before terminating.

Listing 8-10. *The drawBitmap Function*

```
/**
 * Draw bitmap.
 *
 * @param p avi player.
 * @return result code
 */
int drawBitmap(avi_player_t* p) {
    int result = 0;
    jobject canvas = 0;

    /* Lock and get canvas */
    canvas = (*p->env)->CallObjectMethod(p->env, p->surfaceHolder,
            p->lockCanvasMethodId);
    if (0 == canvas) {
        LOG_ERROR("Unable to lock canvas");
        goto exit;
    }

    /* Draw bitmap */
    (*p->env)->CallVoidMethod(p->env, canvas, p->drawBitmapMethodId, p->bitmap,
            0.0, 0.0, 0);

    /* Unlock and post canvas */
    (*p->env)->CallVoidMethod(p->env, p->surfaceHolder,
            p->unlockCanvasAndPostMethodId, canvas);

    result = 1;

exit:
    (*p->env)->DeleteLocalRef(p->env, canvas);

    return result;
}
```

Opening the AVI File

The openAvi function, shown in Listing 8-11, provides the necessary call to
AVILib to open the AVI files. This function takes a Java string as a parameter. It
first converts it to a C string in order to be able to use it as a parameter to the
AVI_open_input_file function. It releases the C string before terminating.

Listing 8-11. *The openAvi Function*

```
/**
 * Opens the given AVI movie file.
 *
```

```
 * @param movieFile movie file.
 * @return avi file.
 */
avi_t* openAvi(avi_player_t* p, jstring movieFile) {
    avi_t* avi = 0;
    const char* fileName = 0;

    /* Get movie file as chars. */
    fileName = (*p->env)->GetStringUTFChars(p->env, movieFile, 0);
    if (0 == fileName) {
        LOG_ERROR("Unable to get movieFile as chars");
        goto exit;
    }

    /* Open AVI input file. */
    avi = AVI_open_input_file(fileName, 1);

    /* No need to have the file name. */
    (*p->env)->ReleaseStringUTFChars(p->env, movieFile, fileName);

exit:
    return avi;
}
```

Rendering the AVI File

The last code segment is the actual implementation of the native render method. As shown in Listing 8-12, it initializes the environment using the helper functions discussed earlier. In a loop, it goes through the AVI frames, populates the bitmap object with the frame data, and draws the bitmap on the surface using the `drawBitmap` function. After each frame, it checks the value of the `isPlaying` flag, and terminates if the player is already stopped. Since the `isPlaying` flag can be accessed from two threads, it uses the JNI's monitor functions to synchronize on the object instance before checking the value of the `isPlaying` flag. Depending on the frame rate of the AVI movie, it sleeps after each frame to match real playback time.

Listing 8-12. *The Java_com_apress_movieplayer_AviPlayer_render Function*

```
void Java_com_apress_movieplayer_AviPlayer_render(JNIEnv* env, jobject obj,
        jobject surfaceHolder, jstring movieFile) {
    avi_player_t ap;
    avi_t* avi = 0;
    jboolean isPlaying = 0;
    double frameRate = 0;
    long frameDelay = 0;
    long frameSize = 0;
```

```
char* frame = 0;
int keyFrame = 0;

/* Cache environment and object. */
memset(&ap, 0, sizeof(avi_player_t));
ap.env = env;
ap.obj = obj;
ap.surfaceHolder = surfaceHolder;

/* Cache surface holder and canvas method ids. */
if (!cacheAviPlayer(&ap) || !cacheSurfaceHolderMethods(&ap)
        || !cacheCanvasMethods(&ap)) {
    LOG_ERROR("Unable to cache the method ids");
    goto exit;
}

/* Open AVI input file. */
avi = openAvi(&ap, movieFile);
if (0 == avi) {
    LOG_ERROR("Unable to open AVI file.");
    goto exit;
}

/* New bitmap. */
ap.bitmap = newBitmap(&ap, AVI_video_width(avi), AVI_video_height(avi));
if (0 == ap.bitmap) {
    LOG_ERROR("Unable to generate a bitmap");
    goto exit;
}

/* Frame rate. */
frameRate = AVI_frame_rate(avi);
LOG_DEBUG("frameRate=%f", frameRate);

frameDelay = (long) (1000 / frameRate);
LOG_DEBUG("frameDelay=%ld", frameDelay);

/* Play file. */
while (1) {
    /* Lock the bitmap and get access to raw data. */
    AndroidBitmap_lockPixels(env, ap.bitmap, (void**) &frame);

    /* Copy the next frame from AVI file to bitmap data. */
    frameSize = AVI_read_frame(avi, frame, &keyFrame);
    LOG_DEBUG("frame=%p keyFrame=%d frameSize=%d error=%s",
            frame, keyFrame, frameSize, AVI_strerror());

    /* Unlock bitmap. */
    AndroidBitmap_unlockPixels(env, ap.bitmap);
```

```
        /* Synchronize on the current object. */
        if (0 != (*env)->MonitorEnter(env, obj)) {
            LOG_ERROR("Unable to monitor enter");
            goto exit;
        }

        isPlaying = (*env)->GetBooleanField(env, obj, ap.isPlayingFieldId);

        /* Done synchronizing. */
        if (0 != (*env)->MonitorExit(env, obj)) {
            LOG_ERROR("Unable to monitor exit");
            goto exit;
        }

        /* If there is no frame or player stopped. */
        if ((-1 == frameSize) || (0 == isPlaying)) {
            break;
        }

        /* Draw bitmap. */
        drawBitmap(&ap);

        /* Wait for the next frame. */
        usleep(frameDelay);
    }

exit:
    if (0 != avi) {
        AVI_close(avi);
    }
}
```

Updating Android.mk

The MoviePlayer module in the Android.mk file needs to be updated with the C source file names and the system libraries that are required for both the bitmap and log functions. Update the MoviePlayer module in the Android.mk file as follows:

```
#
# Movie Player
#
include $(CLEAR_VARS)

# Module name
LOCAL_MODULE := MoviePlayer

# Source files
```

```
LOCAL_SRC_FILES := com_apress_movieplayer_AviPlayer.c

# Static libraries
LOCAL_STATIC_LIBRARIES := avilib

# System libraries
LOCAL_LDLIBS := -llog -ljnigraphics

# Build as shared library
include $(BUILD_SHARED_LIBRARY)
```

In this version of the file, the `LOCAL_LDLIBS` variable defines two additional
system libraries to link against during the build process.

Defining the AVI Player Activity

The AVI player class needs a surface to play back the AVI files. The AVI player
activity will wrap the `AviPlayer` object and provide a surface as well as the
movie path.

Defining the Layout

Choose **File ➤ New ➤ Other… ➤ Android ➤ Android XML Layout File** from the top menu
bar to add a new layout file to the project as `avi_player.xml`. The layout will
contain only a `SurfaceView` object that fills the entire screen. Listing 8-13 shows
the content of the layout file.

Listing 8-13. *The avi_player.xml Layout File*

```xml
<?xml version="1.0" encoding="utf-8"?>
<LinearLayout xmlns:android="http://schemas.android.com/apk/res/android"
    android:layout_width="fill_parent"
    android:layout_height="fill_parent"
    android:orientation="vertical" >

    <SurfaceView
        android:id="@+id/surface_view"
        android:layout_width="fill_parent"
        android:layout_height="fill_parent" />

</LinearLayout>
```

Defining the Activity

Choose File ➤ New ➤ Class from the top menu bar to launch the New Java Class dialog. The new class will extend the `Activity` class, and it will implement the `SurfaceHolder.Callback` interface, as shown in Figure 8-6.

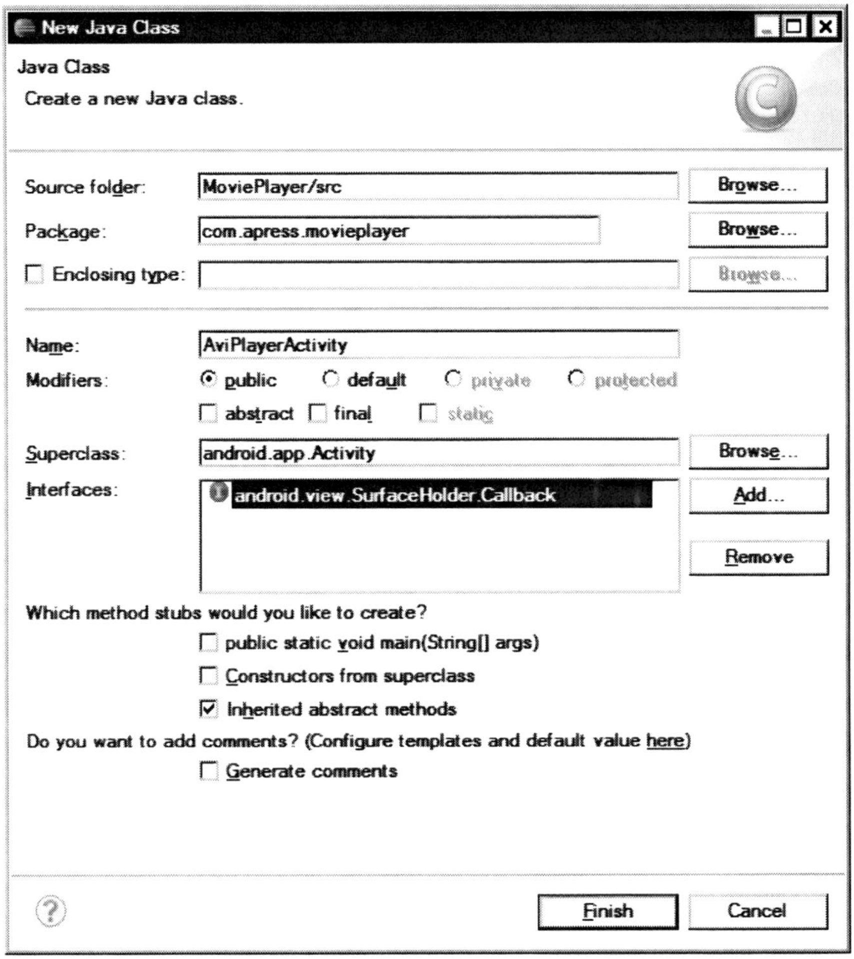

Figure 8-6. *The New Java Class dialog for the AVI player activity*

The implementation of this class file is shown in Listing 8-14. As seen in the `onCreate` method, the AVI player activity will receive the AVI movie file name as a part of the launching intent. It will configure the AVI player with the given movie file, and it will rely on the `SurfaceHolder` callbacks to start and stop the AVI player.

Listing 8-14. *The AviPlayerActivity.java File*

```java
package com.apress.movieplayer;

import android.app.Activity;
import android.os.Bundle;
import android.view.SurfaceHolder;
import android.view.SurfaceHolder.Callback;
import android.view.SurfaceView;

/**
 * AVI movie player activity.
 *
 * @author Onur Cinar
 */
public class AviPlayerActivity extends Activity implements Callback {
    /** AVI player. */
    private AviPlayer aviPlayer;

    /**
     * On create.
     *
     * @see Activity#onCreate(Bundle)
     */
    protected void onCreate(Bundle savedInstanceState) {
        super.onCreate(savedInstanceState);

        setContentView(R.layout.avi_player);

        SurfaceView surfaceView = (SurfaceView) findViewById(R.id.surface_view);
        surfaceView.getHolder().addCallback(this);

        aviPlayer = new AviPlayer();
        aviPlayer.setMovieFile(getIntent().getData().getPath());
    }

    /**
     * Surface changed.
     *
     * @see Callback#surfaceChanged(SurfaceHolder, int, int, int)
     */
    public void surfaceChanged(SurfaceHolder holder, int format, int width,
            int height) {
    }

    /**
     * Surface created.
```

```
 *
 * @see Callback#surfaceCreated(SurfaceHolder)
 */
public void surfaceCreated(SurfaceHolder holder) {
    aviPlayer.setSurfaceHolder(holder);
    aviPlayer.play();
}

/**
 * Surface destroyed.
 *
 * @see Callback#surfaceDestroyed(SurfaceHolder)
 */
public void surfaceDestroyed(SurfaceHolder holder) {
    aviPlayer.stop();
}
}
```

Modifying AndroidManifest.xml

We would like to make `AviPlayerActivity` the systemwide default player for AVI movie files. We will modify the `AndroidManifest.xml` file with the proper intent filters to achieve this. Immediately after the definition of `MoviePlayerActivity`, define a new activity as follows:

```
<activity android:name=".AviPlayerActivity"
android:label="@string/avi_player_label">
    <intent-filter>
        <action android:name="android.intent.action.VIEW" />
        <category android:name="android.intent.category.DEFAULT" />
        <category android:name="android.intent.category.BROWSABLE" />
        <data android:mimeType="video/avi" />
    </intent-filter>
</activity>
```

The intent filter provides the `VIEW` action for movie files with the `video/avi` MIME type. Android will now present AVI Player as an option when the user selects an AVI movie file.

Updating the String Resources

The label for the AVI player activity should also be added to the string resources, in `res/values/strings.xml`.

```
<?xml version="1.0" encoding="utf-8"?>
<resources>
    ...
```

```
    <string name="avi_player_label">AVI Player</string>
</resources>
```

Scanning AVI Files into the Media Store

The Android platform has a default media scanner that updates the media store with the list of audio, video, and picture files. Since AVI files are not supported directly by the Android platform, the media scanner will not add them to the media store automatically. We will add the scanning capability to the MoviePlayerActivity class that we created earlier.

```
/**
 * Goes through the external movies directory and scans the AVI files into
 * the movies.
 */
private void scanAviFiles() {
    LinkedList<File> queue = new LinkedList<File>();
    queue.add(Environment.getExternalStorageDirectory());

    while (!queue.isEmpty()) {
        File dir = queue.poll();
        Log.i(LOG_TAG, "Scanning " + dir.getPath());

        File[] files = dir.listFiles();
        if (files != null) {
            for (File file : files) {
                if (file.isDirectory()) {
                    queue.add(file);
                } else if (file.getName().endsWith(".avi")) {
                    scanAviFile(file);
                }
            }
        }
    }
}
```

The scanAviFiles method goes through the external storage directories and searches for AVI files.

```
/**
 * Scans the given AVI files into movies.
 *
 * @param file
 *            AVI file.
 */
private void scanAviFile(File file) {
    ContentValues contentValues = new ContentValues();
```

```
    String data = file.getPath();
    Log.i(LOG_TAG, "scanAviFile " + data);

    contentValues.put(MediaStore.Video.Media.TITLE, file.getName());
    contentValues.put(MediaStore.Video.Media.DATA, data);
    contentValues.put(MediaStore.Video.Media.MIME_TYPE, "video/avi");

    ContentResolver contentResolver = getContentResolver();

    if (0 >= contentResolver.update(
            MediaStore.Video.Media.EXTERNAL_CONTENT_URI, contentValues,
            MediaStore.Video.Media.DATA + "=?", new String[] { data })) {

        contentResolver.insert(MediaStore.Video.Media.EXTERNAL_CONTENT_URI,
                contentValues);
    }
}
```

When the `scanAviFiles` method finds an AVI file, it calls the `scanAviFile` method. The `scanAviFile` method populates the media information for the AVI file and either updates it or inserts it into the media store. We will call the `scanAviFiles` method right before populating the movie list.

```
public void onCreate(Bundle savedInstanceState) {
    super.onCreate(savedInstanceState);
    setContentView(R.layout.main);

    scanAviFiles();

    ...
}
```

For the sake of simplicity, we call the `scanAviFiles` method within the UI thread; however, in real life, an `AsyncTask` should be used as a wrapper around this operation to prevent blocking the UI thread with extensive IO operations.

Running the Application

Prior to starting the application, you will need to deploy an AVI file to the device. Navigate to `http://zdo.com/galleon.zip`, and extract the `galleon.avi` file. The `galleon.avi` file is an uncompressed raw AVI file with frames in RGB565 color space. Using the command prompt on Windows, or the terminal window on Linux and Mac OS X, upload the AVI file to the SD card on the device using the following command:

```
adb push galleon.avi /sdcard/
```

Starting the Movie Player

Start the movie player application on the device using Eclipse. The movie player will first scan the SD card, and then list the AVI file, as shown in Figure 8-7.

galleon.avi
00:00:00.000

Figure 8-7. *Movie player activity listing AVI movies*

Click the AVI movie file, and the movie player will launch the default AVI movie player on the system, which is the AVI player activity we developed in this chapter. The AVI player will immediately start playing the AVI file, as shown in Figure 8-8.

Figure 8-8. *AVI player activity playing an AVI movie*

Viewing the Gallery

The AVI player is now the default movie player application for AVI files. If you choose the Gallery from the Applications list, you will see the AVI file in the list as well. Click the AVI file, and Android will present a list of available players, as shown in Figure 8-9.

Figure 8-9. *Gallery presenting the list of AVI players*

Checking the Logs

During the movie playback, the LogCat view will show the log messages from both the Java application and the native functions, as shown in Figure 8-10.

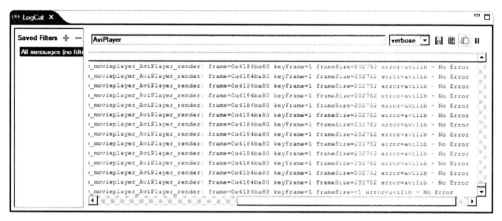

Figure 8-10. *LogCat view showing AVI player logs*

Homework

To further explore the concepts and tools introduced in the previous chapter, you may want to experiment with the project code to add these features:

- **Thumbnail support**: As you will remember from Chapter 6, the movie player list can show thumbnails from movie files. You will need to implement a native method to extract thumbnails from AVI movie files, and also modify the AVI media scanner to add the thumbnails to the media store. Instead of having the native code read the entire AVI file and make callbacks for each frame, you can modify the logic so that the Java code can request frames one by one. This can allow the Java code to extract only the first frame as the thumbnail. Upon obtaining the thumbnail, the bitmap can then be converted to a proper image format, and it can be saved through the media store content provider interface.

- **Player controls**: The AVI player automatically starts playing the AVI movie file, and it stops after the whole movie is played. It does not provide any controls for the user to pause, stop, or restart the playback. Implementing these features will allow you to explore the interaction between Java and the native layer. By refactoring the native code and separating the reader code into multiple functions, you can allow the Java code to control the flow to implement these features.

Summary

In this chapter, in order to better understand the Android NDK and the JNI technology, we expanded the movie player application that we built in Chapter 6 to support AVI-formatted movie files. We integrated an open source AVI library into our project. While implementing the native code, we reviewed method and field access, static and instance method execution, and thread synchronization using monitors from the native code using the JNI functions.

Chapter 9

Android Scripting Using Eclipse

Developing a full-scale Android application using the Java programing language may become a big overhead for simple tasks such as automation and prototyping. Android scripting becomes a very handy tool for such simple tasks. Scripting languages support dynamic typing, automatic memory management, and multiple programming paradigms, and they provide an easy programming environment. Compared to Java, scripting languages are interpreted programming that do not require compiling, linking, packaging, and deployment in order to be executed. Scripts are interpreted and executed on the fly as they are typed on a console or read from a script file.

Multiple scripting solutions are available for the Android platform based on different scripting languages. In this chapter, we will explore the R5 version of the Scripting Layer for Android (SL4A)open source project. SL4A provides a more generic solution to Android scripting. It allows editing and executing scripts directly on the Android device itself, as well remotely from a host machine. It provides access to Android APIs through a set of façades, and relies on script interpreters for processing the actual script files. SL4A supports most popular scripting languages.

Scripting Layer for Android

SL4A has three main components:

- **Script interpreters**: These execute the scripts in a sandbox either on the actual Android device or the host machine.

- **Android RPC client**: The client allows the scripts that are being executed by the interpreters within the sandbox to communicate with SL4A.

- **Façades**: These are exposed to the scripts through the Android RPC client. They are extensive set of APIs that are provided for scripts to interact with the Android platform.

In this section, we will explore each of these components in detail.

Script Interpreters

SL4A provides a scripting host and relies on script interpreters for executing the actual scripts. SL4A provides interpreters for most popular scripting languages, such as Python, Perl, Ruby, Lua, BeanShell, JavaScript, and Tcl. New scripting languages can also be incorporated into SL4A dynamically by developing a new SL4A interpreter for that scripting language.

SL4A runs each script sandboxed in its own interpreter instance. This allows multiple scripts to run simultaneously without affecting each other.

Android RPC Proxy Client

Scripts that are running within their interpreter instance communicate with the SL4A application through the Android proxy RPC client. The client establishes a remote procedure call (RPC) connection to SL4A, and allows scripts to interact with the Android framework through the use of SL4A façades. SL4A enforces per-script security by requiring all scripts to authenticate with the SL4A RPC server by sending a shared handshake secret prior to gaining access to the façades. This handshake secret is provided to the RPC client through the AP_HANDSHAKE environment variable.

Android RPC clients are provided for every supported scripting language. When executing scripts directly on the Android device, these client modules are already available in the script interpreter's path. The client modules need to be present on the host machine interpreter's path when the scripts are being executed remotely. The client modules can be obtained from the SL4A web site at http://code.google.com/p/android-scripting/wiki/AndroidFacadeAPI.

Although their implementations are different, RPC clients provide the same interface in every scripting language. The RPC client module provides an Android object to the script environment and encapsulates the RPC internals. The instance method calls on this object are translated into RPC method calls and executed remotely on the Android device through SL4A. This allows new API methods to be introduced without modifying the RPC client modules.

Façades

SL4A exposes the Android framework API to scripts through an extensive set of façades:

- `ActivityResultFacade`: Allows scripts to return results when triggered by the `startActivityForResult` call. The resulting intent contains the script result in the `SCRIPT_RESULT` attribute.

- `AndroidFacade`: Provides general-purpose Android routines such as starting an activity, broadcasting an intent, toast notifications, vibrating the device, queries for user input through dialogs, sending e-mail, logging, and clipboard operations.

- `ApplicationManagerFacade`: Allows managing Android applications, such as getting a list of launchable activity class names, starting an activity by class name, getting a list of currently running activities and services, and forcing an application package to stop.

- `BatteryManagerFacade`: Exposes the battery manager, and allows tracking battery status, health, type, level, voltage, temperature, and technology.

- `BluetoothFacade`: Exposes the Bluetooth API, and allows controlling the Bluetooth connectivity, making the device discoverable, querying for Bluetooth devices and their information, connecting to another Bluetooth device, and exchanging data over Bluetooth. This façade requires at least API level 5.

- `CameraFacade`: Allows taking a picture using the device's camera and saving it to a specified path.

- `CommonIntentsFacade`: Exposes easy access to common Android intents, such as opening a list of contacts, making a map search, pointing the browser to a local HTML page, starting a bar code scanner, starting an activity by an action, and displaying content to be picked by URI.

- `ContactsFacade`: Allows access to contacts, such as providing the contact list for picking a contact, querying the contact list by attributes, and getting a list of all contacts with their IDs and attributes.

- `EventFacade`: Allows managing the event queue, such as clearing the existing events, removing older events, posting new events, waiting for events, and blocking the script execution until a specific event. It also allows listing, registering, and unregistering broadcast signals.

- `EyesFreeFacade`: Available on devices below API level 4. It allows scripts to speak using the text-to-speech technology. It is now deprecated by `TextToSpeechFacade`.

- `LocationFacade`: Exposes the location manager, and allows collecting location data and querying for the current location and addresses at the current location.

- `MediaPlayerFacade`: Allows playing media files, controlling the player during the playback, and getting information about the media files.

- `MediaRecorderFacade`: Allows recording audio and video into media files at a specified location and controlling the recorder while recording.

- `PhoneFacade`: Exposes the phone functionality, and allows tracking phone state, roaming status, initiating calls, SIM information, cell location, and reading the phone number and the voice mail number.

- `PreferencesFacade`: Allows access to shared preferences, such as getting the list of existing preferences, and reading, modifying, and adding new preferences.

- `SensorManagerFacade`: Allows tracking the sensor data, such as light, acceleration, magnetic field, and orientation.

- `SettingsFacade`: Exposes the device settings, and allows scripts to modify settings such as screen timeout, brightness, airplane mode, ringer volume, media volume, and vibration.

- `SignalStrengthFacade`: Allows monitoring phone signal strength. It requires at least API level 7.

- SmsFacade: Exposes the SMS functionality, and allows scripts to access the existing SMS messages, mark them as read, delete them, and send new SMS messages.

- SpeechRecognitionFacade: Exposes the speech recognition functionality, and allows scripts to recognize user's speech.

- TextToSpeechFacade: Available on devices above API level 4. It deprecates EyesFreeFacade. It allows scripts to speak using the text-to-speech technology.

- ToneGeneratorFacade: Generates DTMF tones for given digits.

- UiFacade: Exposes the Android UI components to scripts through a variety of dialogs and menus to present content and to query for user input. It also allows interactive use of HTML pages.

- WakeLockFacade: Allows scripts to hold wakelocks to keep the CPU and screen on during script execution.

- WebCamFacade: Allows streaming MJPEG streams from the device camera to the network. It requires at least API level 8.

- WifiFacade: Exposes the Wi-Fi manager, and allows scripts to query the status of Wi-Fi connectivity, search for access points, connect and disconnect to Wi-Fi networks, and hold a Wi-Fi lock during script execution.

For a full list of methods provided by these façades, refer to the SL4A API reference documentation at http://code.google.com/p/android-scripting/wiki/ApiReference.

Installing SL4A

To download SL4A, navigate to the SL4A home page at http://code.google.com/p/android-scripting/. The features section on the left lists the latest versions of SL4A and the interpreters. At the time of this writing, the latest version of SL4A is R5. Choose sl4a_r5.apk from the featured downloads to download the Android package to your machine. The older versions of SL4A can be downloaded through the SL4A download page at http://code.google.com/p/android-scripting/downloads/list by browsing the deprecated downloads.

The APK file can then be installed through the ADB. On Windows-based host machines, open a command prompt window. On Mac OS X- and Linux-based host machines, open a terminal window. Navigate to the directory where the `sl4a_r5.apk` file is downloaded, and enter `adb install sl4a_r5.apk` to deploy it to the emulator or the device, as shown in Figure 9-1.

Figure 9-1. *Installing SL4A using the ADB from command line*

As you may have noticed, the SL4A Android package is not too big—only 857KB. The SL4A package includes only the scripting host and the façades. Other than the ones provided by the Android platform, the interpreters are not included, since SL4A does not know your preferred scripting language at this point. On demand, SL4A downloads and installs the interpreters from the SL4A web site.

Since the interpreters are not downloaded from the Android Market, the "Allow installation of non-Market apps" option should be selected in the device settings in order to allow SL4A to properly deploy the interpreters. On Android devices running Gingerbread and below, this setting can be found by pressing Menu key and choosing **Settings ➤ Applications**. On newer devices, it can be found by pressing Menu key and choosing **Settings ➤ Security,** as shown in Figure 9-2.

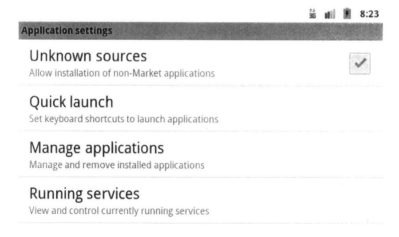

Figure 9-2. *Setting a device to allow installation of non-Market applications*

> **TIP:** You do not need to set the device to allow installation of non-Market applications if the interpreter is deployed manually using the ADB. The installation of interpreters happens in two phases. First, SL4A installs the interpreter installer Android package to the device, and then the interpreter installer downloads a set of compressed ZIP archives containing the actual interpreter depending on the target machine architecture. You can download the interpreter installers from the SL4A web site under the featured downloads section, and manually install them using the ADB.

Next, start the SL4A application. The first time you start SL4A, it will ask your permission to collect usage statistics, as shown in Figure 9-3. You can decline this request; however, accepting usage tracking is strongly recommended. Collecting usage statistics allows the SL4A project to align its road map to areas and features that are frequently used by SL4A users.

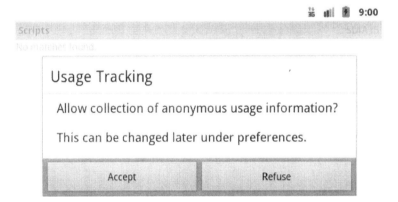

Figure 9-3. *SL4A asking permission for collecting usage statistics*

The SL4A UI provides a set of menus for working with the application. Press the Menu Key to expand the menu bar, as shown in Figure 9-4.

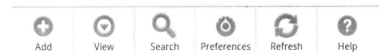

Figure 9-4. *SL4A application menu bar*

Adding Interpreters

Before you can start writing scripts, you need to install a script interpreter. From the application menu bar, select **View ➤ Interpreters**. SL4A will show the list of installed script interpreters. Only the Shell interpreter comes bundled with the SL4A installation.This interpreter provides console access to the Android device. Using the Shell interpreter, you can navigate through the file system and execute the native applications.

From the application menu bar, select **Add**. SL4A will present a list of installable interpreters, as shown in Figure 9-5.

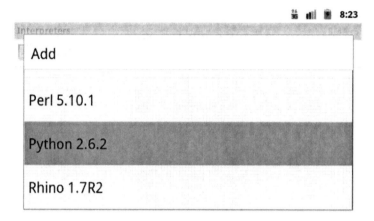

Figure 9-5. *SL4A installable interpreters*

From the list of interpreters, choose the one that you are planning to use for scripting. In this chapter, to demonstrate the capabilities of SL4A, we will use the Python programming language. Choose the Python interpreter, and SL4A will download the Python interpreter installer. From the Android notification bar, expand the download icon to see the status, as shown in Figure 9-6.

Figure 9-6. *Python interpreter installer download notification*

When the download is complete, click the Install button to start installing the Android package, as shown in Figure 9-7.

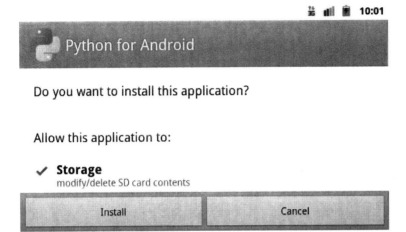

Figure 9-7. *Installing Python for Android*

The Android package contains only the interpreter installer, not the actual script interpreter. After the package is installed, click the Open button to launch the interpreter installer. Then click the Install button to deploy the actual interpreter application, as shown in Figure 9-8.

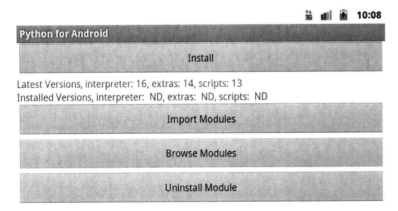

Figure 9-8. *Installing the interpreter application*

The installer will download the Python interpreter based on the device architecture, and then deploy it on the device. In order to efficiently use the device memory, the resource part of the SL4A interpreter is installed in the external storage, and the actual binaries go into the device's internal memory. If you are running the SL4A on an emulator, make sure to follow the configuration settings provided in Chapter 5. If the installation fails, check to make sure that you have enough space in both storage locations.

After a successful installation, the Install button changes to an Uninstall button. Go back to the SL4A application, and you will see Python 2.6.2 added to the list of available interpreters.

Executing Scripts

SL4A supports multiple ways for developing and executing scripts. In this section, we will review these methods in detail.

Executing Scripts Locally on a Device

With the necessary interpreter for your favorite scripting language installed, SL4A is ready to execute scripts directly on the device. SL4A provides two options for developing and running scripts locally: the interactive console mode and the script editor.

Using the Interactive Console

The interactive console mode is launched when you select an interpreter from the list of available interpreters. This mode occupies the entire screen and provides console access to the actual script interpreter, as shown in Figure 9-9. Interpreters run in landscape mode to better use the available display area. If you are running SL4A on the emulator, you can use the key combination Ctrl+F11, or key 7 on numeric keypad to rotate the emulator display to landscape mode. Using the device's keyboard, you can start typing commands, and they will be executed interactively.

Figure 9-9. *Python interpreter running interactively on the virtual console*

The advantage of interactive mode is that you can progressively execute script commands without having a fully developed script in place. It is a great tool for experimenting with the APIs.

Using the Script Editor

In addition to the interactive console mode, SL4A provides a script editor for editing and storing scripts. From interactive console mode, using the Back key, go back to the Scripts view, and choose **Add** from the application menu bar. SL4A will present a list of available script types based on the installed interpreters, as shown in Figure 9-10.

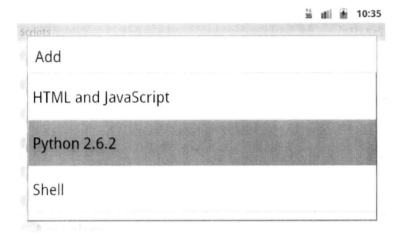

Figure 9-10. *Launching the Python script editor*

Choose Python 2.6.2 from the list to launch the Python script editor, as shown in Figure 9-11. The top pane of the editor allows you to name the script file. The bottom pane is the script editor. The script editor area will be populated automatically with boilerplate script code based on the selected scripting language.

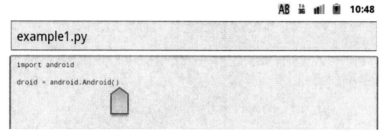

Figure 9-11. *Python script editor*

Using the editor, you can develop and test your scripts, store them on your device, and share them through e-mail. These tasks are accessible through the script editor application menu bar, as shown in Figure 9-12.

Figure 9-12. *Script editor application menu bar*

The API browser is one of the most powerful features provided by the script editor. As shown in Figure 9-13, it allows you to browse through the methods provided through the SL4A façades to streamline script development.

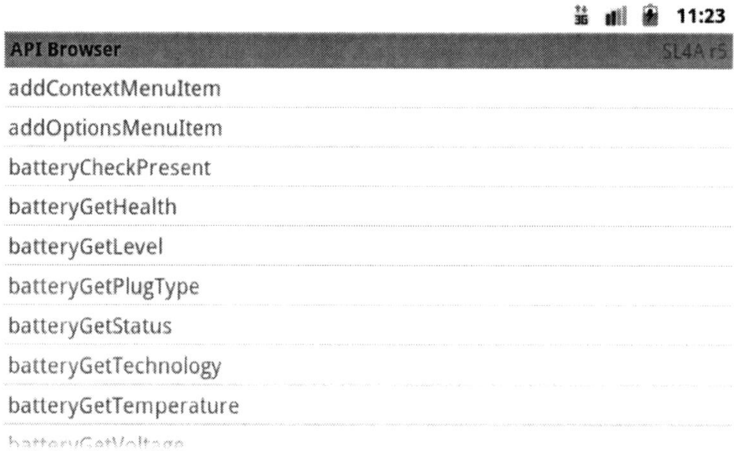

```
API Browser                                          SL4A r5

addContextMenuItem

addOptionsMenuItem

batteryCheckPresent

batteryGetHealth

batteryGetLevel

batteryGetPlugType

batteryGetStatus

batteryGetTechnology

batteryGetTemperature

batteryGetVoltage
```

Figure 9-13. *Script editor API browser listing available methods*

Executing Scripts Remotely

SL4A is not only a device-based scripting environment. It also supports remote execution of scripts that are developed on a host machine. This allows you to take advantage of integrated development environments while still executing your scripts on the Android device.

Starting Scripts Through the ADB

Scripts that are developed on a host machine can be copied over to the Android device, and then executed directly through the ADB on the command line. This allows automating the deployment and execution of scripts.

To copy scripts to the SD card on an Android device, on Windows-based host machines, open a command prompt window, or on Mac OS X- and Linux-based host machines, open a terminal window, and enter the following ADB command:

```
adb push script.py /sdcard/sl4a/scripts
```

This places the `script.py` file into SL4A's `scripts` directory.

After the scripts are copied onto the device, you can execute them in the foreground or the background, as needed. To execute the script in the background, issue the following ADB command at the command prompt from the host machine, all in one line:

```
adb shell am start -a
com.googlecode.android_scripting.action.LAUNCH_BACKGROUND_SCRIPT -n
com.googlecode.android_scripting/.activity.ScriptingLayerServiceLauncher -e
com.googlecode.android_scripting.extra.SCRIPT_PATH
/sdcard/sl4a/scripts/script.py
```

The Activity Manager (am) launches the SL4A application with the `LAUNCH_BACKGROUND_SCRIPT` intent and with the path to the script.

To execute the script in the foreground, the intent changes, and the ADB command becomes the following, all in one line:

```
adb shell am start -a
com.googlecode.android_scripting.action.LAUNCH_FOREGROUND_SCRIPT -n
com.googlecode.android_scripting/.activity.ScriptingLayerServiceLauncher -e
com.googlecode.android_scripting.extra.SCRIPT_PATH
/sdcard/sl4a/scripts/script.py
```

Using Remote Procedure Call

Scripts can be hosted and executed on the host machine, using the script interpreter running physically on the host machine. This allows scripts to benefit from the high CPU power of the host machine and its extensive debugging environment, while still being able to do Android-specific operations remotely. Android-related API calls are executed through RPC on the Android device.

By default, SL4A does not listen for remote RPC connections. The SL4A RPC server needs to be started first in order to allow scripts running on the host machine to communicate with SL4A. To start the server, choose **View ➤ Interpreters** from the application menu bar to see the interpreters list. Then select **Start Server** from the application menu bar, as shown in Figure 9-14.

Add   Start Server   Preferences   Help

Figure 9-14. *Start Server menu item in the Interpreters view*

Next, SL4A will ask you to choose the type of server you would like to launch, as shown in Figure 9-15. SL4A supports two server types:

- **Private:** This server listens on a loopback network adapter, and is reachable only from within the device or from a host machine attached to the device through USB.

- **Public:** This server listens on either Wi-Fi or a data network adapter, and is reachable through the public network.

When you're executing scripts from only one host machine that is physically attached to the Android device, using a private server is recommended.

Figure 9-15. *Selecting a script server type*

SL4A will start the server, and place its icon on the notification bar to indicate that a script server is active. If more than one server is running on the device, SL4A will show the number of active servers next to the icon within a circle, as shown in Figure 9-16.

Figure 9-16. *SL4A active servers shown on the notification bar*

You can select the SL4A icon and drag it to expand the notification. Tapping the notification will take you to the Script Monitor activity, where SL4A lists the running servers, as shown in Figure 9-17. The server list provides the address, port number, interpreter process ID, and duration for all active servers. You can use the address and port number to remotely connect to the servers.

Figure 9-17. *Script Monitor activity listing the active servers*

Using an Attached Device

To remotely execute scripts from a host machine that is directly connected to the Android device through a USB cable, start a private server. Expand the notification icon to launch Script Monitor to find the port number. The port is opened on the loopback device that is only reachable from the device itself. In order to connect to this port from the host machine, it needs to be forwarded through the ADB.

To set up port forwarding, on Windows-based host machines, open a command prompt window, or on Mac OS X- and Linux-based host machines, open a terminal window, and issue the following command (replace *<server port>* with the server port number):

```
adb forward tcp:9999 tcp:<server port>
```

The ADB starts listening on TCP port 9999 on the host machine, and forwards the communication to the script server that is running on the device.

The SL4A RPC module that is running on the host machine needs to know the script server port number in order to communicate with the server. Supply the port number while initiating the Android object in your script:

```
# Connect to port 9999
droid = android.Android(('localhost', 9999))
```

If you prefer not to change your script files, you can inject the port number through the environment variables. The SL4A RPC module reads the AP_HOST and AP_PORT environment variables if the destination host and the port number are not supplied implicitly. These environment variables can be set on the command line or through the system environment variables list prior to starting the interpreter.

Using a Network Device

To remotely execute scripts from a host machine that can reach the Android device through the network, start a public server. Expand the notification icon to launch Script Monitor to find the public IP address and the port number. The SL4A RPC module that is running on the host machine needs to know the server port number in order to communicate with it. Supply the IP address and the port number while initiating the Android object in your script:

```
# Connect to IP adress 10.0.2.15 and port number 47176
droid = android.Android(('10.0.2.15', 47176))
```

If you prefer not to change your script files, the port number can be injected through the environment variables, as described in the preceding section.

Adding a User Interface

Depending on their functionality, scripts may sometimes need to interact with the user. Although scripting languages support text-based input and output on the console, mobile users are much more familiar with graphical and touch-based UI. SL4A provides a set of UI façades to allow developers to use the Android GUI from their scripts. SL4A provides dialog-based, web-based, and full-screen native UI options. In this section, we will implement a simple calculator application using each of these UI types to demonstrate how these façades can be employed from scripts.

Dialog-Based UIs

The easiest way of interacting with the user is through dialogs and menus. The UI façade comes with a set of predefined dialogs for most common tasks. Our first version of the calculator application will use this façade with a script written in the Python scripting language. We start by initializing the SL4A Android RPC client.

> **NOTE:** If you are new to Python, make sure that you are copying the indention of the code as shown. Python relies on code indention to define the boundaries of the code sections.

```
#
# SL4A Dialog based UI
#
# @author Onur Cinar
```

```
#
import android

# Initialize the SL4A Android RCP Client
droid = android.Android()
```

Getting the Two Numbers

We would like to have our script execute as long as the user wants to make calculations, so we enclose it in an infinite loop:

```
# Title of our dialogs
title = "Calculator"

# We will calculate recursively
while True:
```

The script first asks for the first number through an input dialog:

```
    # Get the first number from the user
    result = droid.dialogGetInput(title, "Enter the first number:").result

    # Check if user answered it
    if result is None:
        break

    # Convert the text input to an integer
    first = int(result)
```

As you can see in the example, it is always good practice to check the result of the dialog, since user may cancel the dialog without providing any input.

When the script is executed, the input dialog is displayed, as shown in Figure 9-18. The application loops as long as the user provides a number, and stops when the user selects the Cancel button.

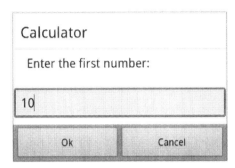

Figure 9-18. *Dialog for the first number*

The script then asks for the second number using these methods:

```
# Get the second number from the user
result = droid.dialogGetInput(title, "Enter the second number:").result

# Check if user answered it
if result is None:
    break

# Convert the text input to an integer
second = int(result)
```

Getting the Operation

With both numbers now available, the script next asks for the operation using a list dialog:

```
# List of possible operations
operations = [ "+", "-", "*", "/" ]

# Open a generic dialog
droid.dialogCreateInput(title, "Select operation")

# Set the items to make it a list
droid.dialogSetItems(operations)

# Make the dialog visible
droid.dialogShow()

# Get the user's response
result = droid.dialogGetResponse().result

# Check if user answered it
if (result is None) or (result.has_key("canceled")):
    break
```

```
# Get the index of selected operation
index = result["item"]

# Find the operation at that index
operation = operations[index]
```

The `dialogGetInput` method that we use here to obtain the numbers is a convenience method for getting the user's input. The UI façade provides multiple methods to shape the dialogs. To present the list of available options, we are starting with a generic input dialog box created through the `dialogCreateInput` method call, and then we supply the list of items through the `dialogSetItems` method call to generate a list dialog. After customizing the dialog, we call the `dialogShow` method to make it visible. The `dialogGetResponse` method blocks until the user responds to the dialog, and returns the response. When the script is executed, the operations list dialog appears, as shown in Figure 9-19.

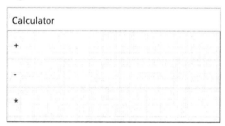

Figure 9-19. *Dialog showing calculator operations*

Based on the user's selection, the script does the necessary operations using the given two numbers.

```
# Do the calculation
solution = {
  "+" : first + second,
  "-" : first - second,
  "*" : first * second,
  "/" : first / second
}[operation]

# Show the solution and ask if user wants
# to do more calculations
droid.dialogCreateAlert(title, "The solution is %d. New calculation?" %
solution)

# Set the answer options
droid.dialogSetPositiveButtonText("Yes")
droid.dialogSetNegativeButtonText("No")
```

```
# Show dialog
droid.dialogShow()

# Get the user's response
result = droid.dialogGetResponse().result

# Check if user answered it
if (result is None) or (result.has_key("canceled")):
    break

# If user answer saying no
option = result["which"]
if option == "negative":
    break
```

Showing the Result

The result is presented to the user in the form of an alert dialog, with Yes and No buttons at the bottom, as shown in Figure 9-20. The user can choose either of these buttons to control the flow of the script. The script first checks if the dialog was dismissed or canceled. Otherwise, the result indicates the user's response as positive or negative, depending on the button clicked. If the user wants to continue with calculations, the script repeats the same flow.

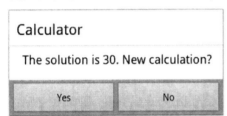

Figure 9-20. *Dialog showing the calculation result*

Before terminating, the script shows a toast using the makeToast method call:

```
# Terminating script
droid.makeToast("Thank you")
```

The closing "Thank you" toast message is shown in Figure 9-21.

Figure 9-21. *Toast message on script termination*

Dialog-based interfaces require a minimal amount of programming. However, from the user's perspective, it's more difficult to input information and navigate in this UI than in native Android applications. SL4A does not provide any functionality to style these dialogs for customizing the application's look and feel. Dialog-based interfaces are the best option for quick automation tasks that do not require too much user interaction.

Web-Based UIs

SL4A provides web-based UI support as an alternative to dialog-based interfaces. Web-based UIs run within an embedded web browser, and can be styled using the CSS support already provided by the browser. Similar to native Android applications, with web-based UIs, multiple UI components can share the same screen. From the user's perspective, the navigation is much easier than with dialog-based interfaces.

Using a web-based interface does not mean that all scripts must be written using JavaScript and HTML. SL4A provides an extensive event queue mechanism that makes it possible for developers to mix and match the JavaScript-based web interface with any scripting language acting as a back end for the application. This architecture is very similar to the way web-based applications are developed these days. For example, you can develop your Android application using a JavaScript/HTML-based UI and Ruby-based back-end code, using SL4A.

UI Layout Through HTML and CSS

In this section, we will redo the calculator example using the web-based UI. The entire UI will be implemented using generic HTML code. Listing 9-1 shows the source code of the `webview.html` UI file.

Listing 9-1. *The webview.html File*

```
<html>
<head>
    <title>Calculator</title>

    <style type="text/css">
        label {
            display: block;
        }

        #solution {
            margin-top: 0.6em;
```

```
            font-size: 2em;
        }
    </style>
</head>
<body>
    <form onsubmit="return calculate();">

    <fieldset>
        <legend>Calculator</legend>

        <label for="first">First number:</label>
        <input type="number" id="first" />

        <label for"second">Second number:</label>
        <input type="number" id="second" />

        <label for="operation">Operation:</label>
        <select id="operation">
            <option value="+">+</option>
            <option value="-">-</option>
            <option value="*">*</option>
            <option value="/">/</option>
        </select>

        <input type="submit" value="Calculate" />
        <div id="solution"></div>
    </fieldset>

    </form>
```

As you may have noticed, at the top of the code, we are styling the UI using CSS. Each HTML element that the application will be accessing or updating has a unique ID.

Manipulating the UI Through JavaScript

The dynamic portion of the UI is implemented through JavaScript. SL4A provides an Android RPC proxy client for JavaScript as well. This RPC client allows the web-based UI to communicate with SL4A and the platform.

```
<script type="text/javascript">
    // Initialize the RPC client
    var droid = new Android();

    // Get elements by id
    var first = document.getElementById("first");
    var second = document.getElementById("second");
    var operation = document.getElementById("operation");
    var solution = document.getElementById("solution");
```

The JavaScript code then registers a callback listener to handle events coming from the SL4A event queue. It registers for only the solution event that will be generated by the Python code:

```
// Register a callback listener for solution
droid.registerCallback("solution", function(data) {
    solution.innerHTML = data.data;
});
```

The calculate function will be triggered when the user chooses the Calculate button. It handles delivering the request to the Python code.

```
// Calculate function
function calculate() {
    // Put parameters into a dictionary
    var request = [
        parseInt(first.value),
        parseInt(second.value),
        operation.value
    ].join();

    // Post request as an event
    droid.eventPost("calculate", request);

    return false;
}
</script>

</body>
</html>
```

Application Logic Using Python

The back end of the application is implemented using the Python scripting language as webview.py. Similar to the dialog-based interface example, the Python code starts by initializing the Android RPC proxy client.

```
#
# SL4A WebView based UI
#
# @author Onur Cinar
#
import android

# Initialize the SL4A Android RCP Client
droid = android.Android()
```

The JavaScript/HTML code is loaded by using the webViewShow method call:

```
# Show the HTML page
droid.webViewShow("file:///sdcard/sl4a/scripts/webview.html")
```

Prior to making this method call, the HTML file should be available on the device. Using the ADB, push the file to the Android device.

```
adb push webview.html /sdcard/sl4a/scripts/
```

> **NOTE:** Due to a known bug in the Android emulator, you can run the web-based UI example on only an Android device. The Android emulator is not supported.

In this example, the HTML file is located in the SL4A default script directory `/sdcard/sl4a/scripts`; however, the HTML file can be located anywhere on the device. SL4A starts an embedded web browser and loads the web-based UI, as shown in Figure 9-22.

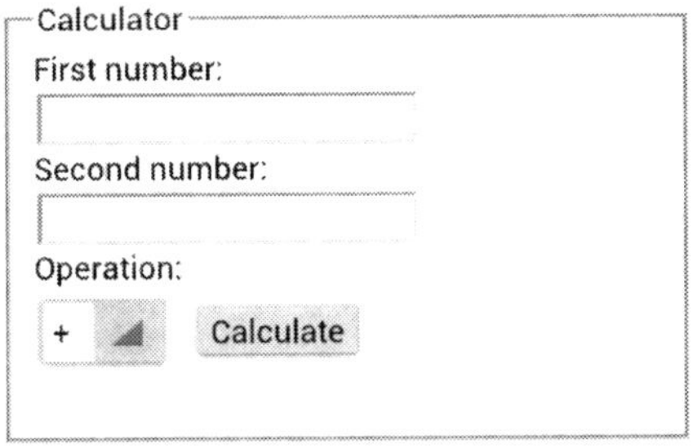

Figure 9-22. *Calculator interface within the embedded browser*

As seen in the JavaScript code, when the user clicks the Calculate button, the web portion of the application posts a `calculate` event with the numbers and the operation. The Python code receives this event through the SL4A event queue:

```
# We will calculate recursively
while True:
    # Wait for calculate event
    result = droid.eventWaitFor("calculate").result

    # Make sure that event has data
    if result is not None:
        # Data comes as a comma separated list of values
        request = result["data"].split(",")

        # Extract parameters from request array
        first = int(request[0])
        second = int(request[1])
        operation = request[2]
```

```
# Calculate solution
solution = {
    "+" : first + second,
    "-" : first - second,
    "*" : first * second,
    "/" : first / second
}[operation]
```

The script can run on the device or the host machine. The SL4A RPC client allows the script to access the main SL4A event queue to receive this request. Upon receiving the request, it first extracts the parameters and does the requested calculation. The solution of the calculation is also sent to the web-based interface through the SL4A event queue:

```
# Post the solution to event queue
droid.eventPost("solution", str(solution))
```

The JavaScript code that is already registered to handle the solution event receives the solution and updates the UI, as shown in Figure 9-23.

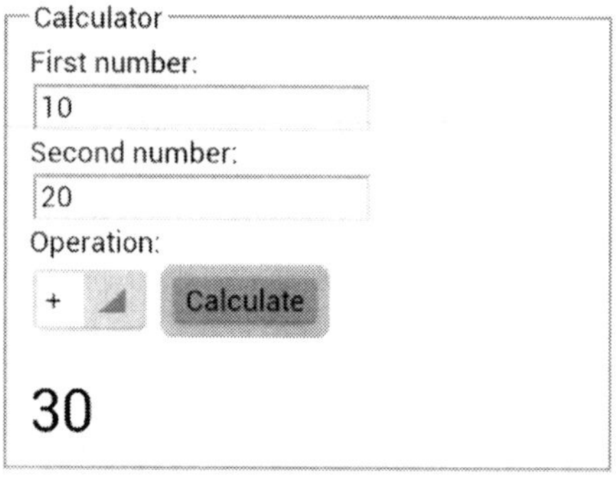

Figure 9-23. *Solution shown in the web interface*

Compared to the dialog-based UIs, web-based UIs are much more flexible. Since the Android RPC proxy client is also accessible through the web code, the entire application can also be developed in JavaScript.

Full-Screen UI

The full-screen UI allows XML-based Android layout files to be used in scripts. In this section, we will redo calculator example using the full-screen UI.

The script starts by initializing the Android RPC proxy client, and then defines the Android layout XML through a string variable.

```
#
# SL4A Full screen UI
```

```
#
# @author Onur Cinar
#
import android

# Initialize the SL4A Android RCP Client
droid = android.Android()

# XML layout
layout = """<?xml version="1.0" encoding="utf-8"?>
<LinearLayout xmlns:android="http://schemas.android.com/apk/res/android"
    android:layout_width="fill_parent"
    android:layout_height="fill_parent"
    android:orientation="vertical"
    android:background="#ffffffff">

    <TextView
        android:layout_width="fill_parent"
        android:layout_height="wrap_content"
        android:text="First number:" />

    <EditText
        android:id="@+id/first"
        android:layout_width="fill_parent"
        android:layout_height="wrap_content"
        android:numeric="integer"
        android:inputType="number" />

    <TextView
        android:layout_width="fill_parent"
        android:layout_height="wrap_content"
        android:text="Second number:" />

    <EditText
        android:id="@+id/second"
        android:layout_width="fill_parent"
        android:layout_height="wrap_content"
        android:numeric="integer"
        android:inputType="number" />

    <TextView
        android:layout_width="fill_parent"
        android:layout_height="wrap_content"
        android:text="Operation:" />

    <Spinner
        android:id="@+id/operation"
        android:layout_width="fill_parent"
        android:layout_height="wrap_content" />
```

```
<Button
    android:id="@+id/calculate"
    android:layout_width="fill_parent"
    android:layout_height="wrap_content"
    android:text="Calculate"
/>

<TextView
    android:id="@+id/solution"
    android:layout_width="fill_parent"
    android:layout_height="wrap_content" />
</LinearLayout>
"""
```

By default, SL4A renders the layout on a transparent background. This example defines a background with a solid color. Since the strings cannot be provided by the string resources, the layout file contains the hard-coded strings. Every UI component has an ID for the script to use.

```
# Show layout
droid.fullShow(layout)
```

The script calls the fullShow method to display the layout, as shown in Figure 9-24.

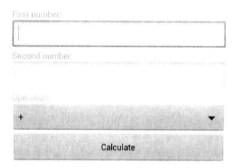

Figure 9-24. *Full-screen UI displaying Android layout XML*

The spinner items are set to the list of available operations using the fullSetList method.

```
# List of possible operations
operations = [ "+", "-", "*", "/" ]

# Set operation spinner items
droid.fullSetList("operation", operations)
```

The script waits for the click event, and then checks the ID of the clicked component to make sure that it is the Calculate button.

```
# We will calculate recursively
while True:
    # Wait for click event
    event = droid.eventWaitFor("click").result

    # Check if it is the calculate button
    if event["data"]["id"] == "calculate":
```

The script first finds the UI components using the `fullQueryDetail` method, and then gets the values for the first and second numbers. If the numbers are not supplied, the script does not do the calculation.

```
        # Get the first number
        field = droid.fullQueryDetail("first").result["text"]

        # Check if field is empty
        if field == "":
            continue

        # Convert field to integer
        first = int(field)

        # Get the first number
        field = droid.fullQueryDetail("second").result["text"]

        # Check if field is empty
        if field == "":
            continue

        # Convert field to integer
        second = int(field)
```

The script calls the `fullQueryDetail` method to find the operations spinner, and then uses the `selectedItemPosition` attribute to determine the selected operation.

```
        # Get the operation index
        index =
int(droid.fullQueryDetail("operation").result["selectedItemPosition"])

        # Get operation
        operation = operations[index]

        # Do the calculation
        solution = {
          "+" : first + second,
          "-" : first - second,
          "*" : first * second,
          "/" : first / second
        }[operation]
```

The result is then displayed using the `fullSetPropery` method to set the `text` attribute of the solution text view.

```
# Show solution
droid.fullSetProperty("solution", "text", "Solution is %d" % solution)
```

Figure 9-25 shows an example of the result display. Compared to the dialog- and web-based alternatives, the full-screen UI is the only one that delivers a platform look and feel. It allows scripts to benefit from all existing Android UI components.

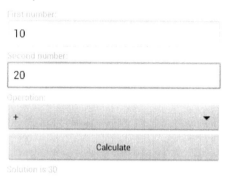

Figure 9-25. *Updated display showing the result*

Packaging Scripts As APKs

SL4A can also be used to package a script as an installable Android package. This allows distributing scripts as ordinary Android applications. The installable Android package contains only the script and resources; the script interpreter should still be installed separately on the target device. In this section, we will go through the steps to set up such an Android project, integrating the script files and deploying it to the Android device.

Downloading the Project Template

To facilitate packaging the script as an installable Android package, the SL4A project web site provides a template Android project. Point your browser to `http://android-scripting.googlecode.com/hg/android/script_for_android_template.zip` and download the template project as a compressed ZIP archive file.

Before importing the template project into Eclipse, you need to make sure that Android API level 4 is installed. If not, use the Android SDK Manager to download it, as described in Chapter 5. As an alternative, you can change the project's build target based on your target platform's API level. To do so, right-click the project and choose **Properties** to launch the Properties dialog. Choose Android from the list on the left, and change the project build target to an API level greater than or equal to 4.

Now we are ready to import the template project into Eclipse. Open Eclipse and choose **File ➤ Import…** from the top menu bar to launch the Import wizard, as shown in Figure 9-26.

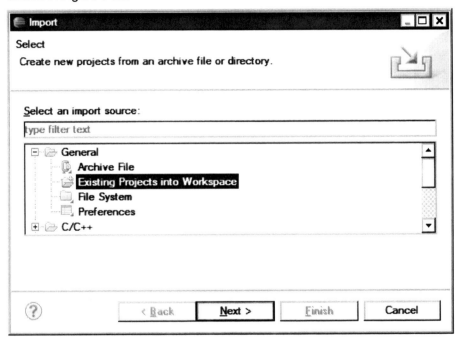

Figure 9-26. *Eclipse project Import wizard*

From the list of sources, select Existing Projects into Workspace, and then click the Next button. Eclipse will ask for the location of the project files. Select the Select archive file radio button, and using the Browse button, point it to the `script_for_android_template.zip` file that you downloaded, as shown in Figure 9-27. Then click the Finish button to start importing the project.

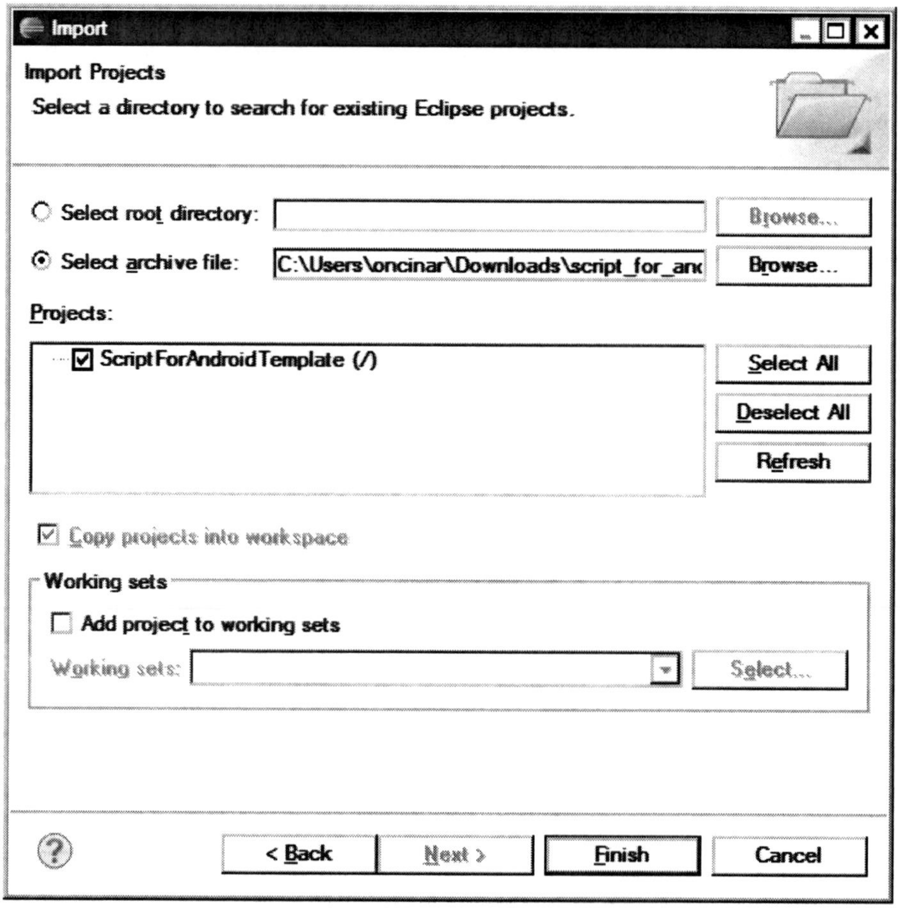

Figure 9-27. *Importing a project from a ZIP archive file*

Configuring the Project

Eclipse will import the template project into your workspace under the name
`ScriptForAndroidTemplate`. To rename the project, right-click its name, and then
choose **Refactor ➤ Rename** from the context menu to launch the Rename Java
Project wizard, as shown in *Figure 9-28*.

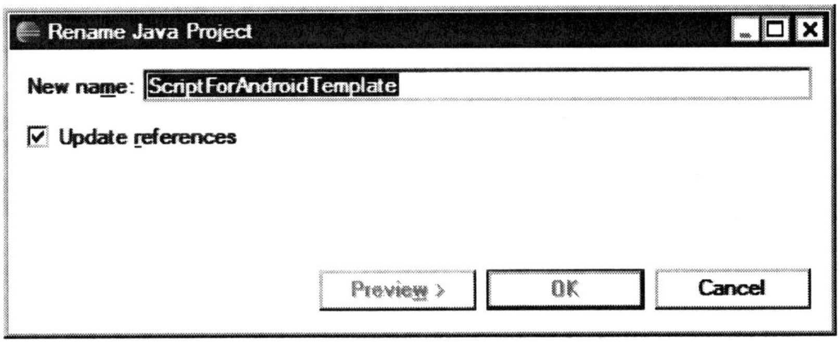

Figure 9-28. *Renaming the template project*

In addition to renaming the project, we should also change the package name to prevent any naming conflicts when the application is deployed. We need to rename the package in the `AndroidManifest.xml` file prior to renaming the Java package itself. Open the `AndroidManifest.xml` file and change the Android package name accordingly.

```
<?xml version="1.0" encoding="utf-8"?>
<manifest
    package="com.apress.chapter9"
    android:versionCode="1"
    android:versionName="1.0"
    xmlns:android="http://schemas.android.com/apk/res/android">
```

Next, to rename the Java package, right-click the package name `com.dummy.fooforandroid` and choose **Refactor ➤ Rename** from the context menu to launch the Rename Package wizard. In the New name field, enter the new package name `com.apress.chapter9`, as shown in Figure 9-29.

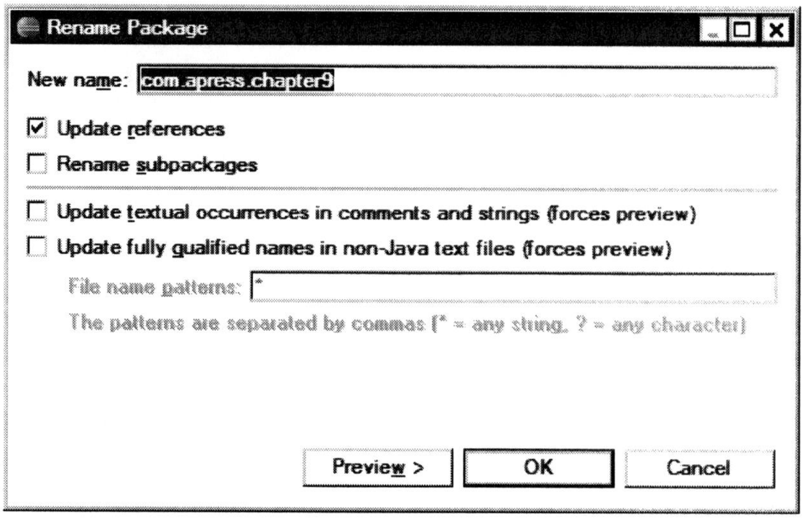

Figure 9-29. *Renaming the package*

Make sure that the Update references option is checked, and then click the Preview button. Eclipse will rename the package, and then it will update all references accordingly. Before making any changes to the files, Eclipse will present the required changes, as shown in Figure 9-30. Upon verifying the changes, click the OK button to apply them to the project files.

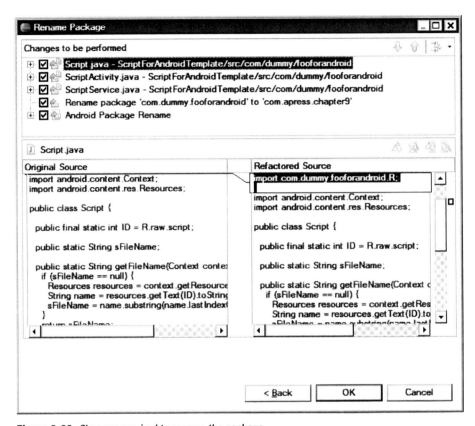

Figure 9-30. *Changes required to rename the package*

Although the template project comes with everything preconfigured, for security reasons, except for the Internet access permission, all permission requests in the AndroidManifest.xml file are intentionally commented out. Uncomment the permissions that are required to execute your script properly.

Incorporating the Script File

Using the Package Explorer view, expand the res directory and then the raw directory to show the raw project resources. The template project keeps the actual script file as a raw project resource.

Although the script file that is provided with the template project is a Python script, the template project can contain virtually any type of script that is supported by SL4A. For example, if you are using the Ruby scripting language, remove the `script.py` reference and insert your script as `script.rb` into the raw resources. The point here is that the script file should be named as `script` with the proper file extension for the scripting language used. If you prefer to rename it differently, you will need to modify the `ID` static field in the `Script` class accordingly:

```
package com.apress.chapter9;

public class Script {
    …
    public final static int ID = R.raw.script;
    …
}
```

This script file is used as the main entry point by the SL4A engine. The Android application may contain multiple script files acting as modules or dependencies for the main script file. These additional script files should also be added into the raw resources. When the application starts, it extracts all script files in the raw resources into the `files` directory, prior to executing the script file.

Deploying and Running the Application

The application can then be deployed and run like an ordinary Android application, as discussed in Chapter 5. When it first starts, SL4A looks for a script interpreter on the platform based on the scripting language used, and automatically installs one if it is not available. This still requires the Android device to be configured to allow installing non-Market applications.

At the time of this writing, SL4A does not directly support bundling interpreters with stand-alone Android applications. Although it is not officially supported, the template application can be modified to include the necessary interpreters by combining the necessary packages from the SL4A source code.

Summary

This chapter provided a quick introduction to Android scripting using the SL4A open source library. We looked at the architecture of the SL4A application, and explored the interpreters and façades provided by SL4A. We also explored the different methods of executing scripts on Android devices, both locally and remotely. We then covered the UI options provided by the SL4A and compared their use with a simple calculator example. Finally, we demonstrated how scripts can be packaged as a stand-alone application that can be distributed as an ordinary Android application.

10

Project: Movie Player Using HTML and JavaScript

In this chapter, we will reimplement the movie player application that we developed in Chapter 5 in HTML and JavaScript by using the SL4A framework. Since the SL4A framework does not provide all of the functionality that is needed for the movie player application, we will go one step further and integrate a new custom façade into the SL4A framework. We will package the resulting application as a stand-alone Android script application that can be distributed and deployed in the same way as an ordinary Android application.

Getting the SL4A Source Code

Our movie player application requires access to the media store content provider in order to query for a list of movie files on the device. None of the existing SL4A version R5 façades provide access to the media store. We will develop a new façade as a part of this example to enable the script application to fetch the necessary information from the platform. The SL4A framework currently does not support dynamic discovery of new façades, and it is limited to using only the built-in façades.

To add a new façade, the SL4A framework source code needs to be slightly modified. In order to achieve that, in this section, we will check out the SL4A source code from the SL4A source repository.

Preparing the Workspace

SL4A R5 source code requires Android API level 3, 4, 7, and 8 platform SDKs to be installed on the host machine. As described in Chapter 5, choose **Window ➤ Android SDK Manager** from the top menu bar to launch the SDK Manager and download these SDKs to the host machine.

SL4A projects rely on the `ANDROID_SDK` classpath variable to be predefined in Eclipse to compile. To define this variable, open the Eclipse Preferences dialog as described in earlier chapters. Using the search box, filter the list of preferences to Classpath Variables. Then click the New button to launch the New Variable Entry dialog. Define the new variable entry as follows and shown in Figure 10-1:

- **Name:** Set the name to `ANDROID_SDK`.

- **Path:** The variable should point to the location of the Android SDK on the host machine. Using the Folder button on the right, choose the Android SDK directory.

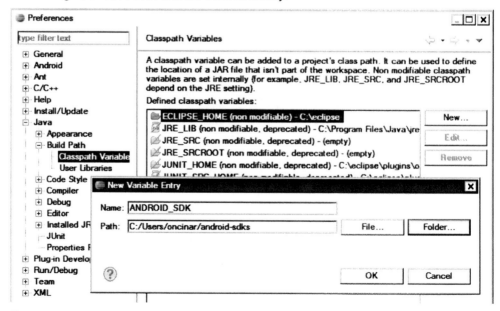

Figure 10-1. *Adding the ANDROID_SDK classpath variable for SL4A source code*

Setting the Java Compiler Compliance Level

SL4A source code is based on Java source version 1.6. If you have installed JDK version 6, as recommended in Chapter 5, no additional configuration is needed. Otherwise, the workspace compiler compliance level needs to be changed to 1.6 for the SL4A source code to compile. To change the compliance level, open the Eclipse Preferences dialog, and using the search box, filter the list of preferences to Compiler. Select the Java Compiler preferences, and change the compliance level to 1.6, as shown in Figure 10-2.

Figure 10-2. *Changing the workspace Java compiler compliance level*

Installing Mercurial

SL4A source code is served as a Mercurial source repository through the Google Code web site. To check out the SL4A source code to a host machine, Mercurial and the Mercurial Eclipse plug-in need to be installed. On Mac OS X and Linux platforms, Mercurial binary needs to be installed prior to downloading the Mercurial Eclipse plug-in. In this section, we will go through the process of installing Mercurial binary on these platforms.

Installing Mecurial on Mac OS X

Using your web browser, navigate to the Mercurial download site at http://mercurial.selenic.com to download the binary for Mac OS X. As shown in Figure 10-3, the Mercurial web site detects your operating system automatically, and provides a Download button for the Mercurial installer.

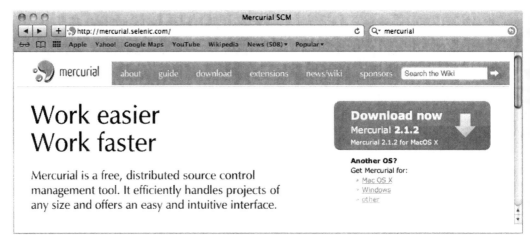

Figure 10-3. *Mercurial download page for the Mac OS X platform*

Click the Download button to download the Mercurial installer ZIP archive file to your host machine. Next, go to your **Downloads** folder. Depending on the version of Mac OS X, the ZIP file may have been extracted automatically, or you may need to extract it manually. This ZIP file contains the Mac OS X installable package for Mercurial binary.

Double-click the installable package file to launch the Mercurial installer, which will guide you through the installation process. Upon completion of the installation, the Mercurial binary can be found at **/usr/local/bin/hg**. To validate the Mercurial installation, open a terminal window and enter **hg** at the command prompt. If you can see the Mercurial basic commands list, as shown in Figure 10-4, your Mercurial installation was successful. You can now proceed to the Mercurial Eclipse plug-in installation.

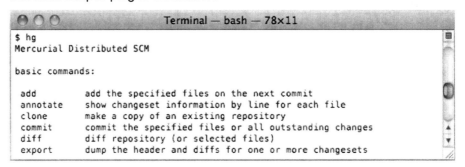

Figure 10-4. *Verifying Mercurial installation on Mac OS X*

Installing Mecurial on Linux

Mercurial binaries are available through the application repositories on most Linux distributions. Open a terminal window, and depending to your Linux distribution, execute the corresponding installation command:

- **Debian/Ubuntu:** `sudo apt-get install mercurial`

- **OpenSUSE:** `sudo zipper in mercurial`

- **Fedora:** `sudo yum install mercurial`

- **Gentoo:** `sudo emerge mercurial`

The Mecurial installation directory may vary depending on your Linux distribution. To find the location of the Mercurial binary, open a terminal window and enter `which hg` at the command prompt. If you can see the installation directory of Mercurial, as shown in Figure 10-5, your Mercurial installation was successful.

Figure 10-5. *Verifying Mercurial installation on Linux*

Installing the Mercurial Eclipse Plug-in

To install the Mecurial Eclipse plug-in, in Eclipse, choose **Help ➤ Install New Software...** from the top menu bar to launch the Install wizard. Mercurial is not part of the official Eclipse software site. Click the Add button and define the Mercurial Eclipse software site with the location `http://cbes.javaforge.com/update`, as shown in Figure 10-6.

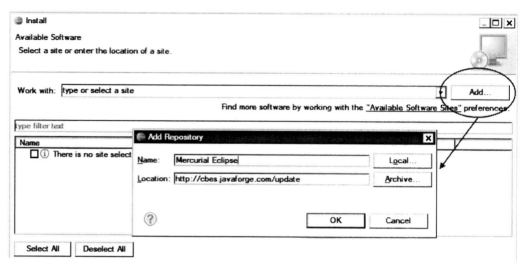

Figure 10-6. *Adding the Mercurial software site to Eclipse*

After you've added the new software site, Eclipse will fetch the list of Mercurial plug-ins and present them within the Install wizard. This process may take some time, depending on your network connectivity. From this list of plug-ins, choose Mercurial Eclipse. For a Windows platform, also choose Windows Binaries for Mercurial, as shown in Figure 10-7.

Name	Version	
⊞ ☐ codeBeamer Eclipse Studio (with Mylyn)		
⊟ ☑ MercurialEclipse		
☑ MercurialEclipse	1.9.1.v201111302231	
☑ Windows Binaries for Mercurial (Recommended)	1.9.3.v201110131844	

Figure 10-7. *Selecting Mercurial plug-ins*

Click the Next button to proceed with the installation. Eclipse will list the plug-ins that will be installed. Click the Finish button to start the installation.

Checking Out SL4A Source Code

With Mecurial and the Mecurial Eclipse plug-in installed, we're ready to check out the SL4A source code. Choose File ➤ New ➤ Other... from the top menu bar, expand the Mercurial category, and select Clone Existing Mercurial Repository, as shown in Figure 10-8.

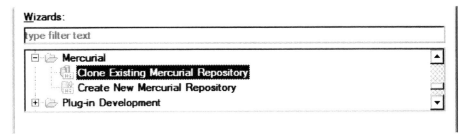

Figure 10-8. *Selecting to clone the existing Mercurial repository*

In the wizard's URL field, enter `https://code.google.com/p/android-scripting/` as the repository location, as shown in Figure 10-9, and then click the Next button. Mercurial is a distributed source control system, meaning that it will clone the entire repository to the host machine. This process may take a few minutes, depending on your network connectivity.

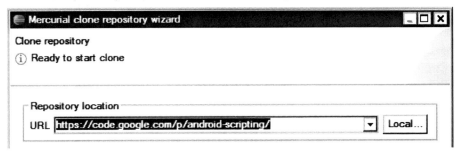

Figure 10-9. *Setting the repository location for cloning*

The latest official version of SL4A is R5. At the time of this writing, SL4A version R5 is not tagged in the source code repository. In order to check out the code base to the R5 version, switch to the Revisions tab, and enter 1214 as the revision number, as shown in Figure 10-10. Click the Next button to continue.

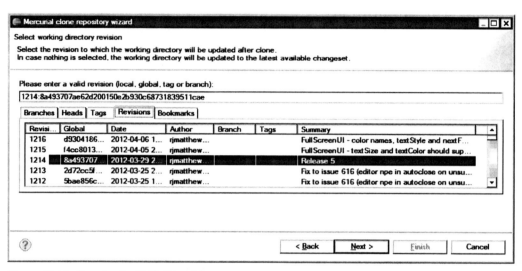

Figure 10-10. *Choosing the SL4A R5 revision*

The Mercurial Clone Repository wizard will present the list of all the projects in the SL4A repository, as shown in Figure 10-11. Although the example project will not use all of the SL4A projects, choose to import all projects except `DocumentationGenerator` into Eclipse.

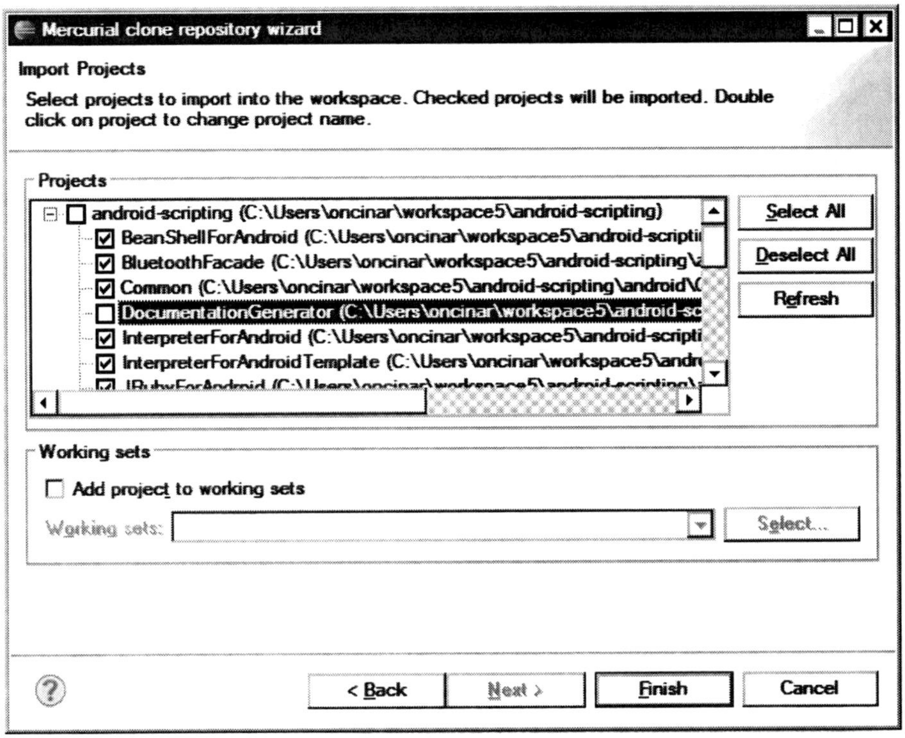

Figure 10-11. *Choosing projects to import*

Eclipse will start building all of the SL4A projects automatically. Check the Problems view and address any reported problems.

Movie Player Script Project

As discussed in the previous chapter, SL4A provides a template project for packaging scripts as stand-alone Android packages. The source code for the template project is called ScriptForAndroidTemplate. The example project will use the template project as its base.

Cloning the Template Project

Instead of modifying the template project directly, we will clone the template project under a different project name. Select the ScriptForAndroidTemplate project, right-click it, and choose Copy from the context menu. Right-click again, and choose **Paste** from the context menu to launch the Copy Project wizard. Name the new project `MoviePlayerScript`, as shown in Figure 10-12.

Figure 10-12. *Cloning the template project as MoviePlayerScript*

Eclipse clones the entire project settings, including the Mercurial metadata. Since the new project is not part of the SL4A source repository, right-click the project name and choose **Team ➤ Disconnect** to detach it from Mercurial.

Linking to SL4A Framework Code

The `MoviePlayerScript` project is an identical clone of the SL4A template. The SL4A template project is a stand-alone project without any external dependencies, except the interpreters.

The SL4A framework code is precompiled and supplied as a JAR file with the SL4A template project. Since we will be modifying the SL4A framework in this example project, we need to remove this JAR file and make the project depend on the SL4A framework project directly. Using the Package Explorer view, expand the `libs` directory under the `MoviePlayerScript` project and delete the `script.jar` file. Eclipse will show a confirmation dialog prior to deleting the file.

Next, right-click the project and choose **Preferences** to launch the project Preferences dialog. Choose Java Build Path from the left pane, and then switch to the Libraries tab. Using the Remove button, remove `script.jar` from the project build path, as shown in Figure 10-13.

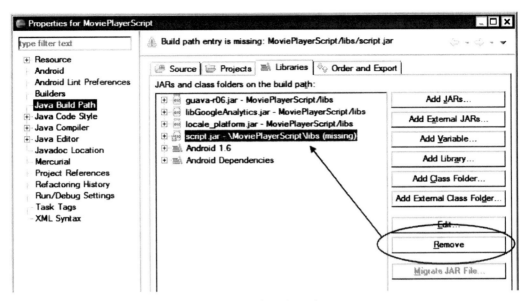

Figure 10-13. *Removing the precompiled SL4A library from the project*

To make the `MoviePlayerScript` project directly dependent on the SL4A framework, switch to the Projects tab and click the Add button. As shown in Figure 10-14, choose to add `BluetoothFacade`, `Common`, `InterpreferForAndroid`, `ScriptingLayer`, `SignalStrengthFacade`, `TextToSpeechFacade`, `Utils`, and `WebCamFacade`. Then click the OK button to save the selections.

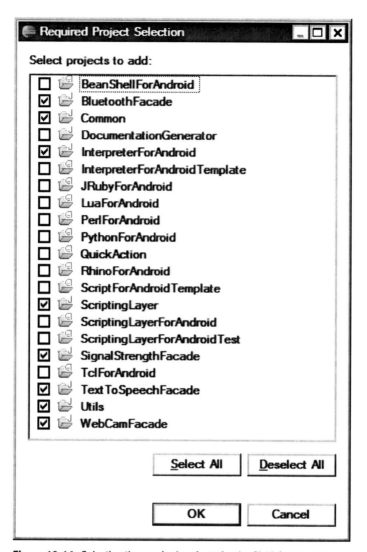

Figure 10-14. *Selecting the required projects for the SL4A framework*

Besides depending on these projects, the output of these projects should also be packaged with the `MoviePlayerScript` project in order to have it execute on the Android device. To do so, switch to the Order and Export tab, and select the same list of projects for exporting, as shown in Figure 10-15. Eclipse will rebuild the project. At this point, try running the project on your Android device to make sure the project configuration was successful.

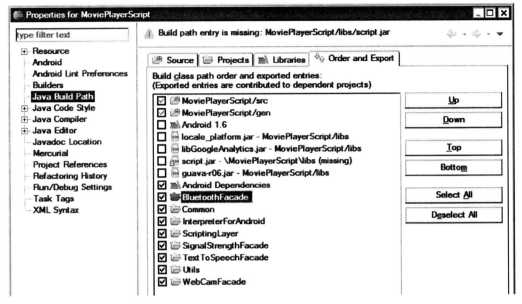

Figure 10-15. *Marking the SL4A projects for export*

Renaming the Project Package

Since the MoviePlayerScript project is a clone of a SL4A template project, it shares the same Android package name. To prevent any possible conflicts while deploying the MoviePlayerScript project, open the AndroidManifest.xml file and change the package name to com.apress.movieplayerscript. To rename the Java package, right-click the com.dummy.fooforandroid package and choose Refactor ➤ Rename.

Adding the Movie Façade

To provide access to the media store, a new façade needs to be developed and added to the SL4A framework. To minimize the amount of change on the actual SL4A framework code, we will create a separate project for the façade implementation.

Choose File ➤ New ➤ Java Project from the top menu bar, and name the Java project MovieFacade, as shown in Figure 10-16. Click the Next button to continue.

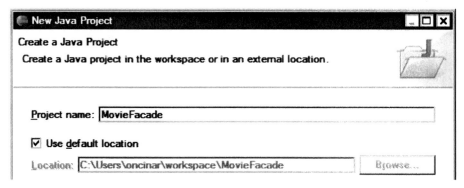

Figure 10-16. *Creating the MovieFacade project*

On the next screen, choose the Projects tab, and add the Common and Utils projects as the project dependencies, as shown in Figure 10-17. `MovieFacade` will be using components from these projects to function as a part of the SL4A framework.

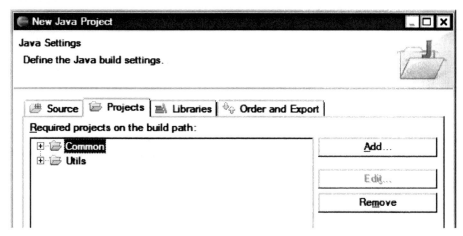

Figure 10-17. *Adding MovieFacade project dependencies*

`MovieFacade` will also be using components from the Android framework; however, it is not an Android project. We need to add the Android framework library to the project. Switch to the Libraries tab, and click the Add Variable… button. Select ANDROID_SDK from the list, and click the Edit button to change its value to `ANDROID_SDK/platforms/android-7/android.jar`, as shown in Figure 10-18. Depending on the Android features you will be using in your façades, you can substitute `android-7` with the appropriate API level required. Click the OK button to save the variable, and then click the Finish button to apply the library changes to the project.

Figure 10-18. *Adding the Android framework as a library to MovieFacade*

Creating the MovieFacade Class

In order to serve as a façade within the SL4A framework, the `MovieFacade` project needs to extend the `com.google.android_scripting.jsonrpc.RpcReceiver` class. Select the `MovieFacade` project and choose **File ➤ New ➤ Class** from the top menu bar. Define the `MovieFacade` class in the `com.apress.movieplayerscript` package, as shown in Figure 10-19.

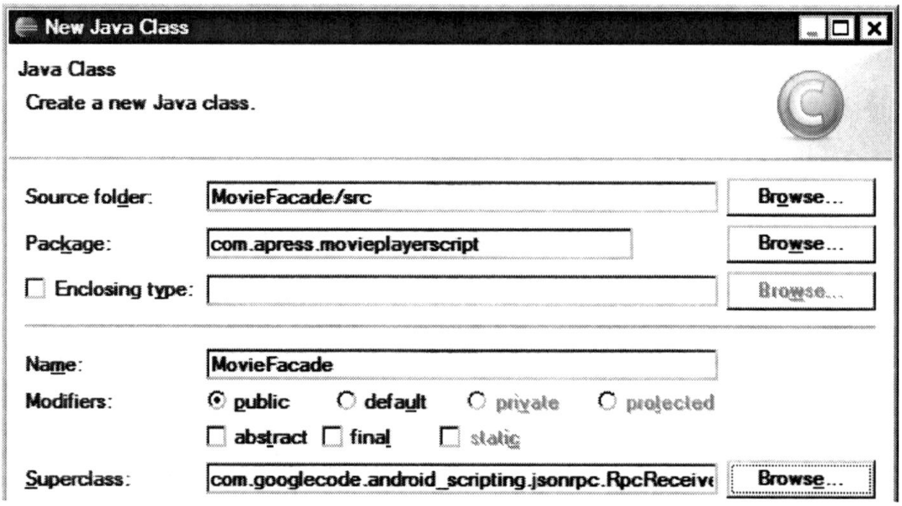

Figure 10-19. *Defining the MovieFacade class*

MovieFacade will contain one method, moviesGet, exposed to the scripts. SL4A expects the exposed methods to be annotated using the necessary RPC attributes. The following RPC attributes are provided by SL4A through the com.googlecode.android_scripting.rpc package:

- Rpc: This attribute is used to mark the method as exposed through RPC. It also provides brief documentation for the method, including its return value.

- RpcParameter: This attribute is used to document the parameters for methods.

- RpcOptional: This attribute is used to mark a parameter as optional.

- RpcDefault: This attribute is used to mark a parameter that has a default value.

- RpcMinSdk: This attribute is used to specify the minimum Android SDK level required to execute the method.

- RpcStartEvent: This attribute is used to mark methods that start event generation.

- RpcStopEvent: This attribute is used to mark methods that terminate event generation.

The source code for the MovieFacade class is shown in Listing 10-1.

Listing 10-1. *The MovieFacade.java File*

```java
package com.apress.movieplayerscript;

import java.util.LinkedList;
import java.util.List;

import org.json.JSONException;
import org.json.JSONObject;

import android.app.Service;
import android.content.ContentResolver;
import android.database.Cursor;
import android.provider.MediaStore;
import android.util.Log;

import com.googlecode.android_scripting.facade.FacadeManager;
import com.googlecode.android_scripting.jsonrpc.RpcReceiver;
import com.googlecode.android_scripting.rpc.Rpc;

/**
 * Movie facade.
 *
 * @author Onur Cinar
 */
public class MovieFacade extends RpcReceiver {
    /** Log tag. */
    private static final String LOG_TAG = "MovieFacade";

    /** Service instance. */
    private final Service service;

    /**
     * Constructor.
     *
     * @param manager
     *            facade manager.
     */
    public MovieFacade(FacadeManager manager) {
        super(manager);

        // Save the server instance for using it as a context
        service = manager.getService();
    }

    @Override
    public void shutdown() {

    }
```

```java
    /**
     * Gets a list of all movies.
     *
     * @return movie list.
     * @throws JSONException
     */
    @Rpc(description = "Returns a list of all movies.", returns = "a List of
movies as Maps")
    public List<JSONObject> moviesGet() throws JSONException {
        List<JSONObject> movies = new LinkedList<JSONObject>();

        // Media columns to query
        String[] mediaColumns = { MediaStore.Video.Media._ID,
                MediaStore.Video.Media.TITLE, MediaStore.Video.Media.DURATION,
                MediaStore.Video.Media.DATA, MediaStore.Video.Media.MIME_TYPE };

        // Thumbnail columns to query
        String[] thumbnailColumns = { MediaStore.Video.Thumbnails.DATA };

        // Content resolver
        ContentResolver contentResolver = service.getContentResolver();

        // Query external movie content for selected media columns
        Cursor mediaCursor = contentResolver.query(
                MediaStore.Video.Media.EXTERNAL_CONTENT_URI, mediaColumns,
                null, null, null);

        // Loop through media results
        if (mediaCursor.moveToFirst()) {
            do {
                // Get the video id
                int id = mediaCursor.getInt(mediaCursor
                        .getColumnIndex(MediaStore.Video.Media._ID));

                // Get the thumbnail associated with the video
                Cursor thumbnailCursor = contentResolver.query(
                        MediaStore.Video.Thumbnails.EXTERNAL_CONTENT_URI,
                        thumbnailColumns, MediaStore.Video.Thumbnails.VIDEO_ID
                            + "=" + id, null, null);

                // New movie object from the data
                JSONObject movie = new JSONObject();

                movie.put("title", mediaCursor.getString(mediaCursor
                        .getColumnIndexOrThrow(MediaStore.Video.Media.TITLE)));
                movie.put("moviePath", "file://" +
mediaCursor.getString(mediaCursor
                        .getColumnIndex(MediaStore.Video.Media.DATA)));
                movie.put("mimeType", mediaCursor.getString(mediaCursor
                        .getColumnIndex(MediaStore.Video.Media.MIME_TYPE)));
```

```java
            long duration = mediaCursor.getLong(mediaCursor
                    .getColumnIndex(MediaStore.Video.Media.DURATION));
            movie.put("duration", getDurationAsString(duration));

            if (thumbnailCursor.moveToFirst()) {
                movie.put(
                        "thumbnailPath",
                        "file://" +
thumbnailCursor.getString(thumbnailCursor

.getColumnIndex(MediaStore.Video.Thumbnails.DATA)));
            } else {
                movie.put("thumbnailPath", "");
            }

            Log.d(LOG_TAG, movie.toString());

            // Close cursor
            thumbnailCursor.close();

            // Add to movie list
            movies.add(movie);

        } while (mediaCursor.moveToNext());

        // Close cursor
        mediaCursor.close();
    }

    return movies;
}

/**
 * Gets the given duration as string.
 *
 * @param duration
 *            duration value.
 * @return duration string.
 */
private static String getDurationAsString(long duration) {
    // Calculate milliseconds
    long milliseconds = duration % 1000;
    long seconds = duration / 1000;

    // Calculate seconds
    long minutes = seconds / 60;
    seconds %= 60;

    // Calculate hours and minutes
    long hours = minutes / 60;
```

```
        minutes %= 60;

        // Build the duration string
        String durationString = String.format("%1$02d:%2$02d:%3$02d.%4$03d",
                hours, minutes, seconds, milliseconds);

        return durationString;
    }
}
```

MovieFacade gets the FacadeManager instance when initialized. The
FacadeManager enables access to the SL4A Android service instance. The
service instance can be used by façades as the Android context while
interacting with the Android framework. The implementation of the moviesGet
method is partially borrowed from the Chapter 5 example project, and modified
to operate as an RPC method. Since the scripts cannot directly consume Java
classes, the return type of the moviesGet method is changed to a JSONObject list.

Registering the Façade

Although the façade is now properly defined, it is not known to the SL4A
framework yet. The MovieFacade needs to be registered with the
FacadeConfiguration class.

Right-click the ScriptingLayer project and choose Properties. From the
Properties dialog, choose Java Build Path, and switch to the Projects tab to add
MovieFacade as a dependency, as shown in Figure 10-20.

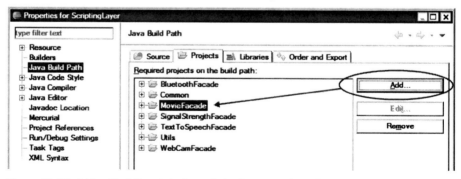

Figure 10-20. *Adding MovieFacade to the scripting layer as a dependency*

Under the same project, using the Package Explorer view, expand the
com.googlecode.android_scripting.facade package under Sources, and open
the FacadeConfiguration class.

The `FacadeConfiguration` class acts as a registry for SL4A façades. SL4A currently only allows façades to be manually registered here. At the top of the class file, within a static context, the façades are added to the `sFacadeClassList` set. As shown in the following code, add the sections marked between the `CHANGES BEGIN` and `CHANGES END` comments to the `FacadeConfiguration` class.

```
if (sSdkLevel >= 8) {
  sFacadeClassList.add(WebCamFacade.class);
}

// **** CHANGES BEGIN ****

// Movie facade
sFacadeClassList.add(MovieFacade.class);


// **** CHANGES END ****

for (Class<? extends RpcReceiver> recieverClass : sFacadeClassList) {
  for (MethodDescriptor rpcMethod :
MethodDescriptor.collectFrom(recieverClass)) {
    sRpcs.put(rpcMethod.getName(), rpcMethod);
  }
}
```

Now `MovieFacade` is part of the SL4A framework and consumable from the scripts.

Exporting the Movie Façade

Although `MovieFacade` is properly registered with the SL4A framework, it is not still declared in the export list of the `MoviePlayerScript` project. Right-click the `MoviePlayerScript` project, choose Java Build Path, add the `MovieFacade` project to the Projects list, and mark it in the Order and Export tab for export.

Adding the Script

The actual UI and the application logic for the `MoviePlayerScript` project will be implemented using HTML and JavaScript. The SL4A framework relies on the Android framework for both rendering HTML and interpreting embedded JavaScript code, and it will not need to download an interpreter.

The SL4A template project comes with an example Python script. Open the `MoviePlayerScript` project, expand the resources, and delete the `script.py` Python script file from the raw resources directory, `/res/raw`. Choose File ➤ New

➤ File from the top menu bar, and add a `script.html` file. You can open this script file for editing by right-clicking it and choosing **Open** ➤ **Text Editor** from the context menu. During runtime, the SL4A framework will detect the file type using its extension, and automatically start an embedded web browser to execute the script.

The HTML Part

The HTML part of the script is very short and basic. As shown in the following code, it defines only an HTML `div` element with the `id` of `movies` to hold the list of movies. The CSS defines how the movie items will be rendered by the browser.

```
<html>
<head>
    <style type="text/css">
        .movie {
            border: 1px solid #000;
            padding: 0.4em;
        }

        .thumbnail {
            width: 4em;
            height: 4em;
            float: left;
            margin-right: 0.4em;
        }

        .title {
            font-size: x-large;
        }

        .clear {
            clear: both;
        }
    </style>
</head>
<body>

    <div id="movies"></div>
```

The JavaScript Part

The script will use JavaScript to communicate with `MovieFacade` through the SL4A framework to fetch the list of movies and the related information. As with

all other scripting languages, the script begins by initializing the Android proxy
RPC client.

```
<script type="text/javascript">
    // Initialize the RPC client
    var droid = new Android();

    // Movie element
    var moviesElement = document.getElementById("movies");
```

The `populateMovies` JavaScript function uses `MovieFacade` to get the list of
movies through SL4A, loops through them, and calls the `addMovie` function to
populate the UI.

```
    /**
     * Populate movies.
     */
    function populateMovies() {
        // Get movies
        var movies = droid.moviesGet().result;

        for (var i = 0, e = movies.length; i < e; i++) {
            var movie = movies[i];

            addMovie(
                movie["title"],
                movie["moviePath"],
                movie["mimeType"],
                movie["duration"],
                movie["thumbnailPath"]);
        }
    }

    populateMovies();
```

The `addMovie` function simply defines the necessary set of HTML elements to
render the movie item, and appends it to the movie list. Besides the visible
information about the movie, the `addMovie` function also saves the movie path
and MIME type into the movie element in order to be able to retrieve it when
necessary.

```
    /**
     * Add movie.
     *
     * @param title movie title.
     */
    function addMovie(title, moviePath, mimeType, duration, thumbnailPath) {
        // Movie element
        var movieElement = document.createElement("div");
        movieElement.setAttribute("class", "movie");
```

```
        movieElement.setAttribute("data-moviepath", moviePath);
        movieElement.setAttribute("data-mimetype", mimeType);
        movieElement.onclick = onMovieClick;

        // Thumbnail element
        var thumbnailElement = document.createElement("img");
        thumbnailElement.setAttribute("class", "thumbnail");
        thumbnailElement.src = thumbnailPath;
        movieElement.appendChild(thumbnailElement);

        // Title element
        var titleElement = document.createElement("div");
        titleElement.setAttribute("class", "title");
        titleElement.innerHTML = title;
        movieElement.appendChild(titleElement);

        // Duration element
        var durationElement = document.createElement("div");
        durationElement.setAttribute("class", "duration");
        durationElement.innerHTML = duration;
        movieElement.appendChild(durationElement);

        // Clear element
        var clearElement = document.createElement("div");
        clearElement.setAttribute("class", "clear");
        movieElement.appendChild(clearElement);

        // Append movie to list
        moviesElement.appendChild(movieElement);
    }
```

Click events on movie items are handled through the onMovieClick function. The onMovieClient function extracts the movie path and the MIME type that were saved by the addMovie function, and relies on the view method provided by CommonIntentsFacade to send an intent to the Android platform to launch the default player for the selected movie item.

```
    /**
     * On movie click handler.
     *
     * @param e UI event.
     */
    function onMovieClick(e) {
        // Get clicked movie item
        var movieElement = e.currentTarget;

        // Movie path
        var moviePath = movieElement.getAttribute("data-moviepath");

        // MIME type
```

```
            var mimeType = movieElement.getAttribute("data-mimetype");

            // View movie
            droid.view(moviePath, mimeType);
        }
    </script>
</body>
</html>
```

Running the Application

The movie player script application is now ready to be deployed, as described in Chapter 5. Due to a known bug in the Android emulator, the example code can currently run only on an Android device. Since the example application will look for video files in external storage, make sure that the Android device contains an SD card with video files on it, and disconnect the Android device from your host machine to release the SD card. When you run the application, you will see the movie list, as shown in Figure 10-21.

Figure 10-21. *Movie player script application showing the movie list*

Summary

In this chapter, we went deep into the SL4A framework and explored its internals, including the façade registry and the project structure. SL4A is an open source project, and it is highly extensible. You can follow the same steps described in this chapter's example to extend the `ScriptingLayerForAndroid` project, the main SL4A application, to include new façades, and later use them locally or remotely through any scripting language.

In this book, we have explored the fundamentals of the Android platform to better understand its foundations. We studied the Android application architecture, and we applied these new concepts to our first Android application, a movie player. Then we augmented the movie player application to support other video formats by integrating the native code library. At every stage of development, we have employed the advanced development features provided by Eclipse, such as fast navigation, Content Assist, code generators, and debugging and troubleshooting features, to streamline the development process.

Resources

The following resources are available for the topics covered in this chapter:

- Scripting Layer for Android (SL4A),
  `http://code.google.com/p/android-scripting/`
- Mercurial Eclipse, `http://javaforge.com/project/HGE`

Appendix A

Testing Android Applications

Testing is one of the most important phases of the application development cycle. The Android SDK provides a powerful test framework for defining and running a variety of tests to validate different aspects of Android applications. The Android test framework is built on top of the popular JUnit test framework. The Android test framework extends JUnit by incorporating Android-specific instrumentation functionality to allow tests to control the environment surrounding the Android applications. This makes it easy to test all possible use cases.

JUnit Basics

JUnit is a testing framework for the Java programming language. JUnit provides a set of classes to define, organize, and run test cases. The most important class provided by JUnit is `junit.framework.TestCase`, which is the base class for all test cases. Android test classes are also built on top of this class, and they follow the same code structure and flow. A basic test case class is shown in Listing A-1.

Listing A-1. *Basic Test Case Class*

```
public class MyTest extends AndroidTestCase {
    /**
     * Sets up the text fixture before each test is executed.
     */
    protected void setUp() {
```

```
    }
    /**
     * Test method.
     */
    protected void testSomething() {
    }

    /**
     * Tears down the text fixture after each test is executed.
     */
    protected void tearDown() {
    }
}
```

The following are the key parts of the test case class:

- **setUp**: This method sets up the test fixture before each test. Developers are expected to override this class to properly initialize the test fixture in order to make sure that new test runs are isolated from the preceding test runs.

- **tearDown**: This method tears down the text fixture and releases any resources that were allocated for the test. The JUnit test framework keeps the test case classes around through the execution of entire test cases. Developers are expected to release any resources in the **tearDown** method in order to prevent exhausting the platform.

- **testXXX**: The test case class can contain one or more tests. Test methods have the prefix **test**. The JUnit framework runs all methods with that prefix while processing the test case class.

Assertions

In computer science, an *assertion* is a predicate that is used to indicate the developer's assumptions about the state of the application at that given stage. Assertions are used to test the correctness of the application.

The JUnit framework provides a set of frequently used assertion methods, through the **junit.framework.Assert** class, for use with test cases. The base **junit.framework.TestCase** class extends the **Assert** class and provides direct access to these assertion methods.

The assertion methods that are exposed by JUnit are highly generic. They do not cover the frequent assertion operations that Android test cases cover. The Android test framework comes into play here by providing additional assertion classes with extensive sets of methods specifically designed to address Android testing needs. Despite JUnit's `Assert` class, these additional classes are not a base class of test cases. Developers need to import these classes into the Java code and use their static assertion methods.

The following additional assertion classes are provided as a part of the `android.test` Java package:

- `MoreAsserts`: This class provides a set of generic assertion methods that are not provided by JUnit for testing Java types, arrays, and values.

- `ViewAsserts`: This class provides a set of assertion methods for Android views. These methods can be used to assert the visibility of user interface (UI) components, as well as how they are positioned on the display.

Unit Testing

Unit testing allows developers to test application components in isolation. The Android test framework provides a set of component test classes that facilitate the component-specific testing needs—such as fixture setup, teardown, and life-cycle control—under the `android.test` Java package. Test cases can extend these classes and provide the actual test methods built on top of the functionality provided.

The following are some of the test framework classes that are provided:

- `AndroidTestCase`: This is a generic test case class with methods for accessing context and resources, and testing application permissions.

- `ApplicationTestCase`: This class provides an environment to test the `Application` class in a controlled environment. It allows the test code to control the application life cycle, as well as inject dependencies such as isolated contexts. It delays the initiation of the application until the `createApplication` method is executed, to allow developers to do the fixture setup.

- **ActivityUnitTestCase**: This is a test class for isolated testing of **Activity** classes. In a test, an activity is started with minimal connection to the Android platform. It allows injection of mock context and application instances into the activity prior to testing. To provide a true unit testing environment, it overrides a set of Android methods to prevent the activity from interacting with other activities and the platform.

- **ServiceTestCase**: This is a test class for testing **Service** classes in a controlled environment. It provides basic support for service life cycle management, and also allows developers to inject dependencies and control the environment through the test code.

- **ProviderTestCase2**: This is a test class for a single **ContentProvider** class and for testing the application code with an isolated content provider. Instead of using the system map for providers, it maintains its internal list and exposes those content providers to only the test cases. It deprecates the **ProviderTestCase** class to break the dependency on instrumentation.

Mock Objects

Unit testing is a repeatable process with known inputs and outputs. All dependencies of the component are fulfilled through mock objects to eliminate external dependencies that influence the test outcomes.

To facilitate the dependency injection, the Android framework provides mock objects for core parts of the Android framework under the **android.test.mock** Java package. These mock classes isolate tests from the running system by overriding and stubbing their normal operations. They are nonfunctional except for the portions defined by the developer. All methods that are not overridden throw a **java.lang.UnsupportedOperationException** to inform the developer that the test code is trying to communicate with the environment. The following mock classes are provided:

- **MockApplication**: This class extends the **Application** class and stubs its methods. Developers can extend this mock class to implement the methods necessary for dependency injection. All other methods will raise the **UnsupportedOperationException**.

- `MockContext`: This class extends the `Context` class and stubs its methods. Developers can use the mock context to inject other dependencies into the application.

- `MockContentResolver`: This class extends the `ContentResolver` class and overrides Android's normal way of resolving content providers by authority. Instead of using the system's content provider mapping, the mock content resolver keeps an internal mapping. Developers should register their mock content providers into the mock content resolver during the fixture setup. The mock content resolver isolates the application being tested by resolving only the mock content providers that are registered directly.

- `MockContentProvider`: This class extends the `ContentProvider` class and stubs its methods. Developers should override the necessary content provider methods to provide static data to the consumers of this content provider. Later, through the mock content resolver, the mock content provider can be injected into the application being tested.

- `MockCursor`: This class extends the `Cursor` class and stubs its methods. It is usually used with mock content providers to provide static data to the applications being tested.

- `MockDialogInterface`: This class implements the `DialogInterface` with stub methods. Developers can override its methods to validate UI inputs to dialogs.

- `MockPackageManager`: This class extends the `PackageManager` class and stubs its methods. Developers can override the necessary methods to mock the interaction between the application being tested and the Android system.

- `MockResources`: This class extends the `Resources` class and stubs its methods. It enables developers to do resource injection in the application being tested by overriding the mock methods.

Functional Testing

Functional testing is a type of black-box testing. It tests software components based on their specifications. Functional testing involves feeding input and examining the output; the internal program structure is rarely considered.

The Android test framework allows functional testing of Android applications through the instrumentation. Android instrumentation is a set of control methods and hooks to inject user events and requests into the application, meanwhile managing its life cycle. The instrumentation methods are provided through the `android.app.Instrumentation` class. This class is instantiated before any of the application code runs.

Unlike the unit testing classes, the functional testing classes load the application using the actual system context, and feed events into the application using either its UI or the Android services it exposes to the system. The functional test classes extend the `InstrumentationTestCase` class and provide access to the instrumentation instance through the `getInstrumentation` method. The following instrumentation classes are provided in the `android.test` Java package:

- `ActivityInstrumentationTestCase2`: This class provides methods for functional testing of a single activity. The activity being tested is initiated using the system infrastructure and then can be manipulated using the instrumentation methods. It deprecates the `ActivityInstrumentationTestCase` class by providing finer granularity of configuration options for the tested activity.

- `SingleLaunchActivityTestCase`: This class launches the `Activity` class that is being tested on its `setUp` method and terminates it in its `tearDown` method. Unlike the other test classes, this class runs all test methods on the existing activity instance, instead of setting up and tearing down the activity instance for each test.

UI Operations

The Android framework requires all interaction with the UI components to happen in the application's main thread, also known as the *UI thread*. The `InstrumentationTestCase` class provides these options for running test code in the UI thread:

- `TouchUtils`: This class provides methods for generating touch events from the instrumentation test classed to mimic user interaction with the application through the touch screen.

- `UiThreadTest`: Annotation can be used to mark the test cases that should be executed within the application's UI thread in the test class. In this mode, the instrumentation methods may not be used.

- `runTestOnUiThread`: This method can be used to schedule `Runnable` objects in the UI thread. This allows test cases to inject only a portion of a test into the application's UI thread.

Test Projects

Test projects are no different from generic Android projects. They are generated as a separate project from the actual application. Although they are a separate project, the best practice is to store the test projects in the main project root under the `tests` directory.

Android Development Tools (ADT), introduced in Chapter 5 of this book, provides two options for generating a test project. One approach is to create the test project while creating the actual project. The New Android Project wizard, on its third step, asks you if a test project should also be generated, as shown in Figure A-1. You can first mark the Create a Test Project option, and then configure the test project.

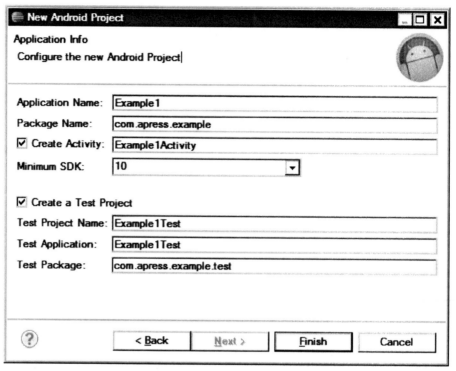

Figure A-1. *Configuring a test project with the New Android Project wizard*

Having a test project at the very beginning of application development is good practice for test-driven programming. However, if the test project is not created at the beginning, it is never too late to build one. ADT provides a New Project wizard specifically to generate a new test project for an existing Android project in the workspace.

To create a new test project, Choose **File ➤ New ➤ Project…** from the top menu bar, expand Android, and select Android Test Project, as shown in Figure A-2.

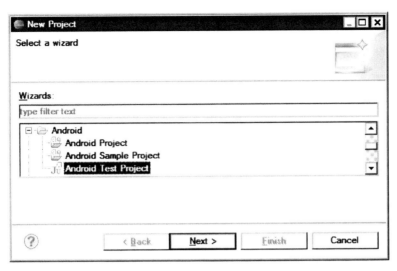

Figure A-2. *Choosing to create a new Android test project*

The ADT New Android Test Project wizard will first ask you for the name of this test project. As the location of the new project, it is recommended to use the `tests` subdirectory inside the project to test. Proceed to the next step by clicking the Next button.

Every test project needs to be associated with an existing Android project. On the next step, the wizard will ask you to choose the target project, as shown in Figure A-3. Select the target project and click the Next button to continue.

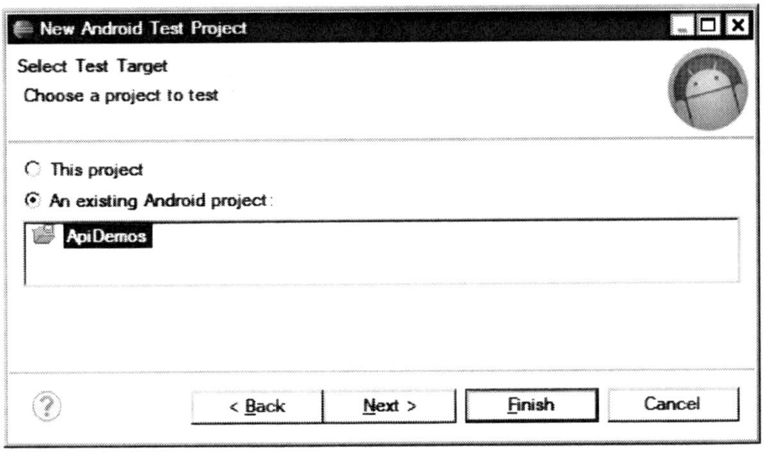

Figure A-3. *Choosing the target Android project for the test project*

As the last step, the New Android Test Project wizard will ask for the target Android SDK version for the new test project. Select the SDK target suitable for the target Android project, and click the Finish button. ADT will generate the test project.

Running Tests

To run the test cases, select the test project and click the Run button. As shown in Figure A-4, Eclipse will ask how the project should be executed. Choose Android JUnit Test from the list, and then click the OK button proceed.

Figure A-4. *Run As dialog for the test project on its first run*

ADT first builds and deploys the actual Android project, and then does the same for the test project itself. While the tests are running on the target device or the emulator, you can monitor them using the JUnit view within Eclipse, as shown in Figure A-5.

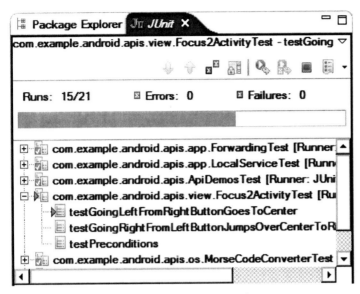

Figure A-5. *JUnit view showing the progress of testing*

The JUnit view has two panes:

- The top pane provides a list of tests that are being executed, along with statistics regarding the number of passing and failing test cases.

- If a test case fails, the bottom pane provides the failure trace showing the location of the error, as shown in Figure A-6.

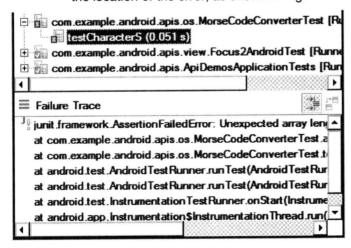

Figure A-6. *Failure trace showing the failed test*

While troubleshooting a failing test case on a large project, it is preferable to run only that test case, rather than the entire test suite. To run only a single test, select the test case class using the Package Explorer, and then click the Run button. Eclipse will display the Run As dialog, as shown in Figure A-7. Select Android JUnit Test, and then click the OK button to proceed. JUnit will run only the tests in the selected test case class.

Figure A-7. *Executing the selected test case class*

Measuring Test Code Coverage

How much testing is enough? This is one of the most frequently asked questions for testing. The number of test cases is not a good measure for the test coverage. The Android SDK comes with EMMA for measuring and reporting code coverage of test cases.

> **NOTE:** Code coverage is currently supported only on the Android emulator and rooted devices.

Although EMMA is an important component of the Android test framework, its use with Android applications is not clearly documented. In this section, we will go through the steps to generate code coverage reports from test projects.

Setting Up EMMA Access

At the time of this writing, the ADT plug-in for Eclipse does not provide access to EMMA directly. The EMMA code coverage tool can be invoked only through the Ant-based build scripts. Eclipse does not generate Ant build scripts when the Android project is created. The build scripts should be manually created for both the application project and the test project.

To create the build scripts, open a command prompt if you are running on a Windows host machine, or a terminal window if you are using a Mac OS X or Linux-based host machine, and invoke the following commands:

```
cd <application directory>
android update project --path .
```

```
cd <test directory>
android update test-project --main <application directory> --path .
```

These commands will generate the Ant build script, `build.xml`, and the other necessary property files in both the application and test directories.

Enabling EMMA for Test Runs

To enable EMMA, using the Package Explorer, expand the test project. If the `build.xml` file is not visible, press F5 to refresh the project directory. Right-click the `build.xml` file and choose **Run As Ant Build**... from the context menu. The Edit Configuration dialog will appear. Switch to the Main tab, and set the arguments to `all clean emma debug install test`, as shown in Figure A-8.

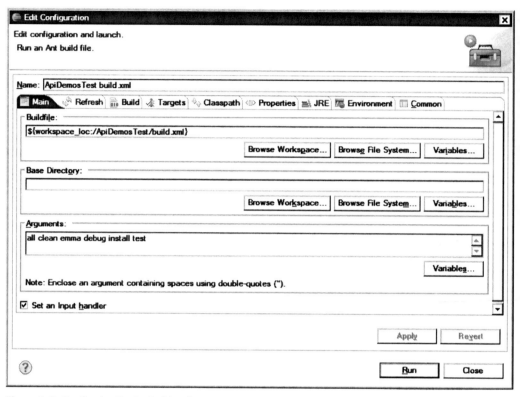

Figure A-8. *Configuring the Ant build script*

Make sure that the Android device is connected to the host machine, and click the Run button to execute the Ant build script. The build script will deploy both the application and the test to the target device or the emulator with EMMA enabled, as shown in Figure A-9.

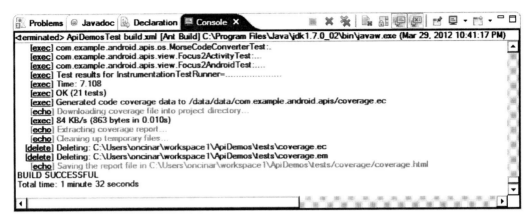

Figure A-9. *Console view showing EMMA being enabled*

Upon completion of the test cases, the script will pull EMMA result files and generate an HTML-formatted report in the `coverage` directory under the test project. Refresh the project directory by pressing the F5 key after selecting the test project using the Package Explorer. Expand the `coverage` directory, and open the `coverage.html` report file, as shown in Figure A-10.

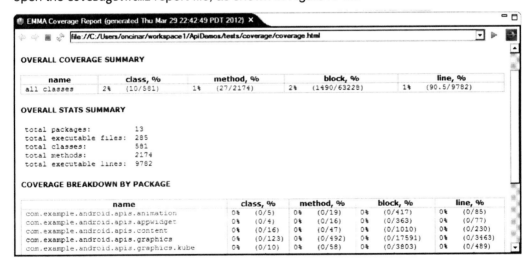

Figure A-10. *EMMA code coverage report file*

The EMMA report HTML file provides extensive information about code coverage of test cases. By clicking the packages and classes, you can navigate into source files and see the portions of the code that are not executed by any test case. Using this information, you can expand the test cases to cover a larger portion of the application code.

Stress Testing

Stress testing is a form of testing that is used to determine the stability of the application by introducing a load beyond the application's operational capacity. The Android SDK provides the Monkey tool to send pseudo-random streams of keystrokes, touches, and gestures to the application. Stress testing is not a repeatable process; however, the Monkey tool allows repeating the stream of events to reproduce error cases.

To launch the Monkey tool, first connect the target device to the host machine or launch the emulator. Open a command prompt if you are using a Windows-based host machine, or a terminal window on Mac OS X and Linux-based host machines, and invoke the following command:

```
adb shell monkey -p <your application package> -v 500
```

This command starts the Monkey tool and sends 500 pseudo-random events to the Android application with the given package name. For more information about the Monkey tool command-line arguments, see http://developer.android.com/guide/developing/tools/monkey.html.

Index

2032401

CPSIA information can be obtained at www.ICGtesting.com
Printed in the USA
LVOW110533190113

316411LV00005B/21/P

9 781430 244434